Lanarkshire's Mining

Matt O'Neill

The No 15 Pit, Cadder, near Bishopbriggs. Scene of the Great Disaster, whereby 22 men lost their lives on Sunday. Aug: 3rd 1913. 4, Pub. by Walter Benton & Co Glasgow.

The Cadder Pit Disaster. Funeral Procession at Lambhill to Lambhill Cemetery. Pub. by Walter Benton & Co Glasgow. 7.

The photographs and illustrations on the upper front cover, this page, and pages 2 and 4 relate to the Cadder Colliery disaster of 1913, a time when picture postcards and other souvenirs were a common way of recording public events.

ISBN 9781840335507

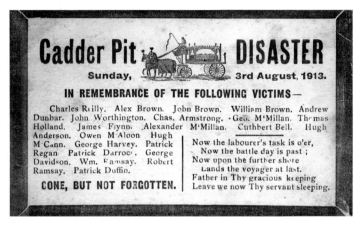

Acknowledgements

No one writes a book of this nature alone and any new study will inevitably stand, at least in part, on the shoulders of those who went before. I would therefore like to take this opportunity to acknowledge the mines inspectors, advocates, commissioners, journalists and authors whose collective endeavours form the basis of this work, and the following people who made the task of research and writing a little easier: George Archibald, Scottish Mining Museum, Newtongrange; Beth Bradley; Lorraine Broderick and Sandra Greatorex, HMSO, London; Alison Cook, editorial, the *Scots Magazine*; Julia Dagg, St George's Library, Sheffield University; John Gordon; Joseph Hackett; Kevin Hall, archives, the *Scotsman*; Tommy Hay; Neville Hill, Health & Safety Executive, Bootle; staff of Kilsyth Library; Frances and Siobhan Logan; John Lynch; Claire McCluskey, production co-ordinator, Caledonia Sterne & Wyld; George McEwan; John McIlvean and Marion Torney, *Kilsyth Chronicle*; Grace McKeown; Christine McPherson, *Kirkintilloch Herald*; Myra Maguire (née Loney); Neil Miller and John Simmons, National Archives of Scotland; staff of the Mitchell Library, Glasgow; Alex Mooney; Daniel Mooney; Kirstie and Scott Nicol; Matt O'Neill Jnr; Dickie Pender; David Pettigrew, Stenlake Publishing; Ian Poynton and John Sims, British Library, London; Jamie Precious, the Stationary Office, Norwich; James Scullion; John Twaddle, deputy supervisor (ret.), Mines Rescue Station, Coatbridge; Hugh Walsh; Peter Wellburn, National Library of Scotland; and last, but certainly not least, Ian Winstanley of the Coal Mining History Resource Centre and Picks Publishing, Wigan, for a wealth of source material.

Contents

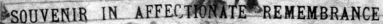

SOUVENIR IN AFFECTIONATE REMEMBRANCE

OF THE

TWENTY TWO MINERS

Who lost their lives in the No. 15 Pit of the Carron Company's Collieries, Sunday August 3rd, 1913.

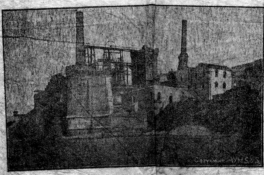

Copyright WHSS

"IN THE MIDST OF LIFE ARE IN DEATH."

TWENTY-TWO miners lost their lives in No. 15 Pit of the Carron Company's collieries, Mavis Valley, near Glasgow, as the result of the fire that broke out on Sunday night, August 3rd.

Known locally as the Cadder Mine, belonging to the Carron Compy, of Falkirk, the scene of the disaster is on the north bank of the Forth-and-Clyde Canal, six or seven miles from Glasgow.

Twenty-six men, finishing the "back shift," on which they started about 3 o'clock on Sunday afternoon, were in the mine at the time. Three of these escaped by a passage to No. 19 shaft, belonging to the same company, and one was found alive after being in the burning mine for 21 hours.

The first alarm of the fire was raised by Fireman William Brown, who descended the shaft about 8 o'clock in the evening to make his customary survey before the next shift began work. When he had walked a few yards along the main road he saw thick smoke and flame raging like a furnace. He at once telephoned to the engineman and banksman at the pithead, and two of his workmates got into communication with the men on duty at the head of No. 17 pit, who immediately reversed the air current.

Hero of the Warning Light.

Another fireman named Charles Riley observed smoke, and he at once hurried in to inform his mates. He was fortunate to find three of them close by, and to these he explained the danger. They were Robert Dunbar, of Lambhill, Michael Keenan, of Possil Park, and Felix O'Neill, Garscube Road.

These were the three who escaped by the communication road to No. 17 pit. They explained later that Fireman Riley, after warning them, seized a lamp and, waving it as a warning, hurried forward through the workings to advise others still at work. He was not again seen alive. His body was in the first group found

by the rescuers. "He might have saved his life," said one of the others later.

The interment of the victims took place on Wednesday, August 6th, 1913.

Names of the Victims.

CHARLES RILEY, married, fireman, Lambhill.
ALEXANDER BROWN, JOHN BROWN, WILLIAM BROWN, brothers, of Mavis Valley.
ANDREW DUNBAR, single, Lambhill.
JOHN WORTHINGTON, married, Summerston.
CHARLES ARMSTRONG, single, Garscube Road.
GEORGE McMILLAN, married, Possilpark.
THOMAS HOLLAND, married, Possilpark.
JAMES FLYNN, married, Possilpark.
ALEXANDER McMILLAN, married, Bishopbriggs.
CUTHBERT BELL, single, Possilpark.
HUGH ANDERSON, single, Lambhill.
OWEN McALOON, single, Lambhill.
HUGH McCANN, married, Lambhill.
GEORGE HARVEY, married, Lambhill.
PATRICK REGAN, married, Lambhill.
PATRICK DARROCH, married, Lochfaulds.
GEORGE DAVIDSON, married, Mavis Valley.
WILLIAM RAMSAY, single, Mavis Valley.
ROBERT RAMSAY, his brother, married, Mavis Valley.
PATRICK DUFFIN, married, Drummond St. Lambhill.

S. Burgess, Printer, 8, York Place, London, W.C.

A Note on the Maps

The maps in this book are contemporary with the events they describe and represent the variety of styles used by accident investigators over the years.

Introduction

Exactly when coal was first used as a fuel in Scotland is largely a matter of conjecture. While it is known that the Romans used brushwood and charcoal for cooking and to heat their bathhouses, archaeologists have also found traces of coal on many Roman sites, suggesting that some coalfields may have had a mining history of almost 2,000 years. But whatever uses the Romans made of coal as a fuel during the years of occupation, they seem to have come to an end with their departure, and many centuries passed before the first references to the coal trade were recorded.

Scottish references go back to the twelfth and thirteenth centuries when coal was mined, on a small scale, on monastic land. The abbeys of Holyrood and Newbattle record mining activity on the south shore of the Firth of Forth at Carriden in Linlithgow and at Preston in East Lothian, and the Cistercian monks of Culross Abbey mined the coal that was readily accessible on the shores of the Forth.

Initially gathered from outcrops lying at or near the surface and followed underground as drift mines, these outcrops were eventually worked out, and when monastic and church lands were broken up following the Reformation, they were distributed among the nobles and gentry who supported the monarchy. In later years these landowners, families such as Elcho, Elphinstone, Bruce, Hamilton, Wemyss and Cunninghame, having exploited such deposits on their estates, began to sink shafts as a more direct method of getting the coal to the surface – and in so doing pushed ever deeper in search of fresh seams. As a result of this, the already hazardous job of mining became even more dangerous.

Scotland's Industrial Revolution is commonly held to have begun around the end of the 1770s. As with the rest of Britain it was powered by coal, but while the technologies of other industries came on in leaps and bounds, mining technology remained static through lack of investment by avaricious coalmasters. Investment, however, would eventually come from the colonial merchants of Glasgow – not for mine safety or the winning of coal, but for its transportation. It was they who financed the Monkland Canal (opened 1793) to relieve Glasgow's growing coal crisis by tapping into the immense mineral riches of Lanarkshire. The Forth and Clyde Canal (opened 1790) became the city's route to the east, built to serve the need of the tobacco houses for a secure and speedy waterway link to their key European markets. With the opening of these vital links the movement of goods (including coal) from the industrial central belt to the east and west coasts was made possible.

With the Industrial Revolution up and running, for the coalmasters there were vast fortunes to be made, and their sole considerations quickly became productivity and profit. In their all-consuming drive to achieve these twin goals all else was left behind, including the health, safety and welfare of the miners. In an industry where accidents were commonplace, the drive for productivity increased risks. Subsequently – perhaps *inevitably* – there were greater tragedies. Some of the tragedies were a result of the unforeseen, for which no one can legislate and for which no blame can be apportioned. Others, however, stemmed either from the 'blind eye' attitude taken by officials intent on keeping production high, or the careless conduct of the miners themselves – having become, over the years, inured to the obvious dangers of their surroundings. On this the historian William Nimmo wrote in 1880: 'Colliers, considering the critical character of their calling, are careless beyond all credence. They may be reasoned with, fined, and even dismissed, for rashly flying in the face of rules specially framed with the object of protecting life and property, but all to no purpose.'

Major accidents claiming many lives captured both the attention and the sympathy of the general public, but while they were mercifully few, accidents involving single or a handful of deaths were many – and non-fatal near misses were an every day occurrence. Speaking to Sub-Commissioner Franks of the Children's Employment Commission in 1842, John Marshall, oversman of the Hirse Colliery, parish of Cumbernauld, said: 'It is not the custom to notice those accidents: we neither give notice, nor do the friends of the parties. The practice is to bury them a day or two after decease.' Kellog Durland, an observer of miners at work in the early 1900s, wrote of the number of hair's-breadth escapes that passed every day without comment, and the acts of real heroism that were performed as a matter of course in the day's work. However, there were many tragedies which simply would never have happened but for the individual company's blind adherence to the dogma of productivity and profit. Lack of investment and the inability – or unwillingness – of company officials to enforce basic safety procedures sometimes wrought havoc in the claustrophobic darkness down below.

Lanarkshire – where the most extensive coal measures were to be found – produced more coal, supported more collieries and employed more miners than any other county. It also accounted for more mining deaths than any other county, and produced the two worst ever Scottish mining disasters.

'The Price o' Coal'

By George McEwan

They fun' Big Tam McGhee's aul' graith bag
A hunner yairds back frae the face,
Ahint an upturned wagon,
That wis the only trace
O' Big Tam McGhee, the hewer
The bare-faced diggers ever fun'
That Tuesday morn the roof cam' doon
A mile ablow the grun'.

Noo Jessie an' her lassies
Rak' the bing fur bits o' shale
Their shaws pu'ed ticht aroon them,
Their faces pinched an' pale
While ayont the miners' raws o' hooses
The winder engine roars an' reeks
An' Wee Tam has quit the schulehoose binch
Tae don the moleskin breeks.

An' sae the wheel keeps tirnin'
Takin' men an' boays ablow the earth
Tae wrestle in the daurk an' damp
Fur the means tae warm yir hearth.
Tae keep ye snug an' blithe an' cheery
Midst winter's froast an' snaw
While Jessie's heart is frozen
Each time she hears the whistle blaw . . .

Chapter 1
No. 2 pit, Commonhead Colliery, Airdrie: Tuesday, 23rd July 1850

Commonhead Colliery, owned and operated by coalmaster James Sneddon and his son John, lay adjacent to the Glasgow–Airdrie railway, a little to the north of the town. With the colliery having not long been in operation, the workings did not as yet extend very far from the pit bottom. The single shaft, split into upcast and downcast divisions by a wooden partition or mid-wall, was over 60 fathoms deep. Whilst the workings were checked for gas using a Davy lamp, the miners preferred to use naked lights – oil-fired 'tally' (tallow) lamps – for everyday working, this despite the known presence of firedamp, a highly flammable gas.

What had long been known among miners was the need for a strong light to work by, particularly useful in checking roofs for potential weak spots, but the safety lamps of the time were not up to the task. This was being pointed out as late as the 1880s by observers like Sir Frederick Abel: 'Vigilance on the part of the miner must often be of little avail, if, as is still very frequently the case, he is dependent upon a source of light, whereby to observe the first signs of an impending fall, which is insufficient to enable him to see distinctly in his immediate vicinity. The utter inadequacy of the light furnished by the safety-lamps hitherto most generally employed, i.e., the Davy, the Stephenson, and the Clanny, has been the chief cause of the frequent yielding to the strong temptation to employ naked lights, even in regions where the possibility of an explosion from the presence of firedamp is scarcely doubtful.'

Shortly after six o'clock on the morning of Tuesday, 23rd July 1850, following a two-day holiday, the day shift force of eighteen men and boys descended the Commonhead shaft to begin work. When they reached the pit bottom they waited while Alexander Willison, the shift fireman, went forward with his Davy lamp to check the various working places for firedamp, as was his duty. Willison had been gone no more than a few minutes when there was a terrific explosion. The blast roared out of the workings and in a matter of seconds had swept the pit bottom and destroyed a large part of the mid-wall of the shaft.

Of the eighteen miners only one survived the blast unscathed. James Willison, brother of the fireman, was talking to his companions near the bottom of the shaft when the explosion took place. He immediately threw himself to the ground and the fireball passed over him, although it tore the coat from his back and he was 'rendered stupid'. When he recovered he tried to reach the bottom of the shaft, but was going away from it when McLuckie, a boy who would not survive, directed him to the pit bottom. There he shook hands with two injured men and promised to send help as soon as he reached the surface, but he then found that the cage had been wrecked by the falling of the mid-wall and by the shattered hutches blasted into the bottom of the shaft by the explosion.

The only chance of escape was by way of the rope connecting the cage to the top of the shaft. The rope was coupled to the chains of the cage with a heavy iron bolt secured by a split-pin, the latter being passed through a hole in the bolt and bent in opposite directions. Willison set himself to disconnecting the rope but found great difficulty in straightening the ends of the pin. At one point he called to his brother to give him a hammer to free the coupling of the cage, but got no answer. Eventually, he managed to bend back the pins with his teeth. He then took the shaft of his pick and, sliding it through the loop at the end of the rope, he sat down on it and began shaking the rope to draw attention. At the top, someone noticed the moving rope and Willison was drawn up the shaft. Still in a dazed state, the survivor managed to tell his story, but he was unable to throw light on the cause of the explosion.

Drawn by the sound of the blast, which had been heard at a considerable distance from the colliery, a large crowd had gathered at the pithead, many of them in the belief that a surface steam boiler had burst. The growing crowd included the wives, children and relatives of those who were working that day, and when they learned that the explosion had happened underground they feared the worst.

Efforts to get down the shaft and recover the dead were hampered until about half past ten by the heavy presence of chokedamp (carbon dioxide) in the workings, about which time it began to clear. From then until around four o'clock in the afternoon operations to get below and begin the task of recovery were carried out successfully, a total of fourteen bodies being brought to the surface at intervals. It was then deemed necessary to suspend recovery operations until the mid-wall of the shaft, destroyed in the blast, had been repaired. When this was completed, it would send a measure of ventilation into the workings and allow the rescuers to carry on without risk to themselves.

There was a certain amount of confusion as to exactly how many miners had descended that morning, officials believing the figure to be nineteen. As they were brought to the surface the bodies were taken to the poorhouse in Airdrie where the governor, Mr Alston, had made the necessary preparations. A medical examination was carried out on each of the victims before they were washed, put into coffins and released to the relatives – those who had relatives. It was reported that, although all had been severely injured by the explosion, the injuries were not such as would have resulted in instantaneous death. It was thus conjectured that the victims must have 'lingered on for some time, till suffocated by the chokedamp'.

By three o'clock the following afternoon the bottom of the shaft had been cleared and most of the bodies recovered. But two victims were still unaccounted for – Wilson McDonald and Andrew Izzat – so the search continued. Although every family's loss was tragic, the story of William Tollson was particularly poignant. This young lad, 20 years old, had only recently arrived from England. He began his first shift at Commonhead on the Tuesday morning and had made his first descent of the shaft with the others. Within a few minutes he was dead.

One of the clearest eyewitness accounts of the disaster was that of William Izzat, brother of the missing Andrew. William had been due to go down the pit with the rest of the shift, but he was late and the cage had gone down without him, leaving him on the bank. He had been standing at the pithead when the explosion happened and was sure that everyone below must have been killed. He ran to find James Sneddon, the colliery owner/manager, and measures were put in hand to rescue those who might still be alive in the pit, but the cage – which had been on its way down the downcast shaft at the time of the explosion – was jammed in the shaft and a delay ensued before anyone could get down the pit.

William saw James Willison brought up, sitting on the pick shaft inserted into the chain, and for nearly half an hour after this he could hear groans and cries from the bottom of the pit, but could not make out what was said. Almost all the bodies of the men recovered were found at the bottom of the shaft. William reported that there had never been any particular air course going through the pit, only what he called 'temporary ventilators'. The pit, he said, had not been worked from the Saturday to the Tuesday and, after 30 years' experience in coal pits, 'he never knew of such a fearful accident'. He was convinced that had due caution been exercised, it would never have happened.

While the work of clearing the wreckage, making safe the workings and searching for the last two victims carried on, gossip circulated on the surface as to the cause of the explosion. The cube, or ventilating furnace, which draws a continual draught of fresh air into the workings, had been allowed to go out on the Saturday and was not restarted until early on Tuesday morning, a short time before the men descended. With the ventilation draught restarted, the fresh air flowing into the workings mixed with a body of firedamp that had been allowed to accumulate over the holiday period. Exactly what caused the gas to ignite will never be known, but the following seems the most likely explanation.

As far as is known the manager's instruction had always been that no one should leave the pit bottom until the fireman had returned from his inspection of the workings and given the all clear. If this was indeed the case, then this instruction in itself was an infringement of the mining rules already in force which stated that men should not descend the shaft *at all* until given the all clear by the firemen. When the workings were searched after the explosion, fireman Willison's Davy lamp was found lying near his body, intact and undamaged. This ruled out his lamp as being the source of ignition for it would have been destroyed. However, given the practice of allowing miners at the pit bottom while the fireman's inspection was in progress, it was not impossible that one of the workmen had gone forward to his workplace without waiting for the all clear; in which case any accumulation of gas he met would have flared at the naked light of his tally lamp and set the explosion rolling.

On the Thursday morning searchers came across the body of young Wilson McDonald, which was brought up and conveyed to Airdrie poorhouse for examination. This left only Andrew Izzat to be accounted for and the efforts to find him were redoubled. Search parties scoured the workings for a further five hours without success, and their failure to find any trace of the man had them baffled. It was then suggested that one of the bodies – which had failed to be identified and was now buried in the New Monkland graveyard – might in fact be the missing man. An exhumation order was obtained and the body disinterred to be at last identified as that of Izzat. The confusion in numbers following the explosion had been resolved; eighteen men and boys had been lost, including one victim (not Izzat) buried yet still unidentified. (No newspaper reported the name; with single Irish immigrants arriving to work, this was a common occurrence).

'There never was any particular air course through the pit; there were only what I would call temporary ventilators.' – The words of William Izzat, who missed the cage and was left at the pithead while the rest of his shift went to their deaths. It would seem that the ventilation system at Commonhead was rudimentary at best. Having established that, according to mining rules, the miners should never have descended at all until the fireman had checked the workings and given the all clear, we have a picture of the fireman with his safety lamp going below in the company of a group of miners wearing their naked flame tally lamps.

The fact that James Willison shook hands with two of the men before coming to the surface, that William Izzat heard groans and cries coming from the bottom of the pit, and that the examining doctor ventured that some of the victims had 'lingered on for some time, till suffocated by the chokedamp' suggests that the atmosphere at the pit bottom, initially clear following the blast, had gradually been engulfed by carbon dioxide shortly after Willison was taken up the shaft. By the time the rescuers broke through the wreckage at the bottom of the shaft the gas had killed those who had survived the explosion.

Having spoken with survivor James Willison shortly after he came up the shaft, Izzat said that Willison had not been long in the pit when he noticed an unusual smell, which he was sure was firedamp. With the ventilation cube shut down for something like three days and only restarted that morning, no wonder he smelled firedamp. The most obvious question is this: why did his brother – fireman Alexander – not notice the smell as soon as he arrived at the pit bottom? Or, for that matter, why did he wander off to inspect the workings for gas when gas was so obviously noticeable at the pit bottom?

At the later inquiry into the Commonhead Disaster, survivor James Willison made this statement: 'The fireman, each morning with a safety lamp, went round the workings and told the men where there was fire[damp] by writing on a shovel. When we saw the shovel we left our naked lights and went [to] waft the fire[damp] out with our coats . . . we made it quite clear by wafting it. I have had to do this twice or thrice in a day, and it would take me about ten minutes. None of the miners had safety lamps. Some of the places were so foul that wafting would not do. The [ventilating] fire was not kept burning night and day, as it should have been. There was no person down the pit from Saturday till the Tuesday morning, the day of the accident. I went down as usual and saw my brother, who was the fireman, go in with a Davy lamp. At the ending, I heard my brother say there was fire[damp], and that my place was filled. He went to another place, and I observed that it fired [in] the lamp. The explosions took place instantly, but not at his lamp.'

On Tuesday, 1st October 1850, ten weeks after the disaster, coalmaster James Sneddon and his son John stood before the bar in the Glasgow Circuit Court of Justiciary to answer charges of culpable homicide and culpable neglect of duty arising from the accident at Commonhead Colliery in July. The accusations levelled against them were numerous, including failure to maintain proper ventilation in the workings, and their failure 'to provide at the bottom of the upcast vent of the shaft, a proper and sufficient furnace, or cube, and to keep a sufficient fire burning in the said furnace while the workings were going on . . . '. In addition, 'it being also their duty to prevent the miners going down when the mine had been unwrought, or without having with them safety lamps – they culpably neglected to take the above necessary precautions, in consequence of which, on the 23rd of July last, an explosion of fire damp took place, and eighteen miners lost their lives.'

The Sneddons put forward a plea of not guilty and the trial continued over the next two days. In summing up, Lord Justice Clerk prefaced his charge to the jury by observing that the defence strategy [of the Sneddons] appeared to be to fasten the blame onto the oversman. It might, he said, be perfectly evident that the overseer had neglected his duty, but that was no excuse for the manager of the pit, whose job it was not only to do his own duty, but to see that the oversman did his. In the eyes of the law, he was guilty if he failed to see that the oversman was doing his duty. The manager must have known, from the frequency with which he was down the pit, that firedamp was present and he ought to have seen that the oversman took every precaution.

The jury then retired to consider the evidence, only to emerge from their deliberations a little over half an hour later: 'they came into court, and gave in a verdict, finding James Sneddon, the father, not guilty; and, by a majority of one, the charge against John Sneddon, the son, not proven.'

The Sneddons carried on in the mining business for at least another 30 years. As for the mining community, they buried their dead and just carried on.

Chapter 2

Nos. 2 & 3 pits, Blantyre Colliery: Monday, 22nd October 1877

In 1871 William Dixon & Co. began operations at High Blantyre in the parish of Blantyre, about two miles to the west of Hamilton, and by 1877 had sunk a total of five shafts from which 700 miners had raised nearly a million tonnes of coal from the Ell, Main and Splint seams. No. 1, a downcast shaft, served the Ell and Main coal seams at 117 and 129 fathoms respectively. No. 2 at 130 fathoms and No. 3 at 155 fathoms were downcast shafts for air and were also used for winding coal from the Splint seam. No. 4 shaft, which was not at that time connected to any of the other workings, served the Splint seam at 133 fathoms. No. 5 shaft, sunk to the Splint seam at a depth of 127 fathoms, served solely as the upcast for Nos. 1, 2 and 3 pits.

Ventilation was produced by a circular furnace (or cube) at the bottom of No. 5 shaft. The furnace, which was kept burning night and day, had three fire grates, only two of which were in operation at any one time. At the top of the shaft a brick chimney rose to a height of 50 feet above the pithead buildings. The furnace consumed about five tons of coal every 24 hours and generated a total flow of around 100,000 cubic feet of air into the workings. About 50% of this volume was directed to the Splint seam by way of Nos. 2 and 3 shafts.

While the workings of Nos. 1 and 2 were connected by blind pits, the workings of Nos. 2 and 3 were connected directly to each other by passages in the Splint seam. Apart from one place where longwall working had been commenced on an experimental basis, the method of extraction at Blantyre was stoop-and-room. The rooms were generally 12 feet wide with the stoops about 20 yards square in No. 2 pit and 25 yards in No. 3.

The Splint seam workings at Blantyre covered an area of about 140 acres. The policy of forging ahead with the rooms or passages and leaving the stoops for later extraction meant that an extraordinary amount of bratticing was used to carry the air to and from the working faces. In some instances the bratticing was up to 90 yards in length and, in total, the bratticing in the Splint workings stretched for well over a mile and a quarter. One of the currents of air travelled a distance of about five miles.

Between the working faces and the shafts lay a labyrinth of temporarily abandoned rooms surrounding the formed stoops which, as stated, were to be extracted later. This vast maze of passageways was ventilated only by a leakage current (a weak current of air allowed to escape from the main current for that purpose). The length of roadway in these deserted labyrinths amounted to many miles.

Blantyre was well known to be a gassy pit and emissions of firedamp were a normal occurrence at the working faces of the Splint seam. In addition, the workings were dry and dusty. In wet conditions gas could be detected coming from the face by the bubbling or hissing sound it made as it percolated through the water, but smell was the only indicator at Blantyre. When the odour grew too strong the men used their jackets to waft (or 'dicht') the gas out from the face into the main air flow. Sometimes firedamp was noticed only when it suddenly fired off at a miner's lamp, and in such cases the miners simply threw themselves to the floor until the flame had passed over them before wafting out any feeders that continued to burn. That done, they simply went back to work. Ordinarily, naked flame tally lamps were used in all parts of the workings except in places where exceptional firedamp was being met. In the workings on the morning of 22nd October 1877 the only place where safety lamps were being used was in a section called 'the Stoopings', where the stoops were being taken out and larger accumulations of gas were being met.

A little before 4.30 a.m. that day, later than was normal, the four dayshift firemen of No. 2 pit – William Black, Alexander Watt, James Wright and Alexander Wood – descended to inspect the workings. It was their duty to examine all the working places and travelling roads in their respective sections and to test for accumulated gas at the various headings before the miners went down to start their shift. Testing for gas had also to be carried out at numerous other places, most of which were bratticed. At about 5.20 a.m., having completed their rounds and found everything to their satisfaction, they met with No. 2 oversman, Joseph Gilmour, at No. 3 pit bottom and signalled for the men to descend.

The two firemen responsible for No. 3 pit – John Little and Alexander McCall – also carried out their examination of the workings and, finding everything to be normal, signalled the surface to send the men down. On reaching the bottom the men dispersed to their regular workplaces. The firemen and John Pickering, oversman of No. 3, went with them.

Work progressed as normal until about 8.45 a.m. when Pickering arrived at No. 3 pit bottom on his way to the surface for breakfast and the customary meeting with the colliery manager, James Watson. (It was Watson's practice to meet all the pit oversmen in the morning and receive their individual reports. On average his duties took him below ground about four times a week, and sometimes twice a day, dealing with particular problems raised at these meetings.) There Pickering met Little and McCall and he invited them to travel up the shaft with him. Also travelling to the surface was young pony driver William Ferguson who was supposed to begin work that morning as a drawer. On reaching the surface they passed James Watson who at that moment was supervising the installation of a new cage at the top of No. 3 shaft.

Two minutes after they stepped out of the cage there was a noise like a steam pipe bursting and a column of flame suddenly roared from the mouth of the shaft, burning Watson about the hands and face and injuring several workmen. This blast of flame was variously recorded as being somewhere between one and four minutes in duration. At exactly the same time thick smoke and dust belched from the mouth of No. 2 shaft, the plume rising high into the air above the pithead buildings. The head frame of No. 3 was wrecked by the blast and No. 2 shaft was also disabled.

Nothing was seen at the top of No. 1 shaft, but the miners in that pit felt the shock of the blast and immediately evacuated the workings. The concussion of the explosion was felt at a considerable distance around the colliery and the smoke hanging over the pithead was seen by miners and managers in other local collieries who at once rushed to the scene. An army of some 2,000 miners were met on the road to Blantyre by local MP Alexander MacDonald, a former miner and a champion of miners' rights, who advised them, on the grounds of safety, not to descend the colliery in a mass rescue attempt.

Having received a telegram shortly after 10.00 a.m., it was about 12 noon that Mines Inspector Ralph Moore and his assistant, Mr Robson, arrived at the colliery. By that time seven bodies had been brought to the surface. Out of an estimated 233 men who had descended Nos. 2 and 3 shafts that morning, only 27 had so far emerged alive.

In No. 3 shaft the cages and ropes were found to have been damaged and some of the woodwork in the shaft had been blown out. A kettle was quickly set up and men sent down to investigate. A depth of 127 fathoms was reached before the kettle was halted by debris blocking the bottom of the shaft. However, a certain amount of air continued to pass down into the workings and, at one point, voices were heard coming from the pit bottom.

Meanwhile, shotfirer Hugh Brown, who had been stemming a hole for blasting in No. 2 workings when the explosion happened, had made his way to the bottom of the shaft. Speaking of his experiences almost 50 years later he recalled of the explosion, 'The whole place shook as if an earthquake had taken place. All sound was gone. I felt as you would feel if you were to put your fingers into your ears. This was due to the fact that the air was cut off.' At No. 2 pit bottom he and other survivors were horrified at what they saw: '. . . men dead and dying all around us. The groans of those who were alive were pitiful to hear and we discovered that the shaft was wrecked and we had no idea as to when it would be repaired.'

Brown also gave a glowing testimonial to William Grant, the Blantyre village doctor. Of this caring and courageous man, Wilma Bolton wrote: 'After the disastrous explosion in Blantyre Collieries in 1877 . . . Dr Grant was not content to wait for the survivors to be brought to the surface. He was among the first rescue parties to go underground to search the workings in indescribably dangerous conditions. He had volunteered because he knew that early medical intervention could make all the difference to the survival of the injured . . . .'

Inspectors Moore and Robson went down No. 2 shaft, accompanied by a team of engineers from the local collieries. Setting out from the pit bottom they managed to travel as far as the South level before they were halted by afterdamp and falls of roof. They noticed that Moor's dook, the incline leading to the blocked No. 3 shaft, was clear as far as could be seen, but they also came across the bodies of several victims lying within 20 yards of the shaft.

With the ventilation of the mine having been disrupted by the explosion and afterdamp found to be widespread, the party returned to the surface where, suspending rescue operations, attempts were begun to reinstate the airflow so that all parts could be entered safely. Considering the amount of bratticing used in the Splint workings – most of which had been either destroyed or displaced in the blast – this would be no mean task. However, although the furnace had been shut down and the fires withdrawn by about noon, the reduced current of air was still passing down No. 3 and along Moor's dook to the No. 5 upcast shaft.

Thanks to this natural through draught the afterdamp had begun to clear on a line between Nos. 3 and 5 shafts. Oversman John Pickering, accompanied by James Gilchrist, manager of nearby Earnock Colliery, and James Malcolm from the office at Long Lee Colliery, descended No. 2 and made their way down Moor's dook and along the Communication road towards No. 3 shaft. To them, the explosion appeared to have come from the south, the debris blown towards No. 2 pit bottom. Beside the stable near the bottom of the communication road they found a man named William Gemmell who, recognising them, called out for a drink. Gemmell was badly burned about the hands and face and told them the explosion had blown him into the sump. He died shortly afterwards. By 10.00 p.m. that night the party had managed to reach the bottom of No. 3 shaft where they found three miners alive but badly injured. One of them, a young boy, died a short time after being dug out of the debris and the other two, although dug out and taken to Glasgow Royal Infirmary, both died later of their injuries.

As the search for survivors continued throughout the night, the full magnitude of what had happened dawned on those waiting on the surface. The search was now for the dead, not the living. In an open field to the west of No. 2 shaft a covered enclosure was erected for the bodies of the victims; this became known as the 'Dead House'.

The next day the *Glasgow Herald* reported on the accident and described the scene at the

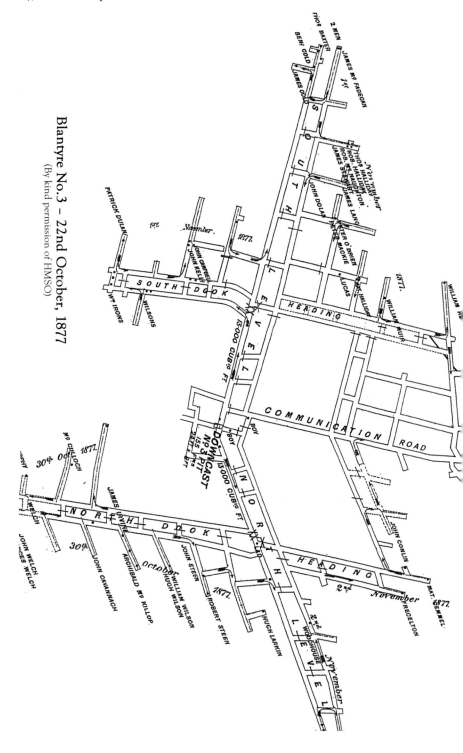

Blantyre No.3 – 22nd October, 1877
(By kind permission of HMSO)

Blantyre No.2 – 22nd October, 1877
(By kind permission of HMSO)

15

surface: 'The arrival of the dead bodies at the pithead created the greatest excitement, which arose to a painful intensity amongst the at all times excitable Irish element. The women sent up a loud wail, tore their hair, and rushed about in a half-crazed state, and strong men had to interfere to prevent them throwing themselves on the corpses.' With sightseers arriving at Blantyre Station in the thousands, 300 policemen had to be drafted in to keep them away from the pithead and tickets had to be issued at the 'Dead House' so that the genuinely bereaved could be allowed in to identify victims while keeping out the morbidly curious. The efforts of the local parish priest, the Rev. Father Donachy, to calm the 'excitable Irish element' was noted, '. . . and a quiet and more resigned air was displayed by the bereaved. These, in their community of grief, went about in companion of threes and fours, weeping piteously, and bewailing in tones which must have touched the most callous heart.'

On Tuesday 23rd steam from four boilers was pumped to the bottom of the No. 5 upcast shaft, which had the effect of improving the ventilation flow. The north and northwest workings of No. 2 were then searched as far as was possible but no bodies were found. It transpired that in the wake of the explosion several miners had been making their way towards No. 2 when they were overcome by blackdamp. Their bodies were found within 200 yards of the shaft.

Unable to venture farther, the search was temporarily suspended until the following Saturday morning (27th) when an opening was made through the rubble at the bottom of No. 3 shaft. This properly secured the ventilation between Nos. 2 and 3 shafts and the No. 5 upcast. Parties then descended No. 2 and made their way to the bottom of No. 3 where they began the task of clearing away the wreckage that had been blown from the workings into the sump, filling it and choking the shaft to five feet above the entrance to the seam.

On Sunday morning (28th) explorers began to send bodies up No. 3 shaft and by Thursday, 1st November, ventilation in No. 3 workings had been fully restored. The victims in No. 3 could now be recovered from every part of the workings.

*

On Monday, 12th November 1877, an official inquiry into the disaster was opened in the County Hall, Hamilton, presided over by advocate Robert MacLean and mines inspector Joseph Dickinson. In the course of the inquiry 44 witnesses would be called and would reply to over 8,000 questions put to them.

First to be called was Frederick Duncan, general manager for William Dixon & Co., who produced the firemen's daily report books. Although it was well known among the local miners that Blantyre was a gassy pit, an examination of the firemen's books revealed that almost no instances of gas had been recorded. Some days contained no entries of any description, not even 'all clear', and some days were found to have been signed by a fireman who was not the owner of the book. When pressed, Duncan could shed no light on these anomalies.

At the conclusion of Frederick Duncan's examination Mr Dickinson addressed the court: 'I have had given to me by Mr Dykes, the procurator fiscal, a list which shows that, at the time of the explosion, it is understood that 110 persons were down No. 3 pit, and 124 down No. 2. Of these, from No. 3 pit, four are surviving, three have died in the infirmary, and 103 were taken out dead, making 106 deaths caused by the explosion in that pit. In No. 2 pit, 23 escaped alive after the explosion, one died in the infirmary, and 100 were taken out dead, and it is supposed that there are still two more bodies in the pit, at all events there are two missing, so that we have a total of 101 dead from No. 2 pit, and 106 from No. 3 pit, making a total of 207 lives known to be lost, and two more that are missing.'

Continuing on the subject of the firemen's books, No. 3 oversman John Pickering, who with firemen Little and McCall had so narrowly escaped the blast, was asked why an explosion of firedamp two months previously in No. 2 – which had killed Joseph McInulty and severely burned his brother Andrew – had also gone unrecorded. He said he could not account for that as he 'had nothing to do with No. 2 then'. He told the court that shotfiring was a fireman's job, but the men would never wait for his arrival and would do the job themselves. He said that if there had been any gas in the old workings it would have been ignited by the explosion as it travelled along. When questioned he agreed that there must have been an 'enormous quantity of gas' collected before the explosion could have been produced.

Miners' agent William Pickard from Wigan, who appeared as an impartial witness to lend his experience to the investigation, managed to find fault with almost everything he had found at Blantyre. He did not hesitate to roundly condemn both the system of ventilation *and* the overuse of bratticing as employed at the colliery. The workings had been opened out too quickly, he said, and too much bratticing had been used. He condemned the use of naked lights in workings that apparently produced gas regularly. He maintained that the Scotch safety lamp, where used, was inadequate for the job. Discipline in the mine had been 'slack'. The furnace having been neglected for two or three hours on Sunday, he said, could have had a serious effect on the ventilation.

He was also of the opinion that the firemen's morning examinations of the workings prior to the men descending had been inadequate, the time stated by the firemen themselves for such examinations being too short. In the wake of the explosion he could not find their daily inspection marks on the various faces – adding that this was probably due to the dry dust having obliterated them during the explosion. 'In some places,' he told the court, 'you can find more than an inch of dust on the face of the coal.'

As for the extensive spread of the explosion, he said it had been of such a speed and intensity that it must have been in some way 'assisted', and this he blamed on 'the vitiated atmosphere' prevalent in the workings due to weak ventilation. All in all he had been involved in the investigation of some 30 mining accidents in England, most of them explosions, and he considered Blantyre to have been one of the most destructive.

Miner William Docherty, who was absent on the day of the explosion, gave the court an insight into the attitude of some officials to the presence of gas. In reply to a line of questioning by Edinburgh advocate R.U. Strachan (representing the deceased miners), Docherty stated he had seen gas in the stoops; it was there nearly every shift. There was one morning, he said, when none of them could get in for gas and they were sent home by fireman Robert Eadie. Docherty told Joseph Gilmour, the overman, of the gas and Gilmour swore at him and said there was no fear. Docherty told him he was afraid the gas would burst the gauze of the lamp and Gilmour swore again. That happened three days before the explosion. Docherty told him that the men would be blown up, and Gilmour replied, '. . . there was damn little fear of that. There will not be a man fall in the pit, I'll guarantee that.'

Docherty told fireman John Sharp on the Friday before the explosion that the air in the stoops was getting bad. He said there was a mist, so much so they could not see to fill their tubs. Sharp told him it was powder reek, but Docherty disagreed, it was more like steam. The working place at the Stoopings was full of gas to within two feet of the floor. Docherty said that was the case nearly every morning. He said Eadie and others were often talking about the gas, and that something would happen.

When called to give evidence William Eadie, son of fireman Robert Eadie, had a tragic story to tell. His father had often spoken to him about the gas in the workings and the carelessness of the men. His father considered the management of the mine to be 'careless', and believed not one of the firemen to be competent. Asked if his father had said there was enough fire (gas) to blow the whirleys (wheels) off the pithead frame, William said 'several times'. He told the court his father said, '. . . so much carelessness used amongst so much gas . . . he had never seen the like of in the world, and it was a disgrace to Blantyre.' He said his father told him if he had not been so long idle and the rent not due, he would never have gone down the pit.

William then related what had happened on the Thursday before the disaster: 'My father told me that this man came out with his lamp open from the stoops. My father asked him why it was open and he said he had had it open firing a shot. My father's blood ran cold, and he said, "You had it open, firing a shot with a naked light?" The man said, "Yes." My father named the number of fathoms of firedamp lying around him, and told him he might have had them all into eternity in a moment. The man said he did not know about the gas. My father then made the man sit down, and kept him there till Gilmour, the oversman, came ben, and Gilmour gave him a swearing, told him not to do the like again, and sent him off to his work.'

Robert Eadie did not go out to work for the next three days. He was easily agitated and William believed his father was afraid to go back down the pit. He told the court: '. . . I think the nerves had got the better of him those two days, for he was afraid every day he went down. He told me he never went down without a grudge on his mind for fear of it. He told me more than once that there would be an England case before long, meaning that there would be as big an explosion as had ever happened in England, and he said there would never [be] a man come out of it alive.'

On the Saturday night before the disaster William Black, the head fireman in No. 3, had come to the Eadie house and 'insisted' that William's father return to work, as a result of which he went back to work on the Monday morning. It was Black's duty to examine the workings in the morning and Eadie descended with the men. Black lost his life in the explosion, his body being found at the top of Speirs' dook. At the time William Eadie gave his evidence to the inquiry – 24 days after the disaster – his father's body had still not been found.

The contentious subjects of ventilation and bratticing also took up a considerable amount of time at the inquiry. The mine officials were confident that the volume of air coursing through the workings had been more than adequate to do the job. As for bratticing, it was universally required in mines to direct air into and out of the working places and to disperse and dilute any gases issuing from the working faces. It also served to clear, when properly directed, the old or disused workings. No one who worked at the colliery, from management down to miner, saw anything wrong with bratticing as used in Blantyre.

The preliminary report on the disaster, compiled by Inspectors Ralph Moore, Thomas E. Wales, and James Willis, was produced and read out to the court by Mr Moore on the last day of the inquiry. The inspectors' main points of criticism lay with the ventilation system, the extensive bratticing and the use of naked lights in a colliery known to produce gas.

Moore also read from Lord Aberdare's speech (as reported in *The Times*) introducing the Bill which would eventually become the Mines Regulation Act. Lord Aberdare was not prepared to increase the present number of mines inspectors – then standing at twelve – to cover the whole of Britain. Instead, he advocated that a system of voluntary inspection by the miners themselves should be introduced.

Part of Moore's testimony concerned his observations on the working operations of the mine in the context of the current regulations and, in reply to Mr Strachan, he said that unless a complaint was made to him, he had no reason to think the rules were being neglected. He had no reason to suspect that men were systematically neglecting the rules, which were laid down clearly and distinctly for their use. It was not his job to manage the colliery, he said. It was the job of the owners and officials to do so, and on those grounds he did not consider it his duty to go into the mine 'to ferret out complaints'.

Mr Strachan asked him if he was not of the opinion that if the regulations prescribed by the current Act of Parliament had been carried out in regard to the stoops – where the explosion was assumed to have originated – that the disaster might have been prevented. Moore replied that was 'supposing the explosion occurred at the stoops'. If Mr Strachan wanted him to say whether the discipline of the mine was good, he could only say that he had been astonished by the statements of the witnesses, and if such statements were correct, the discipline of the mine could not have been worse.

With all the evidence heard and the closing statements made, the inquiry began to wind down. One man, however, came forward and asked to make a statement to the court. His name was William Thomson and, far from being a mines inspector or a mining engineer, he was a joiner from Blantyre. This is what he had to say: 'Mr Moore tells us in his report that the pit is a dry one. It will follow that there must necessarily be a large amount of very fine coal dust. On one occasion Mr Watson, the manager, told me that it resembled a desert. Well, if this were brought into contact with a flame and ignited, and perhaps quantities of loose powder, would it not aggravate the force of the explosion? Whether or not it would increase the choke-damp or carbonic gas, from the large quantity of carbonised coal that was emitted from No. 5 shaft at the time of the explosion, which blackened everything for a long distance, I am impressed with the opinion that much of this dust had been in the explosion. I have made several experiments since then, not sufficient to warrant what I have stated, but enough to arouse suspicion that large quantities of loose coal dust lying in the pit would aggravate the explosion to a great extent.'

The inquiry into the Blantyre disaster was closed amid mutterings of discontent among miners and relatives of the victims. The officials went home; no doubt satisfied that every aspect of the tragic accident had been dealt with thoroughly. Joiner William Thomson also made his way home, possibly unaware that, as far as underground explosions were concerned, he had highlighted the one vital ingredient that all the so-called 'experts' had thus far missed: coal dust.

*

Almost four weeks later MacLean and Dickinson had completed their report on the Blantyre Explosion and on Friday 21st December 1877 the Rt. Hon. Richard Assheton Cross MP presented it to Parliament.

The report said that the explosion had been 'of the most violent kind'. The flame appeared to have travelled through nearly all of the working places except at the north side and the adjoining rise workings of No. 2 pit. The blast in many places 'must have been terrific'. The bodies of some victims had been torn asunder. Props had been driven away bringing down the roof, stoppings blown out, air or trap doors and wooden bratticing shattered to pieces, and tramways torn up with 'rails, sleepers, and debris being mixed together as though shot out of a gun'.

The report continued: 'In one fast place or cul de sac, through which there was no vent, the pressure had evidently been very great. In it was a group of six bodies, as though the men had been at breakfast. There were only slight traces of burning on them. One was lying face downwards, stark naked. Another with his head on one hand, but with the arm to which that hand belonged torn six inches asunder at the elbow. In other fast places, where the pressure had not been so great, bodies were to be seen burnt at a few yards from the face; whilst those within two or three yards off the face, and the face itself were unburned. Some of these bodies were [positioned] with the face outwards, as though the men had been working at the face when the first suck of the explosion came, and, turning round to escape, had perished in the pressure, flame and afterdamp . . . . Part of No. 3 shaft had the timber torn out of it, and hutches and debris, mixed with human remains, blown into it.'

When it came to the cause of the accident the report's authors assumed that, from the evidence given at the inquiry, there had been enough gas present in the workings to account for the explosion. Listing the possible 'contributing causes', they made much of the system of ventilation current in the Blantyre workings at the time of the explosion. For example one of the splits in the airflow, having ventilated all the workings in No. 3 (and undoubtedly collecting firedamp on the way), was allowed to enter No. 2 to ventilate the faces there. This air current was directed into No. 2 for the purposes of passing and ventilating a total of 63 bratticed working places one after another – no doubt still gathering firedamp as it went and carrying it into the next working place where men worked with naked lights.

The mine, they considered, had been opened out too rapidly without throughers being cut between the rooms. This practice had necessitated the erection of extensive lengths of bratticing to carry air from the main flow to the working faces and back – in some cases to within less than two yards of the face (and in one case only four feet). Had throughers been cut regularly, they said, the airflow could have been directed closer to the faces without the need for miles of bratticing. Criticism was also voiced at the cubemen's practice of banking up the fires and leaving their post an hour or more before their shift ended. In addition, when cleaning out the furnaces, the fire was reduced in one while the bars were cleaned. This meant that one of the two furnaces was '. . . at the time of the explosion, not in full operation.'

The firemen's morning examinations of the workings also came in for criticism. The authors noted that, from the individual firemen's own evidence, the times given to complete the task of examining every working face and bratticed place in their particular section was inadequate in the extreme. In many cases the times given, and the distances involved, were incompatible with each other. John Pickering, overseman of No. 3 pit, had stated that such examinations must have been carried out at running pace. Although the firemen's report books showed that the mine was dealt with as one producing firedamp, the ventilation forms that the firemen completed were set out under General Rule 3 of the Coal Mines Regulation Act, 1872 – which applied to mines *not* producing firedamp. That was the reason why so many instances of firedamp at Blantyre went unrecorded. The books issued to the firemen should have been kept under General Rule 2 which contained questions appropriate to mines actively producing firedamp. The blame for this confusion in the report books was laid (lamely) at the door of the stationer who had, apparently, sent the wrong books. The error was not discovered until the inquiry brought it to light.

Where the gas came from and the point where it ignited could not be decided upon with any amount of certainty. Because of the violence of the explosion and the extent of the damage caused it remained a matter of surmise. As it was one of the places in the workings known to produce much gas and was totally destroyed in the explosion, Speirs' dook was considered most likely to have been where the ignition occurred.

The discipline of the workforce in general at Blantyre was considered to be less than it should have been. As far as explosives and blasting operations were concerned, just about every possible instruction in General Rule 8 of the Coal Mines Regulation Act had been systematically ignored. The Blantyre miners, it was pointed out, had not availed themselves of their right to inspect the workings on their own behalf and to their own satisfaction, as they were fully entitled to do under General Rule 30. This particular rule would have allowed them to complain to their superiors about the dangers of gas. Having said that, the inspectors also pointed out that '. . . representations of danger by the miners are said to have been sometimes rudely received by the oversman of No. 2 [Joseph Gilmour]'.

The authors of the report were at pains to assuage public opinion regarding the culpability of the mines inspectors. They believed 'a portion of the public' sought to impose responsibility for such accidents upon the government inspectors themselves. But the inspectors could not be everywhere at once, they said, and a place – once inspected – could deteriorate and an accident occur shortly after their leaving. Instead, the owner, agent, and manager, unless they could prove that the rules had been published and enforced, became answerable not only for their own non-compliances, but for those of subordinates and miners. The colliery manager, they said, was exceptionally responsible. The report concluded: 'The miners as a body are an intelligent and unobtrusive class of men. Being constantly exposed to danger they learn to deal coolly with things which would terrify an inexperienced person. They generally know when more than usual danger surrounds.' But they added that in this instance the miners had failed to make their own inspection of the workings and report, direct to the inspector, any concerns that arose.

In their summing up the authors listed all that had been wrong – all that had been dangerous – about the system in operation at Blantyre, ultimately laying the blame on everyone in general and no one in particular. 'No penalty that could be imposed under the Coal Mines Act,' they stated, 'would be at all appropriate to this awful catastrophe . . . . Nearly every man who had any share in the occurrence lost his life.' Then, having thoughtlessly pointed out that 'The owners are severe sufferers by the wreck of property and the expense of, and delay in, restoration', they proceeded to deliver this chilling warning: 'The most alarming part of the evidence is that which shows that within a radius of two miles of Hamilton West railway station (in which Blantyre Colliery is situated) fourteen new collieries, with 32 pits, varying from 120 to 180 fathoms in depth, are either being sunk or the coal being worked under the same system of stoop-and-room as at Blantyre, and that all of them give off firedamp. One of these collieries, situated at Cadzow, has opened the same seam as that in which the explosion took place at Blantyre, and the issue of gas has at present caused the working to be discontinued.

'Unless warning be taken from what has happened at Blantyre, and such seams be opened out slower, with fewer places and much less bratticing until the gas has been drained, and proper attention be given with respect to discipline and the use of lights and powder, the present explosion may, it is to be feared, be only the first of a series of similar catastrophes, such as have run through several other districts.'

The one startling point that had emerged from the inquiry into the Blantyre disaster was that almost every rule in the regulations relating to safe working practice was being flouted on a daily basis. It would appear that the men chose to ignore the rules in the effort to reach their quota and earn a living wage; and, for the sake of productivity, the firemen allowed it to happen. Some firemen, in their defence, spoke of 'sending men out' in the past because of gas, but they still allowed the rules to be broken as a matter of course.

From the admittedly common practice of using their jackets to waft away and disperse explosive gas, we have a picture of men who were all but inured to danger as they worked with naked lights in what must have been the most hazardous environment imaginable. And while the miners might simply have 'got on with the job' when danger threatened, it was the duty of the on-site company officials, the oversmen and firemen, to enforce those rules designed to avoid such catastrophes. While miners' agent William Pickard told the inquiry that in his opinion the mine was 'too dusty', he blamed the speed and spread of the explosion solely on 'the vitiated atmosphere' prevalent in the workings. He made no mention of coal dust as a factor in the spread of the explosion.

In their report Messrs MacLean and Dickinson included in their summary: 'That the mine being very dry and dusty, and the coal of an inflammable kind, materially helped to spread the flame and blast of the explosion.' This seemingly radical theory was first put forward at the closing of the inquiry by joiner William Thomson and, in a report that placed a great deal of emphasis on the dangers of gas and the importance of proper ventilation, this was the only reference the authors made to coal dust.

But there were those who had already warned of its dangers. In 1830, commenting on an underground explosion at a Jarrow colliery that had taken 42 lives, John Buddle, colliery viewer and inventor, said that coal dust '. . . is deposited in every part of the workings within the range of the fire. This dust flies in all directions in luminous sparks, similar to those discharged from the chimney of an engine, which are frequently propelled by the force of the explosion to a considerable distance beyond where the flame of the ignited gas reaches. They scorch and wound those who may happen to be within their reach, and frequently set fire to any combustible substance they may fall upon – sometimes the coal itself.' Even earlier, in 1828, Robert Bald, Scottish mining engineer and writer, wrote that underground fires in collieries were sometimes caused '. . . by the blast of an explosion, which is a magazine of blue and white flame of intense heat, which sets fire to the small coal dust of the roads in the mines.'

It had long been known in the mining industry that the inhalation of coal dust could be dangerous to health, more often than not leading to respiratory complaints such as black lung. However, what was not generally known (or, for that matter, accepted) at that time was that the same dry coal dust – if caught in the air by the concussion and flame of a firedamp explosion – could turn what might ordinarily have been a local flash-fire into a rolling explosion: a relentless fireball that could traverse a whole seam and its miles of passageways in a matter of seconds. In Blantyre it had claimed the lives of over 200 men and boys. Unfortunately, although it had at last been highlighted, it had yet to be understood and recognised as the silent killer it had always been.

*

The true death toll of the Blantyre disaster was never established. Both reports listed 207 victims with two missing. However, the list recently researched by Andrew Paterson of Blantyre is probably as close as anyone will ever come to the truth. He gives a figure of 215 named victims, corresponding with the death certificates issued in the wake of the disaster – which remains Scotland's worst ever mining accident. About six months after the disaster, William Dixon & Co. – who, in the aftermath of the tragedy, had spared no effort to show the caring side of mine owning – let the mask slip and added their own pathetic footnote to the story. Finding that their tied houses were needed for replacement miners, they evicted the widows and children of men who had lost their lives.

Chapter 3

No. 1 pit, Blantyre Colliery:
Wednesday, 2nd July 1879

'. . . and only on Wednesday, the day of the accident, there was reported in the newspapers, under the heading 'How Explosions are Caused', a prosecution at the instance of Wm. Dixon (Limited) against John McLean, miner, Burnbank, who was charged with contravening the seventh General Rule by unlocking his lamp while working in the splint seam of No. 2 Pit at High Blantyre. Sheriff Spens, who heard the case, referred to the explosion which took place in this pit in 1877, and said that no one had yet been able to explain the cause of that explosion, though he rather took it to have been in some such way as the case under his review had disclosed . . . . As it was, there had been no fire-damp in the mine since April, and a lenient view having been taken of the case, a penalty of £2, with the alternative of three months imprisonment, was imposed.'

– The *Glasgow Herald*, 4th July 1879

It had been almost two years since over 200 lives were lost in Scotland's worst colliery disaster and, to a large extent, Blantyre and the surrounding villages were still in mourning. It seemed that everyone, if not directly related to one of the victims, had known someone who perished on that terrible Monday morning in October 1877, and those who were gone were still spoken of, still remembered.

Charles Thomson was the managing owner at William Dixon's Blantyre Colliery and under him, since the great disaster of 1877, Shenton Thomas had been appointed general manager over all the collieries of Blantyre. James Watson, who had been manager at the time of the disaster, still retained the manager's post with Robert Robson appointed as assistant manager.

At the colliery things appeared much the same as before but, underground, crucial changes had taken place. The system of ventilation, condemned two years before, had been markedly improved. According to the *Glasgow Herald* (4th July 1879) '. . . it [was] generally admitted by all who have personal acquaintance with the working of pits that those at High Blantyre are what might be called models of ventilation.' And, while naked flame (tally) lamps had been widely used in the Blantyre pits in 1877, safety lamps (Clanny and Davy) were now used throughout the workings. The ordinary Scotch safety lamp was no longer in use. Naked lights were allowed only at the bottom of No. 1, which was a downcast shaft, and as far as the lamp station about 100 yards along the level. Beyond that point only safety lamps were allowed and a notice on the wall reminded the miners of that fact. The total underground workforce numbered 660 men, 500 of these working day shift production and 160 on night shift to prepare the workings for the day workers. The Ell coal workforce numbered 100 on day shift and 30 on night shift.

Of the five shafts Nos. 1, 2, 3 and 5 were connected, with No. 4 being separated from the others by a pair of strongly built brick walls. These walls each contained a door, making them available as a second outlet. No. 1, sunk to serve the Ell coal at 117 fathoms and the Main coal at 129 fathoms, carried 3,000 cubic feet of air into the Ell coal workings. The Main coal, which had been worked using the longwall method, was abandoned the previous November and bricked off. No. 5, with the cube located at the bottom of the shaft, still served as the upcast for all the other shafts.

The Ell coal workings extended north from the bottom of No. 1 shaft for a distance of 900 yards and to the south for 770 yards. Both sections had been worked in part by the stoop-and-room and longwall methods. In the north section stoop-and-room was still in operation in a few places, with the longwall places standing idle. In the south the reverse was the case, with the stoop-and-room places idle and the longwall workings – situated beyond the stoop-and-room section – being worked. These workings were reached by way of a road known as the south level.

The longwall workings lay to the west side of the south level and extended over an area of some six to eight acres, with a rise of 1 in 12 from the level to the working faces. The Ell seam was about five feet thick in that area with the roads driven every fifteen yards. Four feet of stone had to be removed from above the coal before it could be extracted and this was done by a back shift brushing squad.

Firedamp – which had been discounted by certain officials prior to the great disaster, but later proved to be rife – was occasionally encountered in the Ell coal workings, but to no great degree. The last instance had been 17th May 1879 when the fireman reported all the workings to be 'in a safe condition between four and five o'clock a.m., with the exception of a little gas in the [No. 2] heading cundy in the longwall.'

Despite the fact six miners had plummeted to their deaths down the shaft in March 1878 as a result of an overwinding accident, No. 1 pit was considered by the men who worked the different shifts as the safest of all the Blantyre pits.

*

Shortly after 9.00 p.m. on Wednesday, 2nd July 1879, those at work around the pithead were startled by a violent explosion, later described as being like 'the report of a dynamite cartridge'. Alexander McMillan, the night shift pithead man at No. 1, heard the blast and witnessed dust coming up the shaft and the cage and pulley wheels shudder. He ran to get John White, the oversman, who lived about 150 yards away and happened to be standing at the door of his house. White went with him immediately to No. 1 shaft and James Malone, fireman at No. 1, arrived at the same time.

Before sending anyone below, White sent the empty cage down the shaft to make certain that all was clear. The cage stopped about six feet short of the Ell coal level and, when they attempted to draw it up again, it became stuck. With access blocked from No. 1 White went down No. 3 shaft and found the men there unaware that anything had happened. John Pickering, oversman in No. 3 splint, along with William Gilchrist, oversman in No. 4 pit, and others who had gathered at No. 3 pit bottom made their way through the communication to No. 1 shaft. They were shortly joined by White, manager James Watson, fireman James Malone, and a host of volunteers.

The immediate task was to find the seat of the explosion and rescue the men who, it was known, were all working in the south side workings. While preparations were made to travel along the level road towards the longwall workings, parties were sent both into the Ell coal north workings and below to the Main coal level. About 20 yards to the north of No. 1 pit bottom the brickwork of an overcast was found to be blown down, but there was no evidence of any other damage to the north workings. The Main coal workings, it transpired, had not been disturbed. Efforts were then concentrated on the south workings.

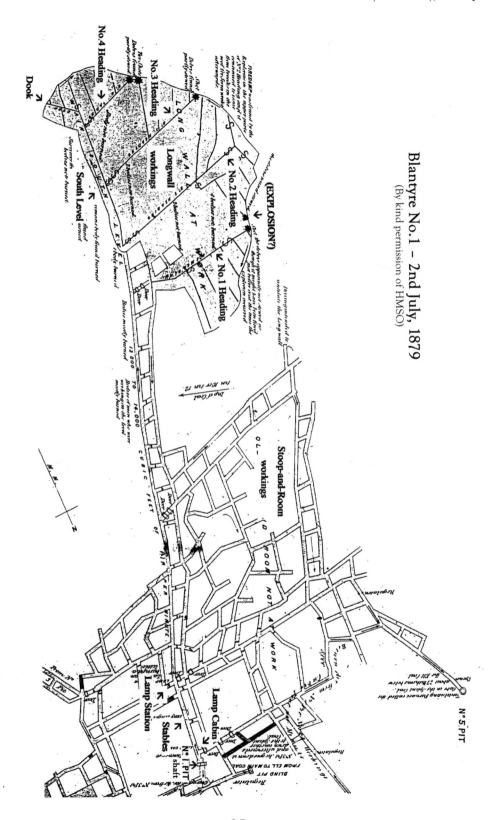

Blantyre No.1 – 2nd July, 1879
(By kind permission of HMSO)

On the south side of No. 1 shaft the explorers found a considerable amount of wreckage. As they followed the air course along the level they passed the lamp cabin, which had been completely destroyed, and farther on found a pony near the stables which, though alive, had been singed by the blast. They came to the lamp station which, with its door blown in, was also destroyed. There, lying in the wreckage, they found Thomas Irvine, the No. 1 pit bottomer who was also authorised to trim the miners' lamps. He was still alive but had sustained serious injuries.

Brandy was sent for and Irvine was able to tell them that the blast had happened abruptly, coming forcibly into the cabin. Leaving brusher Peter Lindsay to comfort Irvine in the wrecked lamp station (he died before he could be brought to the surface), they carried on along the level. Travelling past many falls of roof, the party eventually reached a point about midway between the stoop-and-room and longwall workings, about 400 yards from the pit bottom, where they had to halt due to the strong smell of afterdamp.

On the right hand side of the level all the brick stoppings erected between the intake and return airways had been blown out, destroying the ventilation beyond that point. Being unable to travel farther into the workings without air, brattice cloth was sent for so that temporary stoppings could be erected in an effort to restore the ventilation. The work of replacing the shattered stoppings took up valuable time, but there was no alternative. Travelling deeper into the workings, the necessity of carrying fresh air with them soon became abundantly clear.

Erecting brattice stoppings as they went, they carried on past the longwall workings, finding several bodies lying on the road. As they progressed, some of the explorers inadvertently got ahead of the incoming air. Being overcome by afterdamp, they fell unconscious and had to be carried out by their colleagues. Manager James Watson and oversman John White had become two such casualties when they reached No. 4 heading, just short of the dook at the end of the level. The condition of the former was such that he was reported 'to be dying' and the latter was carried out in a semi-conscious state. As he was being helped out by Lindsay, White heard the cry that living men had been found and told Lindsay, 'Leave me, for God's sake, and go and get out the living men.' Both White and Watson were taken to the surface where they eventually recovered, White returning to the workings three days later and Watson the day after.

That night there was no repeat of the scenes of uncontrolled hysteria that had marked the great disaster of 1877. The accident occurring as late as it did, when few were about except those who were on backshift duty, it was some time before the word of it spread. The news reached Blantyre Police Station about 11.00 p.m., and a message was immediately sent to the County Constabulary at Hamilton. From there, Chief Constable McHardy and a team of men proceeded to the colliery, where comparatively few people had yet assembled. It was after midnight before the news began to pass from house to house through the village, and an anxious crowd quickly gathered round the pitheads of Nos. 1 and 3 shafts.

As the *Glasgow Herald* of 4th July 1879 reported: 'Amongst those people, many of whom had been roused from sleep, and had relatives or acquaintances in the mine, the greatest excitement prevailed; but perfect order was preserved. When the actual extent of the disaster became known, the excitement actually diminished, though in its lessened proportions there was still matter to preserve amongst the onlookers a most uneasy and gloomy feeling. The Irish portion of the population of Stonefield and High Blantyre had special cause to lament the occurrence, for it was known that the greater part of the men in the ill-fated Ell workings were Irishmen; and the grief of the women was very pitiful to witness.'

In the meantime, the explorers had penetrated as far as the top of the dook at the end of the level and came across five men who were still alive. Unfortunately John Newton died as he was being taken out and Bernard Cairns, having reached the surface, died in the engine house. The other three, James Owens, Bernard O'Neill and Charles Lafferty – 16-year-old son of fireman James who lost his life – were taken to the surface in safety.

These men were all treated by local physician Dr William Grant who had treated the injured in the Blantyre workings two years before. Once again he was prepared to risk his life for the sake of others and he immediately requested to be taken down the mine. In the company of several miners, this exceptionally brave family doctor picked his way through the wreckage of the workings until he reached the unconscious rescue party. He treated the men on the spot and then accompanied them to the pithead where, after handing them over to the care of another doctor, he went back down the shaft.

With the blown out brick stoppings temporarily replaced by brattice, ventilation was slowly being returned to the workings and the search was continued. The victims, when found, were carried to the surface. The longwall faces were reached and explored, but the persistence of firedamp prevented entry to No. 1 heading. By Thursday morning, 27 of the 31 men known to have been in the workings had been accounted for, of whom 24 were dead. It was not until around 4.00 a.m. on Friday morning that access was gained to the No. 1 heading and the last four bodies were found and taken out. Ventilation having now been fully restored to the Ell coal level and the gas dispersed, the officials were able to make their inspections of the workings. With all the victims recovered and returned to their families, the mining community of Blantyre was left once again to mourn its loss.

The national press had covered the story from the first day and many of those involved had encountered the reporters who were waiting among the pithead crowd. Despite the fact he had just lost his father in the tragedy, Charles Lafferty was met by a reporter and urged to tell his own story. While no doubt grasping the vital facts, the reporter appears to have tinkered a little with the sixteen-year-old's language (the national press, as usual, being unable to cope with a regional dialect): 'I was working a considerable distance away from the main way at the coalface,' Charles told the reporter. 'There were several other men engaged near me . . . . About nine o'clock we heard a loud explosion coming from the west workings . . . and immediately afterwards there was a rush of gas along the workings. I was thrown violently against the coalface and then hurled on a heap of coal and much bruised and almost knocked insensible, but I managed to pick myself up. The gas was very strong and I could hardly breathe. I tried to get to the main way but I was driven back by the gas. After a little time I made another effort and this time I was able to get to the main way. I found another man who was endeavouring to make his way to the bottom. We went together a little way, but my companion became exhausted and dropped down saying he could go no further.'

Young Lafferty was unconscious when he was found near the top of the dook, but his companion – John Newton, lying just a few yards away – died as he was being taken out.

*

The inquiry into the second Blantyre disaster was held over Thursday 4th and Friday 5th September 1879, in Hamilton Court House. The proceedings were presided over by Mines Inspector Joseph Dickinson who had studied the precognitions of 67 witnesses taken by Mr Dykes, Procurator Fiscal. Before holding the inquiry Mr Dickinson had also studied the earlier report of William Alexander, Mines Inspector for the Western Division of Scotland, and Ralph Moore, Inspector for the Blantyre

District, who had examined the Ell coal workings in the immediate aftermath of the explosion. Their joint findings, dated 12th July 1879, had already been presented to Parliament.

Many of the witnesses testified as to the safety of No. 1 pit, that the ventilation was sound and the general conditions good. Many thought it was the safest pit in the colliery – so safe, in fact, that some thought it almost unnecessary to use safety lamps. Manager James Watson said the stoppings, doors and screens had been rebuilt in the last fifteen months and were made as tight as possible with bricks and mortar. When it reached the longwall workings, the south side ventilation flow (about 13,000 cubic feet per minute) continued on to the face, its course directed by means of pillars of coal, wallings, stoppings, doors and screens. The spent air left the longwall workings, travelling towards No. 5 upcast shaft via the return airway running parallel to the level.

James Owens, one of the three brushers who had escaped, said he had never heard of firedamp being in the pit until about four months previously when he spoke to night shift fireman James Lafferty. Lafferty, who did not survive the blast, told him there was a little firedamp at the top of the brushing in the top of No. 2 heading. Owens had always considered Lafferty to be a careful fireman. Miner John McGhee told the court he had worked in No. 3 heading and had never seen firedamp there. He had been a miner for 44 years and 'had never worked in a better aired pit'. A naked light, he said, would have been quite safe.

William Nallis, a miner who worked in a branch off No. 2 heading, said he never saw any gas in the south section, the air being too strong. That being the case several times he asked oversman John White and assistant manager Robert Robson if his men could be allowed to use open lights, but White and Robson stuck strictly to the rules and disallowed their use. (While the Clanny and Davy were safety lamps, the illumination given out by a naked light was much stronger than either.)

John McMillan, oversman of No. 2 pit, told of how he helped in the exploration of No. 1 Ell coal following the explosion. It was he who found the body of fireman James Lafferty lying on the level just beyond No. 3 heading. The glass of Lafferty's watch was broken and he noted that the hands were standing at ten minutes past nine. McMillan was later overcome by afterdamp and was taken to the surface.

James Owens, Charles Lafferty and Bernard O'Neill each told the court what happened to them between the time of the explosion and the arrival of the explorers at the top of the dook beyond No. 4 heading. At or shortly after 9.00 p.m. fireman James Lafferty, doing his rounds, had come down the dook to check that work was progressing without problems. He spoke to the six men – Owens, O'Neill, John Newton, Tague Boyle, Bernard Cairns and his own son Charles – then left, walking back up the dook to the level.

About two minutes after he left, young Lafferty and Newton, repairing brickwork at the side of the main road about ten or twelve feet from the face of the level, heard a loud report and 'they were thrown down and their lamps extinguished'. Twelve yards from the face of the level Owens, working with Cairns, also heard the report and had their lights blown out. He told Cairns, 'She has blasted', but Cairns thought it was only a shot being fired. O'Neill, working with Boyle farther down the dook, heard nothing, but a strong gust came in and blew out their lights. O'Neill thought it came from a heavy shot.

The men, knowing their surroundings well, came out from their workplaces in the dark and, meeting up, began to make their way out of the dook. They found, however, they could only get so far before they met with afterdamp, which drove them back into the dook. As though to leave them in no doubt that something serious had happened, a piece of burning cloth had been blown into the dook beside them. For around 20 minutes they sat at the top of the dook waiting for assistance, but with no sign of life coming from the level or the longwall workings, they decided they should try to reach the shaft.

They groped their way along the level for a distance of about 20 yards, but meeting with heated afterdamp, they returned to the dook. After a time they tried again to make their way along the level, but again they were unsuccessful. They returned to the head of the dook to await rescue. As they sat in the dark the afterdamp crept slowly towards them and each, in turn, became unconscious. By the time rescuers reached them Tague Boyle had died, and John Newton died as he was being carried out. Bernard Cairns died in the engine house at the surface.

At the inquiry much was made of the absence of discipline among the workforce in the Ell coal workings. Of the 31 men working that evening only two were known to be non-smokers, and many illegal items were found in the pockets of the victims when they were searched. These were listed as pipes, tobacco, lucifer matches and nails adapted to open safety lamps. In the aftermath of the disaster some lamps were found to have been opened and, in No. 1 heading, men were found to have been smoking at the time of the explosion. The lamp book, in which was daily recorded the number of each lamp and the name of the miner it was issued to, could not be produced, having somehow disappeared.

Other matters were covered in some detail including reports of firedamp found in the workings in recent months (some was found but considered not enough to merit a report in the firemen's books). Also covered was the amount of explosive used in different shots and the procedure used in firing those shots.

The main questions laid before the inquiry were: 1) where exactly in the workings was the point of ignition?; and 2) what caused the gas to ignite? The first could not be easily determined due to the various directions taken by the initial blast before it left the longwall workings. The second question had two possible answers, the first being that gas had fired at an open lamp, and the second – more ominous – that gas had fired at a naked flame, possibly a lucifer match struck by someone having a smoke.

*

On Friday, 12th September 1879, Inspector Dickinson concluded the official investigation into the circumstances surrounding the second Blantyre Colliery Disaster, his report being passed to the Rt. Hon. R.A. Cross MP, Secretary of State, for presentation to Parliament.

It was Dickinson's opinion that the explosion took place at ten minutes past nine in the evening. This was arrived at from the statements of the majority of witnesses and the evidence of James Lafferty's watch. He described the findings of the rescuers as they made their way into the Ell coal seam; the wreckage of the workings, the positions of the victims and their injuries, and the finding of the five men alive at the top of the dook, two of whom did not survive.

Ventilation, ventilating power and the quantity of air passing through the workings he considered more than adequate for the mine. Inspection of the workings was also considered sufficient. However, when firedamp was found and dealt with to the satisfaction of the officials, it was not always entered into the firemen's book as required by the rules.

In trying to determine where the explosion originated the testimony of the colliery manager, James Watson, had brought a little order to the confusion. When Watson began to examine the workings he had taken a note of the position of the bodies of the victims. He also paid particular attention to the direction from which the blast appeared to have come. He was certain from his inspection that all the stoppings in the throughers along the level had been blown uphill, and that all the doors to the entrance of No. 1 heading were also blown upwards. The screens at the bottom of No. 2 heading had been blown downwards into the level. Those at No. 3 heading had been slightly damaged, but as to those of No. 4 he could not state as he had been overcome by afterdamp before he could see them, and they had all been put right again by the time he returned.

Following his inspection Watson was of the opinion that, where he found firedamp at the face between Nos. 1 and 2 headings, the force (which had been slight there) became greater as the heat had increased. The blast had gone down No. 2 heading where it blew out the screens at the foot, and some of the force had gone inwards along the level. To a much greater degree, however, the blast had travelled out towards No. 1 shaft, feeding upon the incoming air and the dust. This was indicated by pieces of grit being indented into the faces of the posts. He believed that the explosion must have occurred at a naked light.

General manager Shenton Thomas corroborated his manager's evidence. He thought the explosion occurred at the top of No. 2 heading, where two men were taking down the roof, and who might, as they worked, have liberated a quantity of firedamp. It must have been a sudden outburst of firedamp and was kindled by a naked light. The bodies of the two workmen were found further down, not burned, and their lamps were locked. It was a common thing, he said, for the man who lit the gas to escape burning.

In reviewing discipline in the mine Inspector Dickinson commented that the rules concerning the examination and locking of safety lamps, and the prohibitions on having lamp keys or contrivances for unlocking lamps, lucifer matches and tobacco pipes in their possession, were supposed to be rigidly enforced. Not even the manager, oversman, or firemen were allowed to carry a lamp key, and if anyone required to have his lamp opened he had to go to the man at the lamp station to have it done.

Dickinson also stated that the results of the explosion showed that discipline on the night shift was lax. Beyond the lamp station, in the clothes of the men or in close proximity to where they had been working, there had been found lucifer matches, some of which had been struck and others not, and tobacco pipes, some of which contained tobacco that had been partially smoked. Added to which, although no lamp had been found actually open, some were found unlocked, and some of the men had possessed either lamp keys or contrivances for unlocking the lamps.

Later, agreeing with the statements of Watson and Thomas, Dickinson gave his conclusion: 'Some of the witnesses, I think, judging by the fact that on the level outside the headings where the greatest traces of force were exhibited, seem to have arrived at the conclusion that it was there that the explosion originated; but I may say that that is a fallacy, and that I have seen it demonstrated by experiment that the greatest damage is done nearest to the intake and furthest from the point of ignition.

'That I believe is borne out both by actual results in the inspections generally and by experiment, so that I think those witnesses who stated that the explosion originated up at the top of No. 2 heading, and that it rushed down there and drove out the sheets at the bottom, and then drove everything from it right and left as it went out, have given a correct position for the origin of the explosion.'

It would appear that the ignition most likely occurred at the top of No. 2 heading. The blast from the explosion had travelled down the heading, blowing out the double screens at the bottom of the incline and thereby gaining access to the level and the incoming air. The force of the explosion then split to left and right. Some of the blast force blew down the double doors and penetrated up No. 1 heading. The main blast, however, had travelled along the level, blowing out the brick stoppings between the intake and return one after another, feeding on the incoming air and the dry coal dust as it headed for No. 1 pit bottom. The reason the blast failed to sweep the dook where the survivors were found was probably due to air pressure in the cul-de-sac and the fact it had already found a greater supply of air and a way out in the opposite direction.

Mr Dickinson stated that five shots had been fired that night and an examination of the debris blown down in the five different places showed that three of them had been partially cleared away, indicating that the shots had been fired at some time before the explosion. However, the other two shots showed little or no evidence of being cleared away, indicating they had been fired 'very recently before, if not at the time the explosion occurred'. He also observed that if either of these two shots had been fired at the time the explosion occurred, it could not have been fired by the section fireman, James Lafferty, who, at that time, was on his way out of the dook. Regardless of who fired them, if neither of these shots was responsible for the explosion, then one of them may have been responsible for releasing the gas that eventually ignited and swept the workings.

Exactly what caused the ignition is a question that will now never be answered. In the aftermath of the disaster many of the miners' safety lamps were found to have been unlocked, but as far as is known, none were found to have been opened. Not all the safety lamps taken out at the beginning of the shift were accounted for. Some had gone missing. Thomas Irvine, the man who trimmed the lamps, had died in the wreckage of the lamp station, the subject was not raised at the inquiry, and the lamp book itself mysteriously disappeared.

If the gas did not flare at a shot or an open lamp then the alternative is unthinkable. The only other source of flame found in the workings that night were lucifer matches. Did someone, in what was known to be a gas producing mine, unthinkingly strike a match to have a smoke, only to send himself and his workmates into oblivion?

*

Three years later Robert Galloway would write in his *History of Coal Mining in Great Britain*: 'Much attention has been directed of late to the probability of coal-dust playing an important part in propagating indefinitely the flame arising from a small local explosion, whether of gunpowder or fire-damp. Herein it is supposed lies the secret of the mysterious violence which has characterised some explosions, which have occurred under circumstances where it appeared almost impossible to account for the presence of a volume of fire-damp sufficient to produce the results.' Highlighted by joiner William Thomson at the inquiry into the 1877 tragedy, the danger posed by dry, airborne coal dust in an underground explosion was now being recognised by the powers that be. But it was still not understood, and it would be some time before measures were taken to combat its deadly force.

Chapter 4
Udston Colliery, Hamilton:
Saturday, 28th May 1887

Udston Colliery, owned by the Udston Coal Company, was situated about three miles outside the town of Hamilton. Originally sunk on the lands of Udston Farm in 1874, the royalty covered around 150 acres and was bordered by the collieries of Blantyre on the west, and Earnock and Greenfield on the east.

Udston had two shafts working three seams. No. 1 shaft (the upcast) serviced the Main coal seam at 140 fathoms, and No. 2 shaft (the downcast) serviced both the Ell coal at 125 fathoms and the Splint coal at 150 fathoms. The Splint seam, in which the disaster took place, was first sunk to in 1883/84, and by May 1887 about two-thirds of the property had been driven into. Ventilation for the mine was provided by a 20-feet-in-diameter Guibal fan near the head of No. 1, which was connected to the enclosed shaft by a fan drift. The system used for extracting coal in Udston Colliery was stoop-and-room, with the stoops varying in size from 20 to 40 yards square. The underground workforce at the time of the disaster totalled 185 – 46 in the Ell coal, 66 in the Main coal, and 73 in the Splint coal.

At the beginning of the working day each section fireman would descend to inspect the workings and other places in the seam, this being done to check the safety of the roof and to test for gas. This inspection was normally carried out an hour or so before the shift arrived to start work. It was also an everyday rule of the colliery that the section fireman put his mark on each working face to show he had been there that morning and had made his inspection.

The fireman was next required, when he had signalled for the miners to descend, to examine their safety lamps before he permitted them to travel to their workplaces. Each of the firemen had around 35 lamps to examine and these examinations took place in one of the three lamp rooms in the Splint seam. Safety lamps were obligatory in all sections of the Splint seam except at the bottom of the downcast shaft and in the three lamp rooms, where open gauze lamps were kept for re-lighting and trimming the miners' lamps. Although the lamps were colliery property, the men usually took them home for the purposes of cleaning them.

The type of lamp carried by all the working miners was the Scotch gauze lamp. While these lamps could come in two different sizes with two different gauges of wire mesh screen, what was uniform about them was that they were unshielded. They also had no pricker or any other means of raising or lowering the wick, and that being the case, an occasional visit to the lamp room was necessary to have the wick trimmed. A slot-head screw on the side casing served to lock the lamps and opening them outwith the lamp room was highly illegal.

Physical searches of miners for tobacco, matches, or nails to open their lamps were not authorised by the Principal Act of 1872, current at that time. Searches were occasionally carried out by the firemen, but they were very infrequent and usually provoked complaints from the men. With their daily inspections over, the firemen sent their report books back to the surface with the first lift of coal up the shaft.

The presence of accumulated firedamp in the workings was not held to be common. The manager, James Gavin, stated he had never seen any indication of firedamp being present in the air returning from the Splint seam, and to his knowledge none had ever been reported in the firemen's books. Firedamp was nevertheless being reported periodically by the firemen. Every day from the 4th to the 7th of January gas was found at Quin's stooping by Alexander Torlay, one of the two firemen responsible for the Splint seam. He also made an entry in his daybook on Monday, 9th May – almost three weeks before the disaster – that he had found 'a little gas' in Berrie's stooping in the Blantyre section. In Udston, firedamp was never considered to be enough of a problem that the ordinary ventilation current coursing through the mine could not adequately disperse, and the firemen's entries generally read 'all clear'.

The workings in the Splint seam were, however, very dry and generally dusty – more especially so in the horse roads. The Splint coal in itself was particularly flammable and, although the coal lying at the faces was more round and comparatively free from fine dust, the horse roads tended to become very dusty. This dust was highly combustible and an average of two or three hutches of it was removed from these roads on a daily basis and, added to manual clearing, the roads were sometimes watered to comply with the 1887 Coal Mines Act which stated that dust must be watered for a radius of 20 yards in the vicinity of a gunpowder shot.

*

On the morning of Saturday, 28th May 1887, oversman Edward Torlay descended to the Splint seam at around 5.55 a.m., an hour earlier than he would normally have done on a week day. At No. 2 pit bottom he met his son, fireman Alexander Torlay, who had by that time completed his inspection of the workings, and they both entered their reports in the book before parting company. It would be the last time that Edward would see his son alive.

Leaving the pit bottom, he travelled to the top of the stooping on the east horse road level where he found miners John Wilson and Joseph Neilson. One of the fireman's tasks was to check if a miner's workplace was safe to leave before they moved to another area and Wilson asked Torlay if he would check theirs as they intended to move on after they had tidied up. Torlay examined the place, assured them all was well, and left them filling loose coal into a hutch.

He then walked into the west level and visited every face in the three stoopings where work was being carried out, finding everything to his satisfaction and the men at work as usual. He next toured the rise division of the east section, examining every room in the section whether it was being worked or not. Amongst these places was Denniston's in which blasting was allowed, but the Denniston brothers, William and Thomas, appeared to have made no preparations for shotfiring. Torlay, having tested for firedamp at every face he visited that morning, had so far found no trace of gas.

He next entered Harkness's place which, like Denniston's, had at that time been given authorisation to carry out blasting operations. He met and spoke to John Harkness but, as with Dennison's, he did not notice any preparations being made to fire shots. Harkness had about two hutches of coal lying already worked. As he had done in Denniston's, Torlay went to the face and put his Davy lamp to the head, but did not detect any gas. He finished his rounds by going back to where Wilson and Neilson were working and found them still there and still at work. All places in the Splint seam were clear of gas, the ventilation was flowing as it should, and the roof was good, making no noises.

Miners, from the earliest days, preferred wooden supports – pit props or 'trees' – to shore up the roof over their heads. The reason for that preference was simple. Unlike steel, the trees could 'speak' to them, creaking and groaning when under pressure to warn them of danger.

33

Torlay returned to No. 2 pit bottom, walking the horse road level and arriving there at about 9.00 a.m. His next task was to inspect the shaft; this normally being carried out in some detail three times a week and partially every day. Taking the assistant pit bottomer, James McGurty, with him, they entered the cage and began their slow journey up the shaft, checking the condition of the slides and buntons.

When they reached the level of the Ell coal at 125 fathoms they were joined in the cage by James McKendrick, the overman of that seam, and a lad, Archibald Muir, who were both going to the surface. Torlay and McGurty continued to examine the shaft as they travelled slowly upwards, the cool air passing them as it was drawn down into the workings. After a few minutes they reached the halfway point, and operating on the counterbalance system, the other cage (empty) slowly passed them on its way to the pit bottom. The time was now about 9.20 a.m., and what followed was witnessed by those on the surface.

Without warning, a thick cloud of smoke and dust suddenly belched from the mouth of the downcast shaft. A moment later a roar of flame lasting several seconds erupted from the upcast shaft, engulfing the head frame, setting fire to the wooden shed surrounding the shaft and blowing away the wooden shuttering of the fan drift that prevented air from entering at the top of the shaft. Although the exhaust fan itself continued to operate, it was now drawing only fresh air. Reacting immediately to the explosion, pithead workers brought a water hose to bear on the flames and in about ten minutes they had the blaze under control.

The *Scotsman* of 30th May 1887 contained a vivid report of the explosion: 'Twenty minutes past nine saw Mr Gavin standing in the office doorway . . . . In the shaft of No. 2 the cage was approaching the surface, and was within ten fathoms of it, containing four persons, who were examining the opening [the shaft] as they ascended . . . . Suddenly the air was rent by the dread sound which is instantly recognised in mining communities, even where it has never been heard before, as the signal of a fearful calamity . . . . Simultaneously with the report, columns of mingled fire, dust and smoke ascended from both shafts high into the pithead gearing. The light was sufficiently vivid to show with a fierce glare, in spite of bright sunlight, and the dust fell in clouds all around the pithead, while the smoke rose high into the air and hung over the locality like a pall.'

Those employed in the upper workings described the explosion as having caused what *The Times* of 30th May called 'a fearful rumbling noise'. It was deafening in its intensity and filled the air for a mile or two. It was then, they said, followed by clouds of coal dust; but still they did not realise the gravity of the disaster. Some, who were shut off by doors from the main air course, remained at their work places until informed of their perilous situation. Exactly how startling the explosion was in its intensity was borne out by the fact that it was distinctly heard in the workings of Greenfield Colliery, a mile distant. According to Wilma Bolton in *Black Faces*, 'The sound of the explosion was heard in Greenfield Colliery through a 135-foot barrier of solid coal. In the Blantyre Colliery . . . miners working that morning were temporarily blinded with the dust thrown up by the vibration of the explosion.'

Meanwhile, in the downcast shaft, what was later described as 'blue flames' had also come roaring upwards from the pit bottom in the immediate wake of the smoke and dust. This rush of flames had briefly enveloped the cage in which Torlay and his companions had been travelling. The empty cage that had passed them on its way down only moments before had been lifted by the force of the blast and jammed in the slides, bringing an abrupt halt to winding operations. Torlay's cage could not be raised any further.

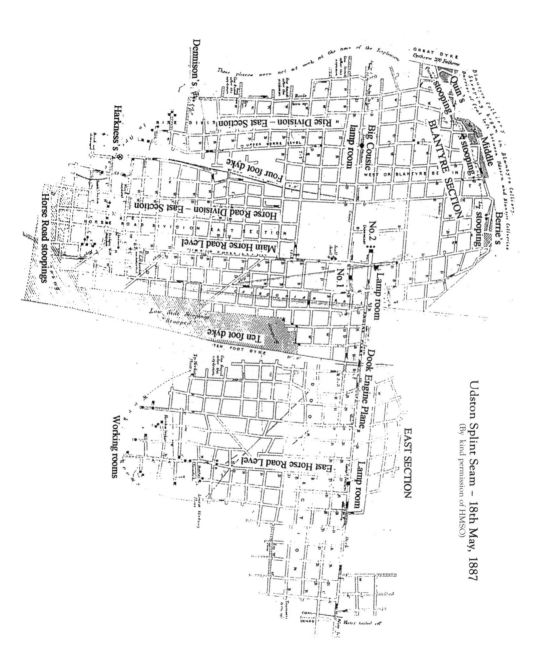

Udston Splint Seam – 18th May, 1887
(By kind permission of HMSO)

Having to first disconnect the rope of the stuck cage from the winding engine, it took the pithead workers almost an hour to make the adjustments and bring the men up. When the cage finally reached the surface it was found that, while three of the four miners were blackened and had received superficial burns, the Splint coal assistant bottomer, James McGurty, was dead. *

With the blaze at the top of No. 1 shaft having now been extinguished, the wooden shuttering was quickly replaced and the ventilation draught restored to the mine. However, what was now being drawn up from the Splint seam was for the most part choking black smoke and afterdamp.

Using the working cage in No. 2 shaft, James Gavin, the colliery manager, along with oversman William Watson, Daniel McPhail, James Gilchrist of nearby Earnock Colliery, and others, descended and brought up some men from the Ell coal who had managed to climb partway up the shaft using the buntons and slides. Once inside the cage, one of the rescued men told them that the slides only a short distance beneath them had been damaged by the blast, so they returned to the surface.

Arriving back at the pithead, the cage was boarded by a joiner called Robertson who, along with miner John McBride and a man named Bowie – the latter an oversman from Blantyre Colliery – travelled down the shaft until they came to the damaged area. Working quickly, they repaired the broken slides and soon evacuation of the rest of the miners from the Ell coal seam began.

Robertson and his companions then turned their attention to the No. 1 shaft, the upcast, where repairs were also carried out. When this was done, an evacuation of the Main coal seam could begin. Sixty-two men were brought safely to the surface, along with the bodies of four others who had been working near the shaft. It would seem that these four had been suffocated when the column of flame from the Splint seam below had roared past the Main coal entrance in the shaft, taking their air.

At 1.00 p.m., with the arrival at the pithead of Mines Inspector Ralph Moore, a meeting was held and it was decided that, as the shaft below the Main coal seam was damaged beyond immediate repair and impassable for the cage, an iron kettle should be lowered on a chain beneath the cage. When the kettle had been set up, Daniel McPhail – who had been one of the first to go down – along with John McBride and a man called Boyd climbed in for the journey below. A short time later they passed by the displaced slides and reached the heap of debris at the bottom of the shaft.

The jumble of rubble and broken timbers all but blocked the entrance to the workings leaving only a narrow space near the roof. They made their way through this space and looked around in the immediate area of the shaft, but found no one. What they did notice was that a brick stopping designed to keep the downcast and upcast ventilation draughts separate had been shattered by the blast. The fresh air passing down No. 2 shaft was now coursing through the break straight to the upcast shaft where it was being drawn back out of the pit. In effect, the Splint seam had no ventilation.

---

* 'At No. 2 shaft the situation did not at first appear to be so alarming, although it was then that those who were above ground witnessed the death of the first victim of the disaster. With great suddenness the cage was blown up the shaft with the force of the explosion, and ahead of it was projected the body of James McGourty, a lad of seventeen years of age. He was caught in the woodwork, had his neck broken and was terribly crushed internally.' – The *Glasgow Herald*, 30th May 1887. This gruesome report proved to be inaccurate. The cage stayed in the shaft and McGurty died *in* the cage.

McPhail and his companions returned to the shaft and went to the surface where they reported what they had found. James Gilchrist, Robert Beith and James Hastie – all managers from surrounding collieries – then descended the shaft, to be followed by James Gavin and others. It was then that the search for survivors began.

Shortly after commencing the search, a pony driver named McLean was found alive in the lamp room situated less than 30 yards from the downcast shaft. Also in the lamp room the searchers found their first body. Another party came across the No. 2 pit bottomer, James Lang, also alive, in an opening on the low side of the west level. Of those who had descended to the Splint seam that morning, only McLean, the pony driver, Lang, the bottomer, and oversman Edward Torlay, who was in the shaft when the pit exploded, would be found to have survived.

The scene that greeted the searchers was one of utter devastation. The explosion appeared to have spread throughout the entire workings of the Splint coal seam – over a hundred acres criss-crossed with roadways and narrow rooms – in a matter of a few seconds. Almost every brick stopping had been shattered. Every wooden stopping and brattice screen had either been blown away or set ablaze.

There were several falls of roof where supports had been ripped out and driven up the roadway. Tramways were torn up and in one place a heavy iron rope wheel had been pushed a distance of ten yards and its iron frame almost flattened by the force of the blast. In many working places throughout the seam the coal at the faces had been coked in the intense heat generated by the fireball.

While the search continued, the rubble was cleared from the bottom of the upcast shaft and work began to repair the slides and buntons, eventually allowing one of the cages to be used to ferry the bodies to the surface. While some of the victims had sustained injuries consistent with having been caught up in the blast – broken limbs, etc. – the greater majority had suffered burning or suffocation, in many cases both. In a few cases the victims had been stripped naked by the force of the explosion.

By 2.00 p.m. on Sunday 29th, the first body from the Splint workings had been sent up the shaft. On reaching the pithead the body was identified by a man as that of his brother Andrew Buddy, and it was sent to his brother's house. But Mrs Buddy said it was not her husband and refused to accept it. The body was taken back to the pithead and later in the day it was recognised as that of John Reid. The bodies were sent up at intervals from below in twos and threes, but they were badly mutilated and burnt. In some cases the clothing had been torn to rags 'and the limbs almost separated from the body'. As soon as they reached the pithead, the bodies were taken to the joiner's shop, placed in coffins, then taken to the smithy for identification.

The attitude of the rescuers at this time was best described by the *Scotsman* of 31st May: 'The operations of the explorers . . . were carried on under the disadvantage of an increasingly vitiated atmosphere the further they penetrated into the workings, and not long after two o'clock one of the searchers named Peter Gibson, residing in Burnbank, was carried up from the pit in an unconscious condition. When taken into the open air, he quickly revived, and afterwards descended the shaft again.'

Using a great deal of volunteer help, by the evening of Tuesday 31st all the bodies of the victims had been found and brought to the surface; with the exception of three, who were later found to have been buried under falls of roof.

*

With the exception of the police and rescuers, the press had been among the first to arrive at the scene, gathering what information they could from those around them and those coming from and going to the shafts. The *Scotsman* of 30th May reported: 'In an incredibly brief space of time, men, women, and children from the surrounding houses, too, came tearing across the fields with terror-stricken faces, and in a few minutes there was a large crowd on the bank . . . while the men worked with an energy which seemed almost superhuman, the women wailed with lamentations which were altogether heartrending. Indeed, the cries of the poor creatures in their frenzied agony in regard to their bread-winners would assuredly have distracted the attention and unnerved the hands of men less stolid in their heroism than those connected with the mining community are on such occasions.'

In those days some newspapermen, while reporting what they heard and assuming it to be fact (which was not always the case), also exhibited a predilection for sensationalism – an ingredient that, unfortunately, has always sold newspapers. Thankfully, however, one device now missing from today's papers (or *most* of them) that was freely indulged in Victorian times was the tendency to describe injuries in a graphic manner. A man struck by a car today would simply be reported as having died at the scene. The Victorian press, on the other hand, would turn the same accident into an anatomical lesson. The following, from the *Evening Citizen* of 30th May, is an example describing the recovery of six victims: 'With the exception of that of Denniston, the bodies were not in the least harmed, death resulting from the after-damp. But the body of Denniston presented a fearful spectacle. It was very much mutilated, and the internal parts were protruding at the back. The bodies, too, emitted an offensive odour, showing that decomposition had thus early set in. Under these circumstances, after identification, they were speedily placed in the coffins. The men handling them had, for their own protection, to use chloride of lime.' It can barely be imagined the shock and horror that must have been felt by the relatives of these men – especially the Denniston family – when they read such reports.

Not every victim was claimed immediately by relatives. One of the bodies, 39th on the list, earlier identified as Thomas Denniston, turned out to be that of Allan Stirling, aged 22, of Harnock. He was unmarried. Again early that morning a body was identified as that of David Crichton and taken to his home. Crichton's relatives, however, returned it about ten o'clock, and at mid-day it was still not claimed. The body lay in the mortuary and remained unidentified.

For relatives waiting at the surface the realisation that all might be lost was described in the *Glasgow Herald* of 30th May: 'Still there was no positive certainty as to the fate of the missing men, although those in a position to form an unbiased opinion could not help by this time making up their minds for the worst. Even among the relatives themselves the sad result of "hope deferred" was beginning to assert itself, and they, too, now feared that even the faintest hope must be abandoned. At seven-thirty-five Mr Ralph Moore returned to the surface after an official inspection of the mine, and no one who saw the sad, ominous shake of the head which he gave in answer to sundry questions could doubt for a moment that the time for hope was now indeed finally past and that the grim truth must at length be faced, however reluctantly.'

Inspector Moore's party, who had explored the workings for a considerable distance, reported seeing two dead bodies in one part of the mine. They also reported that, as the roads were badly blocked by falls from the roof it would still be some hours before the search for the missing could be begun. When this announcement leaked out, the same edition of the *Glasgow Herald* reported that it '. . . damped the spirits of the onlookers not a little, and many, who had no other motive than idle curiosity to be there, began to leave, their decision to depart no doubt being hurried by the fact that, with darkness now beginning to set in, the night was also bitterly cold.'

However, two of those who waited, shivering in the darkness, were not held there by idle curiosity. According to Bolton in *Black Faces*, the Cook family '. . . consisted of the father, Richard, aged 50, three sons, Thomas aged 21, James aged seventeen, both of whom worked underground with him, another son aged eight and a daughter aged twelve. When the two younger children heard of the explosion they ran, panic-stricken, for more than a mile to the colliery. After waiting at the pithead for almost fourteen hours, they were called to the makeshift mortuary to identify the bodies of their father and two brothers. As their mother had died some years previously, these two distraught young children were now orphans.'.

The following morning a party of seven explorers examined the entire mine. The ten victims who were still missing were assumed by the searchers to be buried under the fallen roofs or lying in the sump at the bottom of the shaft. Men worked all day clearing and repairing the sump, after which the mine would be ventilated before the roofs were repaired and made safe. It was supposed that the bodies would not be reached for several days. The crowds had by now dispersed, with only the relatives of those whose bodies had not yet been recovered waiting at the pithead.

The effect of the disaster on the local villages was traumatic. The working population of Auchentibber, for example, was decimated. From the family of farm worker John Boyce alone, a total of seven young men died. He lost his three sons, his two daughters were left widows, a brother of his son-in-law was killed and his nephew also perished. One of his daughters, Mary Harrison, gave birth to twin boys a few months after her husband, William, was killed. Having been left to raise eight fatherless children, Mary herself died six years later and her eight children became orphans.

*

The fatal accident inquiry into the Udston Colliery disaster was held under section 3 of the Coal Mines Regulations Act, 1887, at the County Hall, Hamilton, on Friday, 24th June 1887, and lasted until the following Friday, 1st July. Presided over by Mines Inspector Joseph Dickinson and advocate Charles C. Maconochie, 23 witnesses were called to give evidence, including several miners who had, prior to the explosion, been employed at the colliery. Whilst there were a great many questions to be addressed, including doubts over adequate ventilation and the illegal trimming of lamps by the miners themselves, two main questions concerned the court: 1) In which part of the Splint coal seam did the explosion originate; and 2) what happened to set it off? The former employees had much to say on both subjects.

William Quin worked in the east section up until four days before the disaster, and had previously worked in the Blantyre section. He told of how the firemen 'had a great deal of work to do putting up bratticing, sorting roads, and one thing and another'. Apart from their regular morning inspection, their daily follow-up inspections dwindled to only occasionally – and some days not at all. On the subject of lamp trimming, he said the men had sometimes to wait for an hour or an hour and a half at the lamp station for the firemen to arrive, and sometimes they did not come at all. As a result, the practice of going to the lamp station fell away, and as the lamps could be unlocked with a nail, the men would trim their own lamps. This was usually done in a close place where the fresh air was coming in. He also said he had seen 'a good deal of gas in the Blantyre section'.

John McCallum, a miner for almost 30 years, had worked in the upper part of the rise workings at Udston. When called to give evidence he told the court there had been 'a little gas two or three times a week'. Corroborating what Quin had said earlier, he said that the firemen did not take the time to properly examine the lamps in the morning – the lamps were simply locked and handed back. The roadsman trimmed their lamps at the Big Cousie lamp station, but they had to wait so long that 'an odd one would open his lamp and trim it himself'. David Arkison said that when he had worked up the Big Cousie the roadsman was not regular in attending. Whenever he failed to arrive, the men took their lamps to the pit bottom to be trimmed. He never trimmed his own lamp, he said, and could not say if anyone else ever did. James Eadie, a bottomer, and William Murdoch had both worked in the Splint seam. Corroborating each other's evidence, they spoke of the use of naked lights in the dook engine plane, and Eadie also spoke of the fireman formerly opening his lamp for the purpose of firing shots.

On the subject of what caused the explosion and where it began, various witnesses ventured an opinion. Daniel McPhail, who had been a roadsman in the Splint seam and had left three weeks before the disaster, had gone down in the first cage with manager James Gavin. He thought the explosion had originated in Quin's stooping in the Blantyre section, and he had found gas there after the explosion. He did not think a shot had been fired in Dennison's place because the bodies there had been found hard up against the coalface. During his time as roadsman, he said, he had always been regular for trimming the lamps, but some men had not come to have their lamps trimmed.

James Gavin, the colliery manager, believed that there must have been 'a little gas somewhere, and it must have been fired at an open light'. He thought that the stoopings were the likeliest places to give off gas. The explosion might have begun in the horse road stoops, or in any one of the three stoopings in the Blantyre section, and the dust could have carried the flame to the place near the bottom of the dook, where the marks of coking and charring were most severe. 'Dust prevailed most on the travelling roads,' he said, 'but where the signs of coking and charring were most severe was in rooms not at work'. Edward Torlay, the Splint coal overseman who was injured in the cage, thought that the explosion might have started in the uppermost stoop in the Blantyre section, or from the lower side stoops in the east section. He knew that wood had been drawn at the uppermost of the three Blantyre stoopings on the Wednesday and Thursday prior to the disaster. That, he said, was the only work done after the day shift that week.

Matthew Laird had been a roadsman in the Splint seam up until three days before the explosion. He told the court that he left mainly because his wages had been reduced – but also because he had objections to signing the report book describing the condition of roads he had not inspected.

James Gilchrist, manager of Earnock Colliery, one of the three collieries that bordered Udston, took part in the exploration work after the blast. It was his opinion that the explosion had come from the horse road stoopings in the east section. It originated with gas, he said, and was helped forward by dust – although the signs of burning were in the rooms and not in any of the main roads, where there was the most dust. These opinions were also held by Robert Beith, manager of Clyde Colliery and one of the explorers.

Taking the stand, Inspector Ralph Moore stated that, as Udston was in the neighbourhood of other gas producing collieries such as Blantyre, where the explosion occurred in 1877, he instructed that the colliery be inspected three times a year. It was last inspected by one of his assistants in September the previous year, and was due to be inspected again two weeks after the explosion.

Nothing wrong had ever been reported to him about the colliery. He also added: 'On various bodies found in the pit there were matches, ignited and unignited, tobacco, pipes, lamp keys and nails.'

On the subject of where the explosion began and what had caused it he was less certain, having not quite made up his mind. However, he tended towards the opinion that the explosion began in the rise division of the east section, and that there may have been a little gas in Dennison's place. 'A shot had been fired there which set the thing agoing and kindled the dust, and for the rest it was a dust explosion. That it came out of both levels, and went into the engine dook, where it expanded in the waste, and then came up like out of a bottle neck.'

The consensus of opinion was that the explosion was ignited, in the first instance, by firedamp, which was then aggravated by coal dust. All agreed that it most likely originated in the rise workings, but they could not agree on which section.

*

On Saturday, 30th July 1887, the report on the Udston disaster was completed and in August was presented to Parliament by the Home Secretary, Henry Matthews. The authors, Mines Inspector Dickinson and advocate Maconochie, began with a description of the colliery, the layout of the Splint coal seam, the system of working, the ventilation flow and the numbers of men who worked there. They listed the duties of the various officials and explained the conditions in the seam both before and after the explosion.

They went on to chronicle the events of the disaster; describing in detail the widespread damage done to the workings and the carnage visited upon the workforce when the seam blew up. The earlier inquiry also took up its share, with evidence given by present and former employees, colliery managers, and Ralph Moore, District Inspector, who was early on the scene and would later produce his own, very similar, report.

In beginning to set out their conclusions, the authors said the evidence showed that the explosion began in the Splint seam and, regardless of whatever section, panel, or district it originated, the blast extended throughout the workings without any interval being noticed in the outbursts from both shafts. Following an examination of the workings, the explosion '. . . was found to have extended into every part of the Splint seam, killing altogether 73 persons, being 69 of the Splint men, and 4 in the Main Coal, who were suffocated.'

At the inquiry, the witnesses had unanimously believed that the explosion was caused by firedamp, and was propelled throughout the mine by the ignition of coal dust. On this, the inspectors remarked that if the explosion was begun by the ignition of a small quantity of firedamp and was extended throughout the workings by dust, where did it begin? There had been no evidence of gas in the dook or at the horse road or low-side stoopings.

The mine being dry and dusty and the Splint coal being of a highly inflammable kind gave plausibility to the supposition that the explosion was aggravated by dust. On the other hand the evidence showed that the main roads, and not the rooms, were 'the most dusty part of the mine'. It was, however, in the rooms not cut through and least dusty that the greatest signs of coking were found, extending not quite up to the face, and not in the main roads, some of the principal coking being found in rooms which had not been at work.

Regardless of where the gas had come from, they assumed it must have been ignited by flame passing through one of the Scotch gauze lamps or by ignition at an open lamp or at a match, 'of the possession of which there is abundant evidence.' If it had begun at one of the two places where blasting was allowed (Harkness's or Dennison's), then the drawing out of gas and the lighting would be accounted for by the blasting itself. If it began at the west, or Blantyre stoopings, the gas could have come from the stoopings where it had last been found, and could have been lighted and spread as already mentioned.

On the direction (or directions) taken by the blast the authors thought that the force evident in the dook, where it had been most violent, came mostly from the working faces towards the shafts. In the west, where it had been less violent, it came mainly from the stoopings, where work was ongoing. In the rise division the blast had travelled outwards and downwards from the far workings towards the shaft and the west section. In the horse road division, it went mostly towards the stoopings, 'but from the most eastern cutting through the four-foot dyke it went towards the shafts.'

In trying to determine the place where the blast originated, the authors recalled the evidence given by witnesses at the inquiry. The places pointed out in the east section were in the rise division at Dennison's place, and in the horse road division, either at the stoopings or at Harkness's place. In the Blantyre section, the suggested place of origin was the upper stoopings, known as Quin's stoopings. This was close to the main 200-fathom dyke. It was the only part of the mine where, prior to the explosion, firedamp was recorded as having been found by the firemen.

In closing, Messrs Dickinson and Maconochie turned the spotlight on the 1877 Blantyre explosion and the Scotch gauze safety lamp as used then, and still in use at Udston. The lamp was widely used in the Scottish coalfields and both miners and management continued to 'place implicit faith in it as a safe lamp for experienced colliers in mines of the same class, and ventilated in the same way, as the Udston Colliery.' However, the authors had their reservations about the Scotch gauze lamp: 'We desire strongly to express our opinion that this lamp does not satisfy the conditions met with in such a mine as Udston, where velocities it could not safely withstand were met with at certain points.'

What this meant, in essence, was that the pressure of the ventilation draught in many collieries (including Udston) was such that, in certain circumstances, its strength could penetrate the fine gauze mesh encircling the lamp and reach the flame. That being the case, if the ventilation draught contained too high a concentration of firedamp – or if there was a sudden emission of firedamp from the face – the result could be disastrous. In addition, with both Udston and Blantyre collieries working the same gas-producing Splint seam, the system of stoop-and-room, as used at Udston, also came in for criticism. The seam, they said, had been under-worked and over-extended, with too many rooms standing unused and bratticed and, in effect, slowing down the ventilation to those parts of the mine which were producing coal. The authors then harked back to an unsettling (and somehow prophetic) paragraph contained in the report on the 1877 Blantyre Disaster, repeating it verbatim to enforce the warning.

In conclusion, having no real evidence to a shot having been fired at either of the two places authorised, they stated that, in their opinion, there had been laxness on the part of the management with regard to the following: the safety lamps used were incapable of withstanding some of the currents in the mine; examination of the lamps was perfunctory and, as the lamps needed trimming and some men did not bring them in, it could be assumed that men opened and trimmed the lamps themselves; the stoopings in the horse road division of the east section, being in the midst of the workings, were a source of danger; and there were too many rooms left uncompleted, with bratticing in them contracting the air, instead of allowing it to circulate freely.

Arriving at their conclusions, they found:

1. That the explosion originated either at the stoopings in the Blantyre section, or at Harkness's in the east section, the former being the most likely.

2. That it was primarily caused by the ignition of firedamp at an open light, or at a match, or by being drawn through the gauze of a Scotch safety lamp.

3. That, having commenced, it was reinforced by gas in the ventilation flow, and by dust together with gas drawn out from the solid coal and from cavities by pressure set up by the explosion, and that some issues of gas were ignited separately through the gauze of the lamps, or at open lights.

4. That some of the miners were clearly guilty of contravening the Act, in that they had lamp keys and matches in their possession and had opened their lamps.

Finally, having said all that, '. . . no apparent contravention of the Act is proved against the officials of the mine.'

Strangely, while the authors of the report criticised the colliery owners for 1) issuing safety lamps which, in their opinion, could not be described as such and could, in fact, have been a source of danger, 2) not replacing the former fireman when he left, and 3) for cutting stoops in the heart of the seam, not at the edge, and leaving too many bratticed rooms, which must have been a drain on the available ventilation, they ultimately failed to find them guilty of any wrongdoing.

When Inspector Ralph Moore had given evidence to the inquiry he stated that, as Udston was in what was known to be a gas-producing neighbourhood, he had instructed that the colliery be inspected three times a year. The last time it had been inspected, he said, had been in September of the previous year, and it had been due its next inspection two weeks after the disaster. If that was the case, then why had there been a gap of some nine months between these inspections? And, for that matter, why – as mines inspector for the district of Blantyre and Hamilton – did he himself not criticise the maze of bratticed rooms in the heart of the Splint seam?

When it was eventually published, Inspector Moore's report contained a great many similarities to that of Dickinson and Maconochie – but his earlier indecision at the inquiry was gone and his conclusions were now more definite: 'I confirm my opinion that the disastrous effects of the explosion were due to the ignition of coal dust in the mine and not to an accumulation of firedamp. There had probably been a small quantity of gas in the place where the explosion began and a shot fired surreptitiously which, without an examination for gas, ignited this gas. This raised and ignited a cloud of coal dust and the flame, fed by the dust in the workings, traversed the whole seam.'

Even after such intense deliberation the experts could not entirely agree.

When it came to the rescue efforts of the volunteer miners, inspectors Dickinson and Maconochie gave generous praise: of course, the bravery of the miners was never in doubt. Brothers Richard, Thomas and George Cowan were underground when the explosion happened and had managed to escape – only to put their lives at risk again by volunteering to return to Udston's shattered tunnels to rescue others. Along with Richard Cowan, Thomas and James Weir also went back underground having already rescued twelve unconscious miners before they too had to be rescued.

Impressed by the quiet heroism of the volunteer miners – many of whom rushed to the stricken colliery from their own places of work – an appeal was made to the Home Office by Stephen Mason MP suggesting that the Albert Medal (at the time the highest civilian award for bravery) be awarded to one or more of the rescuers. However, any chance of medals being won by miners was wrecked by a letter from Mines Inspector Moore, who arrived at the colliery five hours *after* the explosion. Showing crass disregard from men who having of their own accord descended into a wrecked and gas-filled mine to rescue others, he said that, in his opinion, 'None of the men in anything they did were subjected to more than the ordinary risks of mining. I have most respectfully to state that there is no cause in my opinion for awarding a medal to anyone.' The medals were never awarded.

And so it ended. The cause of the explosion was still a mystery. Was it a shot fired illegally? Was it air impregnated with firedamp that blew through the gauze on a Scotch safety lamp? Was it a miner opening his lamp illegally to trim the wick? Or was it the striking of a match in some dark corner as one of the miners stole a forbidden smoke? The authors of both reports – Dickinson and Maconochie, then Moore – were careful to point out the damning fact that some of the victims were found to have been carrying nails for opening their lamps. Only two had been in possession of tobacco and only one had been carrying matches.

The exact place of origin of the explosion had also proved impossible to pin down. Had it been at Harkness's place in the horse road division, or in the rise division at Dennison's place? Had it ignited somewhere else in the horse road stoopings? Was it beyond the ten-foot dyke in the dook section? Or was it in the Blantyre section, where they thought it most likely?

The direction of the blast had also been impossible to calculate. At some points – thanks to the myriad of rooms criss-crossing the seam – it appeared to have come from almost every direction, including the dook section. The direction of the blast was, like all the other questions, largely a matter of conjecture.

On the matter of coal dust, Benson in *British Coalminers in the Nineteenth Century* explains: 'Mines were always dark, dirty and dusty. A great deal of dust was inevitably created in cutting the coal, getting it down and moving it to the surface. As pits . . . went deeper, so more and more dust was created by the spread of mechanical haulage . . . . No real success was had in the suppression of this choking, swirling dust until the very end of the century and even then progress was painfully slow. The miner always worked enveloped in dust and sweat . . .'.

While there were witnesses who thought it was solely a firedamp explosion, the majority believed that coal dust had played its part. In the 1850s chemists Faraday and Lyell had experimented with coal dust and, nearer the end of the century, Galloway and Abel also examined its deadly effects. Kerr said in 1902, 'These two authorities have studied the question very closely for years, and after many careful and comprehensive experiments, have come to the conclusion that coal dust is highly dangerous under certain conditions. Others have entered the field of investigation, and the results have placed beyond doubt the statement that coal dust, rather than firedamp, plays the most important part in many colliery explosions.'

Regardless of where it had come from or how it had started, the concussion from the Udston explosion was felt in the bowels of Blantyre Colliery to the west and Greenfield Colliery to the east. The blast not only swept round the rise and horse road divisions, but had entered the dook section down the only two roads that linked one side of the Splint seam with the other. Feeding on dust and sucking firedamp from the waste, it had come roaring back into the west side of the seam like flame from the mouth of a cannon. The enormous pressure generated by the rolling explosion then found the only possible points of escape, the shafts. From ignition to surface blow out, only a few seconds passed – but in that brief time 73 men and boys died.

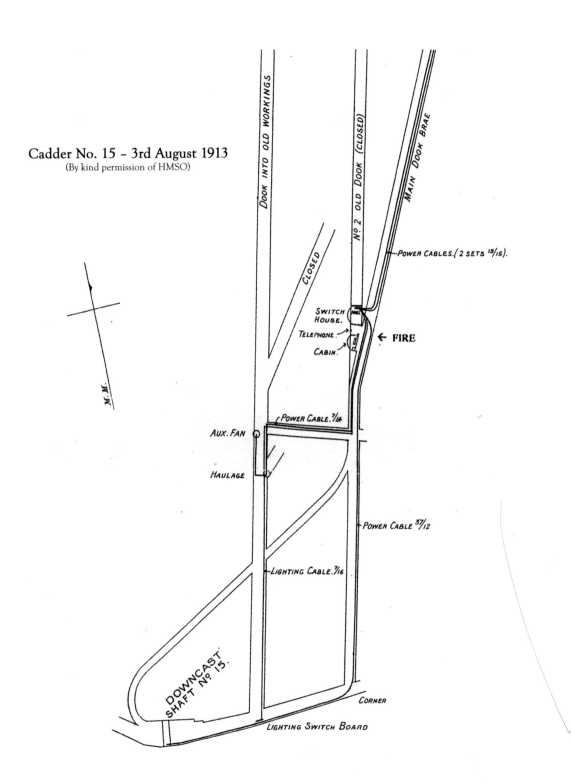

Cadder No. 15 – 3rd August 1913
(By kind permission of HMSO)

which provides that where one of two ways of egress from a mine is along a road not usually travelled, every fireman shall at least once a quarter traverse the whole of such [a] way in order to make himself thoroughly acquainted with the same.'

When Dunbar and his companions reached the surface – a little before eight o'clock in the evening – they raised the alarm and immediately made their way over to No. 15 pit. There, John Marshall, the winding engineman, told them that the night shift firemen, William and Joseph Brown, had just gone down the shaft to carry out a routine check. As opposed to following them, the trio decided to wait for them to return. They did not have long to wait.

When the firemen reached the pit bottom they found nothing wrong. Everything was as it should have been – quiet and in darkness. Setting off towards the workings, it was only when they turned the corner in the main airway that they saw the inferno ahead of them. Returning to the surface, they immediately organised a fire-fighting party and went below to tackle the fire. It was quickly realised that they would be unlikely to defeat the fire in time to save the men below.

William Owens, under-manager of Cadder No. 15 pit, went over to No. 17 and after consultation ordered the air current to be reversed with a view to clearing smoke from the workings. He also sent word of the fire to Archibald Spiers, manager of No. 15, who hurried to the scene. While this was being done rescue parties were organised by Owens to go below at the earliest opportunity. There was, however, no rescue apparatus at the colliery. Although preliminary steps had been taken by the management to form a brigade, it had never come into being, and no rescue apparatus of any description had been provided. Canaries and other equipment had been supplied, but nothing else.

And so it was that the first of the search parties descended No. 17 pit carrying with them caged canaries and no breathing apparatus. The men who made up these parties were not trained rescuers but local miners, many of whom lived in the nearby village of Mavis Valley. With the ventilation having been reversed the draught was now at their backs as they made their way along the main return airway and into the communication road. Unfortunately, the first two parties were eventually forced to abandon their search when they encountered gas, but not before one of them – at about eleven o'clock – had come across two bodies on the inbye side of the regulating door to the south of the air crossing. On their return to the surface a rescue brigade was sent for – three hours after the alarm had first been raised.

At that time the nearest Mines Rescue Brigade was stationed at Bowhill near Cowdenbeath in Fife, some 50 miles to the northeast of Cadder Colliery. On receiving the telephone call the brigade members were quickly gathered together and their equipment checked, and they left the station around midnight. As fate would have it, travelling as they were at night on unfamiliar roads, they lost their way at Kirkintilloch and eventually received proper directions to the colliery from a local policeman.

At about midnight Robert McLaren, Senior Inspector of Mines for the west of Scotland, arrived at the colliery and immediately went down No. 17 shaft. By this time the reversed air current, which had been running for over four hours, had all but cleared the workings of smoke and poisonous gases. A column of smoke rose high into the air above the No. 15 head frame. The inspector and his party, skirting the eastern edges of the workings by way of Connor's, Harrigan's and McLaren's headings, were able to reach Stewart's level at its junction with the Main dook. It was at this point that Robert Dunbar, Michael Keenan and Felix O'Neill had parted company with the main party retreating from No. 1 Machine section.

When the Cowdenbeath Rescue Brigade arrived at the colliery around 3.00 a.m. on Monday morning, James Forrester, captain of the brigade, was informed by firemen at the surface that smoke helmets and bellows were all that would be needed below. Assuming that no one knew the colliery better than the firemen, the brigade took their advice. Carrying these with them, Forrester led the first rescue squad below – but it quickly became apparent that helmets and bellows were useless in the particular situation they found themselves in and they returned to the surface.

Before Forrester and his party went back down No. 17, they discarded the smoke helmet and bellows in favour of the W.E.G. self-contained oxygen breathing apparatus. When they eventually reached the junction of Stewart's level with the Main dook they were met by Inspector McLaren who was waiting for them, unsure as to the safety of the rest of the main intake. To ascertain how safe the road was the inspector asked Forrester to take a caged canary with him and go southward along the intake towards the fire. Forrester put the breathing tube in his mouth, picked up a canary and disappeared into the darkness.

As he made his way down the Main dook he proceeded warily, his attention divided between the road ahead and the canary in the cage. Although the self-contained breathing apparatus would protect him from deadly gas, the bird would warn him of its presence. A few yards short of the junction with the disused No. 3 level he came across six bodies clustered together on the road. As the canary was still showing no signs of distress, he knew that the reversed air current had cleared the workings of gas up to that point and he returned to the party waiting at the junction of Stewart's level to report what he had found.

With the mine now believed to be safe, the local search parties were once again allowed to go below and they spread throughout the workings in search of survivors. At the point where Connor's level crossed the Main dook another six bodies were found, five on the dook just outbye of the level and one, fireman Charles Reilly, on the level itself before the regulating door. Reilly could have saved himself, but he chose to warn the others first, a selfless act for which he paid with his life.

Having been warned of danger by Reilly, the men of No. 2 Machine section had left their workplaces, following the direction of the airflow towards the Main dook. They had varying fortunes. Four of the eight never got out of the section, three of them got to within a few yards of the Main dook, and Owen McAloon – who was that day driving a pony on the western side of the Communication road – somehow managed to get as far as the disused No. 3 level. It is possible he went directly by the No. 3 level which, touching as it did the No. 2 Machine section in the west, crossed the full width of the workings to the other side. To do that would have meant travelling against the ventilation flow and into the oncoming smoke. Regardless of how he got there, his was one of the six bodies found clustered on the Main dook by James Forrester, captain of the rescue brigade. The other five had come from the No. 1 Machine section – also travelling against the ventilation flow.

Of the four who never left No. 2 Machine section, three were found dead and Michael McDonald, who had found his way into a 'dead end' of air on the Cuddy heading, was eventually found alive late on Monday morning. He was brought to the surface in an exhausted state and revived by Dr Miller, who had been in attendance at the colliery from an early stage.

With all the men accounted for and the bodies removed, preparations were made to tackle the fire. The ventilation flow, which had been reversed to remove the smoke and fumes from the workings, was reinstated. This action filled the mine once again with smoke, but cleared the 125-yard passageway between the bottom of No. 15 shaft and the fire. Water hoses were laid down the shaft and teams of men worked round the clock in six-hour shifts, pouring millions of gallons of water onto the inferno. *The Times* of 7th August was able to report, '. . . the fire at the pit has not been completely extinguished, but good progress has been made considering the conditions underground. The men at work describe the pit as like a blazing inferno and state that the operations had been carried out under extreme difficulty.'

Notwithstanding the smoke and heat, and the constant threat of roof collapse, they worked with a purpose, clearing the road as they progressed. Some days later, just when they thought they were winning the battle, the blaze flared up again. It burned out of control for several weeks until, admitting defeat, the management ordered that the fire should be sealed behind brick walls and left to burn itself out.

On Wednesday, 6th August, the funerals of the victims were held. *The Times* described the scene in its report the following day: 'Some 50,000 people congregated around the funeral procession in Glasgow . . . . The largest section assembled in front of St Agnes's Roman Catholic Church where services were conducted for eleven Roman Catholic miners, and amid impressive scenes the eleven coffins were borne on the shoulders of miners and other relatives from the chapel to the cemetery [St Kentigern's], a mile distant. Among the mourners were the widows and fatherless children. Pathetic scenes also marked the funeral of seven Protestant victims . . . [before] the burial a service was conducted in Mavis Valley Hall. Among the dead were the three young brothers Brown and the two brothers Ramsey. The young wife of Robert Ramsey entered the hall and lay over the coffin crying bitterly.' According to Guthrie Hutton in *Lanarkshire's Mining Legacy*, 'An impressive procession of horse drawn hearses took the victims from Mavis Valley, along the road beside the Forth and Clyde Canal to Cadder Cemetery.'

*

On Monday, 22nd September 1913, the inquiry into the Cadder Colliery disaster was opened in the Justiciary Buildings in Jail Square, Glasgow. Presided over by Sir Henry Cunynghame, KCB, 38 witnesses were called to give evidence. Those who worked in Cadder, including three of the four who survived the tragedy, gave evidence on events that day and on the mine in general. Various experts were called to give their opinions, not only on what happened, but also on other points raised by the evidence. These included the origin of the fire, ventilation and the merits and demerits of current types of breathing apparatus.

Concerning the fire, Cadder's underground electrical system was discussed in great detail, but nothing was found which could lead to the conclusion that the fire had been of an electrical origin. While electricity had been used in the colliery since 1906, the system had been 'reconstructed and remodelled' in June 1913 – almost two months before the disaster – and 'no suggestion was made by anyone but that the electrical work was well and substantially done.'

Fireman William Brown, who was one of the first to witness the fire, told the court he saw the cables burning, but was not in the position to say if the fire had been caused by electricity. Professor Thornton of Armstrong College, Newcastle, thought it possible that the fire could have been started by some failure in the electrical system – but it was more probable that it was due in some way to lights or lucifer matches. His opinion was echoed by no less than three mining inspectors. This line of thinking stemmed from the fact that Cadder was a naked light pit and the miners' jackets, hanging on nails near to the scene of the fire, were likely to have been saturated with lamp oil.

The question of whether or not a pit bottomer should have been on duty at the foot of No. 15 shaft also came in for some discussion. The regular weekday bottomer for No. 15 was Patrick Etherson, but on Sundays the fireman usually acted as bottomer, ringing the men down before leaving the pit bottom to examine the workings. The bottom was then left unattended until he returned at the end of his shift. It was also the usual practice on Sundays that, if Etherson did go below, he was sent to work in some other part of the mine. On the day of the accident, he did not go down the pit at all.

The inquiry closed on Saturday, 27th September. Exactly four weeks later – on Saturday, 25th October 1913 – Sir Henry Cunynghame completed his report and passed it to Home Secretary the Rt. Hon. Reginald McKenna, who presented it to Parliament in early November. The author, having first listed the witnesses who gave evidence at the inquiry, went on to describe Cadder Colliery and the underground layout before turning to the accident itself – and the origin of the fire.

He found that, 'In the first place it appears that the origin of the fire must have been either some failure of the electrical apparatus, or else a misadventure due to the accidental ignition of clothes, or a lamp wick or some timber.' However, in light of the available evidence he felt he had to agree with Professor Thornton and the inspectors that the fire was more likely to have been started by 'lights or lucifer matches' rather than any electrical fault. He also conceded that the cause of the disaster was uncertain.

While concluding that an electrical fault would be the least likely cause, it could not be entirely ruled out, and here Sir Henry reiterated an earlier concern that had been brought up at the inquiry: '[A] question arises whether the electric lighting cables should have been armoured. They would have been better armoured.' With the legal position on armouring at that time being largely a matter of 'interpretation of the Act of 1911 and [its] regulations', he would speculate no further, turning instead to the subject of pit bottomers.

Should there have been a regular bottomer at the bottom of No. 15 on the 3rd of August, and if there had been one, would he have seen the fire? That question had been discussed at the inquiry and Sir Henry concluded – as did most of those who gave an opinion – that the fire would most likely *not* have been seen by a bottomer standing at the foot of the shaft. Anyone on duty there would have to have gone to the corner, some 45 yards away, before the fire would have become visible. The report stated: 'All the witnesses who saw the fire concur in saying that you could not see it except by going to the corner, and this would have taken the bottomer out of hearing of the signal bell.'

According to Sir Henry, if Patrick Etherson, the regular weekday bottomer, had been on duty on that Sunday, '. . . his duties might have been to clean up any coal that might be about near the pit bottom, but, as no coal was being drawn, he would probably not have had anything to do.'

If that had been the case then Etherson would have spent a long and boring shift indeed, although with nothing but his own thoughts for company, he might have noticed something in the silence. If not the flickering glow of flames at the corner, then perhaps a distant roar as fire engulfed the cabin and the switch-house? Perhaps he would have noticed the ventilation flow down the shaft become stronger as the inferno sucked in more air? With a man on duty at the foot of the shaft, the lights would certainly have been switched on. As the flames rose they would have quickly melted the two unarmoured lighting cables, plunging the pit bottom into darkness. Surely Etherson would have noticed that?

Sir Henry continued: 'Prior to the coming into force of the Act [of 1911] in July 1912, it seems to have been usual in many mines in Great Britain not to have a bottomer if men and coal were not being regularly raised. The Royal Commission on Coal Mines, however, recommended that in all cases a bottomer should be stationed at the pit bottom as long as there were persons in the mine, and this recommendation was carried into effect in the Act of 1911. This Act . . . requires (Section 53 (2)) that so long as persons are below ground, other than mine officials or persons authorised to give signals, a bottomer shall be in constant attendance for the purpose of receiving and transmitting signals.

'In addition to this section, however, a set of rules was in force at the colliery made under the Coal Mines Regulation Act of 1887, which provided that, in the absence of a bottomer, the signals might be given by the fireman if duly appointed for that purpose. By virtue of Clause 126 of the Act of 1911 these rules remained in force till they were supplanted by new regulations, which came into force on September 10th, 1913, after the date of the accident. These new regulations do not allow the fireman to act as bottomer.'

So it was that Clause 126 of the Act of 1911 created a loophole that allowed colliery managers the option of not having to pay a man to stand idle all day at the bottom of the shaft. Although the Royal Commission on Coal Mines had already recommended that in all cases a bottomer should be stationed at the pit bottom as long as there were persons in the mine, it was no more than a recommendation and, as such, open to interpretation.

Next to be dealt with were the interconnected subjects of rescue brigades and rescue apparatus. In 1910 an Act of Parliament had been passed designed to make regulations for the supply and maintenance of rescue apparatus. Under this Act an order was made in April 1912, requiring that a rescue brigade be set up at every mine unless the men were unwilling to form them, or the apparatus could not be obtained owing to lack of supply. The rescue apparatus recommended was to be 'portable breathing apparatus'.

The regulations of April 1912 remained in force until they were incorporated in the new regulations which came into force in September 1913, at which time there were several varieties of rescue apparatus on the market. Some, known as 'self-contained apparatus', were a type that enabled the wearer to be completely isolated while in a dangerous atmosphere. Another type consisted of a helmet connected by a flexible pipe to a large pair of bellows 'worked by hand by a person in rear of the person wearing the helmet'. As such, it was necessary that the man working the bellows should be in good air himself, added to which the wearer of the helmet could only go beyond him by the length of the flexible pipe – and this length depended entirely on how much pipe he could carry or drag behind him.

Sir Henry then went on to discuss five documents (given in the appendix of his report), the contents of which clearly revealed how the Lanarkshire Coalmasters' Association was dealing with the urgent matter of miners' safety. The first was a circular from R.A.S. Redmayne, Chief Inspector of Mines, pointing out that although the order to train rescue brigades and supply them with breathing apparatus had been in force for almost a year, nothing had yet been done by them in this regard. He reminded them of the penalties for non-compliance with the order (a fine of £20 and a further fine of £1 for every day during which the failure to comply continued).

Along with the above threat came the advice that a 'smoke helmet', which was supplied with fresh air by means of a tube and bellows, was *not* a portable breathing apparatus within the meaning of the order. According to the order, the phrase 'portable breathing apparatus' meant a *self-contained* apparatus which would enable the wearer, in the event of a rescue, to visit any part of the mine. On the other hand a 'smoke helmet', which would allow the wearer to travel only a very limited distance in advance of the fresh air, did not meet the requirement.

Following the implementation of the Act of 1912, the management of Cadder had collected the names of miners willing to form brigades. But that was as far as it went. They neither trained the volunteers in rescue procedures nor provided them with any kind of rescue equipment – other than oxygen reviving apparatus and ambulance boxes, as required by Regulation (4) (c).

On 19th April, in the wake of Mr Redmayne's circular, the Lanarkshire Coalmasters' Association sent out their own circular advising its members to form brigades and supply them with reviving apparatus. But the circular was careful to point out '. . . that the kind of breathing apparatus required by the Act was being discussed with the provincial inspectors of mines for Scotland, and that a test case would be raised to determine the matter.'

But the Act of 1912, being quite specific on the subject of breathing apparatus, had already determined 'the matter'. The proposed 'test case' referred to in their circular appeared to be no more than a less-than-subtle delaying tactic, possibly because the 'self-contained breathing apparatus' as defined by the Act was more expensive than their more favoured smoke helmet and bellows.

In April Robert Baird, secretary of the Lanarkshire Coalmasters' Association, wrote to Mr W. Walker, Divisional Inspector of Mines, on the subject of Mr Redmayne's circular. In the letter Mr Baird readily acknowledged that '. . . sections (3) (a), (b), and (c); and (5) (b) and (c) and the five subsections under the latter . . .' must be complied with. Along with this admission, however, came two startling statements.

In the first he said that '. . . in the area covered by this Association the question of 'Rescue and Aid' is not one of urgency in the interests of safety . . .'. He also stated: 'With regard to the principal question raised as to the kind of 'portable breathing apparatus' required by section (5) (a), my Executive are of [the] opinion that for the mines within this Association, smoke helmet and bellows apparatus will be found to be the safest and most suitable, and that they comply with that section.'

In closing the subject of smoke helmet and bellows versus self-contained breathing apparatus, Sir Henry said that it was not necessary for him to decide the legal question of whether or not smoke helmets complied with the letter of the Act. What was certain, he said, was that however useful they might be in dealing with fires which were restricted to small areas, they were not safe, suitable, or sufficiently portable to be of real use in an accident such as happened at Cadder. 'Their uselessness,' he emphasised, 'in cases where considerable lengths of roadway are filled with smoke or fumes is not in dispute, and this was frankly admitted by the agent and manager of the Cadder Mine.'

As to whether or not the self-contained apparatus – had it been available on site at the earliest moment – would have saved lives, he thought it '. . . as certain as any fact can be that depends on circumstantial evidence', that before the first alarm of fire was given on the surface about 7.55 p.m., Reilly and all the men in No. 1 Machine section and at the pumps were dead.' As for those who had been working in No. 2 Machine section, he did not think that a brigade, even if it had possessed the necessary apparatus, could have been gathered in time to save them.

Having had almost a year during which to organise rescue brigades and supply them with the proper equipment, the owners and management of Cadder Colliery – and the Lanarkshire Coalmasters' Association – came in for some well-earned criticism. Sir Henry accused the Cadder Company of being in default in the provision of rescue apparatus as required by the regulations in force at the time of the accident. Not only that, they had failed even to provide their favoured smoke helmets and bellows, or made any arrangements to call for them from a rescue station within ten miles distance. As for the Lanarkshire Coalmasters' Association, they had failed to set up any form of rescue station in that part of Scotland.

Concerning the interminable delay in complying with the Act of 1912, Sir Henry made it clear that the association's indecision over the type of breathing apparatus required to comply with the Act was no excuse. The colliery masters of Lanarkshire '. . . do not seem to have been delayed by this consideration, for the association to whose decisions they adhered took the view that no self-contained oxygen rescue apparatus of any sort was necessary, and that smoke helmets and bellows were the safest and most suitable for the mines within the association.

'If a similar case were to arise tomorrow,' he continued, 'and lives were lost for want of self-contained apparatus, what would be the position of owners who, in spite of every remonstrance, and in spite of the warning afforded by this case, failed to provide it? I shall be surprised if, after the experienced gained in this accident, the Colliery Masters of Lanarkshire will be found still to maintain the position they took up. I can hardly believe that they will take their stand on legal grounds, even if they were valid, and decline to recommend to the members of their association the use of the only apparatus proper to deal with all difficulties that may arise.'

Coming to his recommendations, Sir Henry had several points to make. He first dealt with the underground telephone system as it was in Cadder at the time of the accident. The circuit consisted of a single wire leading from No. 17 pithead overland to No. 15, then down the downcast shaft and into the workings via the Main Dook Brae. Telephones were fixed to this wire at various points with earth returns, but the system did not extend as far as the upcast, No. 17 shaft. One of the disadvantages of such a system was that an accident to one part of the line might put the telephones on the rest of the circuit out of action. The fire probably destroyed the system at an early stage.

It was his understanding that a new telephone system had been devised for use in mines, which would be independent of accidents to the wires. If such a system turned out to be practicable, he thought it ought to be extremely useful, and might, in such cases of disaster, '. . . be invaluable in ascertaining the position of men in the pit, and of assisting in the direction of the operations of the rescue parties.'

The two cabins and, in particular, the timber packing placed above them was also criticised. 'Above the cabin,' he said, 'there was a pile of timber exactly in the position most calculated to burn fiercely if lighted. It would have been better if there had been a stone packing instead.'

Sir Henry then closed his report by recommending that firemen – or at least one man working in each group – should be well acquainted with the layout and roadways of the mine and should be aware of what to do in case of emergency. Feeling it likely that most firemen did not know enough about the by-products of fire, he suggested they should also be trained to the dangers of smoke containing carbon monoxide: 'I do not think they all understand the difference between carbon monoxide and carbonic acid and other gases found in ordinary smoke, and it appears to me doubtful whether they are all sufficiently acquainted with the best methods of dealing with the dangers arising from it.'

*

And so the book was closed on the Cadder disaster with no answer having been provided for the first question asked – how did the fire start? Was it possible that one or more of the miners renewed their lamp wicks in the area of the cabins? Had someone been careless with fire in a colliery where the naked flame was an accepted sight? In the area where the fire started there had been spilled lamp oil, saturated jackets, pipes and matches. Had there been a guttering wick left against dry wood, or had an unseen spark been left to smoulder on a jacket left behind them? In his report, Sir Henry stated: 'The pit was a naked light pit. The firemen had safety lamps, the miners carried the small tin oil lamps usually employed in Scottish mines . . . . The flash point of the compound [the mixture of oils] is high and I could not learn that it is specially inflammable or dangerous.'

Then again, could it have been what they thought it was not – a fault in the electrical system? Despite their inquiries, they did not know then. Now no one will ever know.

On the contentious subject of what did and what did not constitute self-contained breathing apparatus, the Lanarkshire Coalmasters' Association seemed determined to defy the lawful regulations and the advice of the mines inspectors. They instigated a delaying 'test case' to prove what they already knew. Self-contained breathing apparatus such as the W.E.G. system (as recommended by Mr Redmayne, Chief Inspector of Mines) gave almost unlimited access to mine workings, while their favoured (and less expensive) smoke helmet and bellows was, in its very design, self-limiting. In the face of the blindingly obvious, they continued to back a horse that would always be second best. After all, did they not themselves say that the subject was not a matter of 'urgency in the interests of safety'? Indeed no. *It was more a matter of fiscal policy.*

In a postscript to the Cadder tragedy the *Scotsman* of 5th August 1913 said this: 'As happens on all such occasions, there have not been lacking noble examples of heroism and self-sacrifice. Human nature never seems to display itself better than in these mining accidents. The call for volunteers to go to the rescue of entombed men is never made in vain, although those who come forward know well the risk they are taking. The task of the rescuers, as the experience of former disasters has shown, is scarcely less dangerous than the plight of those caught in the first onset of the calamity. At the Cadeby Pit, where 87 lives were lost last year, the death roll was made up mostly of those who had gone down to succour their comrades and were killed by the second explosion. Happily in this case the work of rescue has not exacted an addition to the heavy toll of life taken by the fire; but the courage of those who went down on their unavailing errand of mercy should not pass without its need of recognition.

'The little that is known of what happened among the doomed men shows that the heroism which can sacrifice itself in the effort to save others was exhibited among them also. One at least of them proved himself a true hero. This was the fireman Reilly, who could have made his own escape, but gave up his life in an effort to warn the others of the danger of whose approach they were unaware.'

*

On 27th March 1914 miner Robert Dunbar was awarded the Edward Medal, Second Class, by King George V for courage shown in the saving of life during the Cadder Disaster. Having led two of his companions through the dark maze of passageways to safety, he then returned underground and succeeded in saving one of the rescue party who had been overcome. There appears to be no evidence of a posthumous award for the courageous fireman Charles Reilly who left a widow and seven children.

In 1920 Cadder closed its gates forever.

Chapter 6
Stanrigg & Arbuckle Colliery, Airdrie: Tuesday, 9th July 1918

To let, for a number of years as may be agreed upon, the coal and ironstone in the farm of Stanrigg, about two miles from Airdrie. The coal, which has been wrought, is an excellent smithy coal; the other seams have not been ascertained. The ironstone consists of one seam of fourteen inches and the other of 26 inches. Apply to James Waddell, Stanrigg.

– The *Glasgow Herald*, 20th November 1818.

While mining operations in the area of Stanrigg in the parish of New Monkland had taken place prior to the placing of the above advertisement, they had been of limited scope. The advertisement, however, would generate a wider interest, leading to the first major development at Stanrigg. In February 1832 Baird of Gartsherrie took out a lease to work the blackband ironstone seams. In 1854 the Stanrigg lease was taken over by William Black and Sons who operated until 1902, when they were succeeded by United Collieries who worked the site for four years.

In 1908 the royalty was taken over by the McCracken Brothers and further large-scale developments were undertaken. The McCrackens held the lease until 1927 and it was during their term of ownership that the worst ever accident at Stanrigg Colliery took place. Up until 1903 accidents had been infrequent and, in each case, limited to one fatality only. Despite the presence of gas in the Stanrigg workings, it was never considered to be of such quantities as to constitute an overwhelming source of danger. To the miners who worked underground the greatest perceived source of danger had always been the moss that overlay the colliery workings. The existence of a substantial pump engine at the pithead testified to the fact that there was water in the mine, but since the early days of development the heavy moss had never encroached into the workings.

In 1861, following a lengthy period of heavy rain, the moss became unstable and a phenomenon referred to as 'the great moving bog' occurred. Eyewitnesses reported that the moss was moving westwards at the rate of five or six miles per hour. For a time the village of Slamannan, lying beyond the eastern boundary of the parish, was under threat, but was saved when the moss drained into the River Avon. When the moss stopped moving and was once again stable, it lay over roads, the railway, and on a number of fields, destroying crops.

By July of 1918, three seams had been worked at Stanrigg: the Humph coal at a depth of 82 feet, the Splint coal at 117 feet, and the Virgin coal at 126 feet. Three shafts were employed at the colliery. The downcast No. 1 shaft with its adjacent fan drove over 14,000 cubic feet of air into the workings to ventilate the three seams. The No. 2 (Arbuckle) shaft – the upcast – lay 950 feet to the west of the downcast. The No. 3 (Stanrigg) shaft was situated about 70 feet to the northeast of the downcast. No. 3 was used solely to deliver men and materials below and to raise the hewn coal to the surface. It was not connected to the ventilation system.

All the haulage roads leading to and from No. 3 shaft were in the Virgin Seam and two drift mines had been driven from that level through the barren ground to access the Humph Seam above. On the day of the accident only the Humph and Virgin seams were being worked. As was the custom

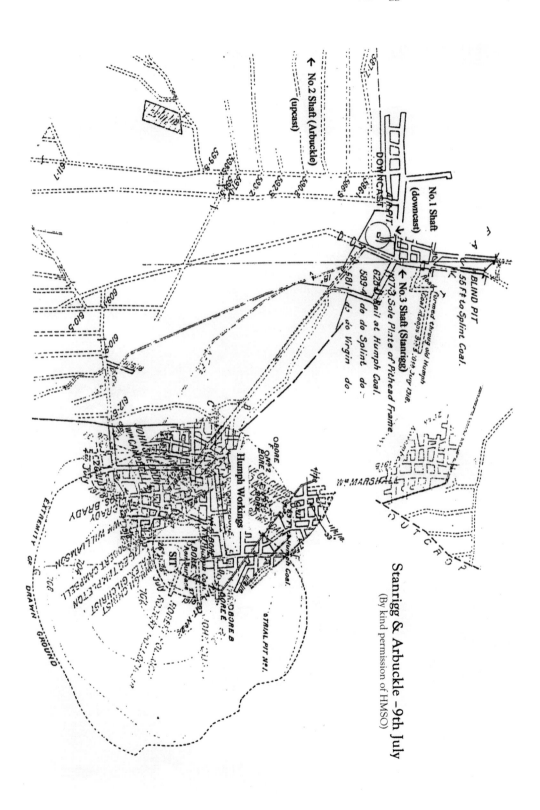

Stanrigg & Arbuckle -9th July
(By kind permission of HMSO)

59

at Stanrigg Colliery, both surface and underground staff worked a single shift per working day; in the case of the underground workers, beginning their shift at 6.45 a.m. and ending at 3.15 p.m.

The method of extracting coal in Stanrigg had always been stoop-and-room, but in April of 1918, with a view to improving productivity, longwall working with coal-cutting machines had been introduced by George Johnston, the colliery manager. The experiment did not last long and in June of 1918, as working longwall was proving to be less than cost effective, the new method was abandoned and stoop-and-room was reintroduced. The Humph Seam ran through several faults, and one of them in particular – an upthrow of one foot inbye – lay close to the longwall face when that method of extraction was halted.

*

About 6.00 a.m. on the morning of Tuesday, 9th May 1918, William and Edward McCracken, the firemen in charge of the working seams, stepped into the cage and descended No. 3 shaft. It was part of their normal daily routine – and also their statutory duty under Section 64 (1) of the Coal Mines Act of 1911 – to carry out a preliminary inspection of the workings prior to the shift of miners going below. They parted company when William McCracken left the cage at the Humph seam level to walk the slow gradient to the coalface. Edward McCracken continued on to the pit bottom and the Virgin coal where he made his way to the upper section of the workings, known to the men as 'the Sour Milk'.

Later, with their inspections completed and everything found to be satisfactory, they returned to the surface. Waiting for them at the pithead were the 77 men and boys who would go below that day. The firemen passed them into the mine before also descending to return to their workplaces and their normal duties. Of the 77, 58 were employed either in the Virgin coal or in other parts of the mine and nineteen in the Humph seam. There should have been 22 miners working that day in the Humph seam, but three failed to turn out. Work progressed normally in the two seams until around ten o'clock when, as was their usual practice, the two firemen met and went to the surface to have their breakfast in the firemen's station.

The first indication that something was wrong came when it was noticed that the ventilating current had suddenly grown stronger. James Rafferty, one of the No. 3 pit bottomers, went immediately to the surface to report the change. In the meantime another miner, a drawer who had been working near the bottom of the drift mine leading to the Humph seam, had seen a flood of moss and water coming through a break in the workings and came running towards No. 3 shaft shouting, 'The moss! The moss! It's coming down!' He then sought safety at the surface.

At the same time John McCabe, a fifteen-year-old drawer, arrived at No. 3 pit bottom pushing a full hutch. He had been there only a matter of moments when the warning came that the moss had broken into the workings. While the first drawer made for the surface, young McCabe immediately left the pit bottom and ran the quarter of a mile to where his brothers, Thomas and Joseph, were working to warn them of the danger. His selfless action was to save many lives that day. All 58 of those who were not working in the Humph workings that day escaped to the surface, seven by way of the eastern shaft and the rest by an emergency shaft.

It was shortly after ten o'clock, in the firemen's station on the surface, that William and Edward McCracken were disturbed at their breakfast by James Rafferty, who burst in to tell them that the ventilating current at the pit bottom was 'coming out very strong'. The firemen immediately rushed to No. 3 shaft and went below, each heading for their respective sections.

60

As William McCracken made his way through the Virgin lower workings towards the drift mine leading to the Humph seam, he had reached a point some 90 yards distant from No. 3 shaft when he was brought to a halt. Coming slowly towards him he saw a flood of mud and moss moving along the haulage road, pushing a hutch before it towards the shaft. Finding no other way forward he returned to the pit bottom and went to the surface.

Edward McCracken was not only able to reach the 'Sour Milk' section of the Virgin seam, but travelled as far as the drift mine that led to the machine section before he was stopped by a thick flow of moss moving towards him. Realising that the seam would shortly be flooded he gathered his men and took them to No. 2 shaft. When they arrived, however, they had to endure an anxious wait until enough steam could be raised to operate the winding engine for the cage. He and his men were eventually raised safely to the surface.

While all others in the mine had now reached safety, the nineteen men and boys who worked in the Humph seam had no chance of escape. They were cut off and entombed by the sudden inrush of mud, clay, stones and moss that had quickly flooded the coalface and blocked the only two roads by which they could have escaped. They were trapped behind a wall of sludge that flowed down the drift mine towards the Virgin seam and immediate rescue from any direction was now impossible.

At 11.35 a.m. the colliery manager, George Johnston, having consulted with the firemen from both sections and been appraised of the situation, phoned the Mines Rescue Station at Coatbridge. The rescue brigade arrived at the pithead fifteen minutes later and immediately went down No. 2 shaft; travelling the communication road towards No. 3 pit bottom and the Virgin seam. The squad was accompanied by manager Johnston and William Black, the manager of nearby Ballochney Colliery.

As the full extent of the inrush was unknown to them at that time, Johnston posted men at regular intervals along both levels of the road to prevent their line of retreat from being cut off by the moss. Running out of sentinels, he sent to the surface for 20 volunteers to extend the lines. When they eventually found that the Humph seam could not be reached by way of the communication road, they retraced their steps, picking up the sentinels on their way to the surface.

In the company of Thomas Thomson, manager of Whiterigg Colliery, George Johnston then descended No. 3 shaft. Although it was not connected to the regular ventilation system, he knew from experience that a small proportion of air had always managed to make its way from No. 3 shaft through a fault into the Humph workings. It occurred to him that a road might be driven through these old workings and into the section where the men were trapped. Work was immediately begun on this road from the bottom of the blind pit in the Splint seam.

At 3.00 p.m. Johnston returned to the pithead where James Crawford and Ian Allan, the manager and under-manager of Darngavil Colliery, had organised a squad of men to work on a new pit shaft at the surface. The excavation, about five feet square, was begun at a point considered to be immediately above the northwestern edge of the Humph workings. By this time the men below had been trapped for almost five hours.

That same day Henry Walker, Divisional Inspector of Mines, and Frederick Wynne, Senior Inspector of Mines, were giving evidence concerning another incident at Kilmarnock Sheriff Court. They received a telephone call about 12.20 p.m. from Divisional Headquarters in Edinburgh informing them of the situation at Stanrigg. They took the first available train and arrived at the colliery between four and four-thirty. On their arrival they were met by manager Johnston and Leslie McCracken, one of the colliery owners, who briefed them on what had happened and brought them up to date on what measures were being taken to reach the entombed men.

Three operations were underway at that time. Apart from the new shaft begun by James Crawford's squad and Johnston's attempt to drive a road through the old Humph workings, work was begun on clearing out an old surface borehole put down some time before. The first of the three to encounter difficulties was the borehole. Not satisfied with the rate of progress in clearing it James Pollock, the borer, declared that he could sink a new hole as fast, if not faster, than the present operation. A new borehole was immediately started.

In attempting to sink the five-foot shaft through the soft surface moss, Crawford's men soon discovered that normal shoring was useless and that some kind of boiler shell would be required. The search to find a suitable shell was begun, ending eventually at Stewart and Lloyd's steel fabricating yard in Motherwell. The first section arrived at the pithead about ten-thirty that evening and the second length sometime later.

Meanwhile, Pollock's attempt to put down a new borehole had to be abandoned at a depth of 44 feet following the breakage of the lining tubes due to the movement of the moss. A second attempt to drive a new borehole was then begun but also failed, for the same reason, around midnight. The second attempt had reached a depth of 48 feet. With the Humph seam no more than 60 feet below ground at that point, drilling had been suspended a mere twelve feet from the place where the men were thought to be trapped. Notwithstanding these setbacks, Pollock began work on two further boreholes.

With Crawford's men having toiled in shifts throughout the night, by 11 a.m. the following morning (Wednesday 10th) work on the new shaft was progressing steadily and the boiler shell had been sunk to a depth of 22 feet through the liquid moss and into the bed of soft muddy clay lying beneath. It was during the afternoon, as the liquid material within the shell was being pumped out, that fate once again turned against the rescuers. With the removal of this material the shell itself began to move, pushed aside by the relentless pressure of the moss around it. Unable to keep the boiler shell plumb, the attempt to sink a shaft had to be abandoned.

Later in the day the hopes of the large crowd gathered at the pithead were briefly raised when one of the two ongoing boreholes (the fifth) at last broke through into the Humph workings. Hope was crushed, however, when it was found that the depth of water in the seam at that point was sixteen and a half feet above the pavement. Not only that but blackdamp had been detected, which, had they managed to survive the flood, would have suffocated the men in a very short time. Another borehole was begun within the abandoned boiler shell, but operations had to be halted due to the lateral movement of the moss bending the lining tubes.

In the meantime George Johnston's attempt to clear a road through the old Humph workings was being continued by relays of men. The distance to be cleared, measured in a straight line, was 462 feet before the nearest part of the workings could be reached. Added to the normal dangers of mining was the risk that their only exit could be blocked by an inrush of moss up No. 3 pit from the Splint seam. Regardless of the dangers they carried on until the fifth borehole reached the Humph seam; but, in the knowledge that the water level ahead of them was standing too high above the pavement for the miners to have survived, Johnston's attempt had to be halted.

Early on Thursday morning, 11th July, the moss was found to be still advancing through the underground workings at a steady pace and all idea of getting to the victims from below ground had to be abandoned. Moving some twelve to fifteen feet to the east of the boiler shell, yet another borehole was started, eventually reaching the Humph workings between six and seven that evening. This last sinking crushed all remaining hope of finding any of the nineteen miners alive, for the depth of water at that level – the highest point in the seam – was found to be almost nine feet above the pavement. The search for survivors was over.

Paul McKenna, the miners' agent, announced the terrible news to those relatives who waited around the pithead, and the dreamed-of miracle dissolved in bitter anguish. Among the nineteen victims were the three Gilchrist brothers, leaving their elderly father – who had stood vigil at the pithead for almost two and a half days – to go home to an empty house. Two fathers had died with their sons. Three other victims – George Templeton, William Williamson and Robert Campbell – were married to three sisters. Fourteen-year-old James Sneddon had worked in the pit for only three days. Bernard McAdams, also fourteen, had worked in the pit for little over three hours on his first day as a working man.

The results of the final bore brought all operations to a halt. Inspector Henry Walker consulted with management officials and rescuers on what should be done next and it was decided that efforts to recover the bodies of the victims should nevertheless go ahead. To that end a new shaft was begun late on Thursday evening at the site of the fifth borehole, which had earlier reached the Humph seam and measured the water level at sixteen and a half feet.

All the next day (Friday 12th), while work on the new shaft continued, miners and scores of volunteers threw all kinds of materials, including the branches of trees, into the large hole which had opened up on the surface above the point of the inrush. This was done in an attempt to stabilise the moss and prevent it from further sliding into the workings – for wide cracks had opened up, radiating away from the opening, indicating that the surface was unstable.

On Saturday 13th, with volunteers still bringing materials to throw into the yawning hole, men worked to lay rails from an old bing of blaes towards the crater so that hutches might be used to carry this material to fill the breach. As it was then the beginning of the Glasgow Fair holidays and a fine sunny day, hundreds of people found their way to the scene to watch the comings and goings. Work had also begun at the top of No. 3 to remove the liquid moss that had found its way into the shaft through the workings. At its height this flood had come to within 32 feet of the surface. In addition to pumping operations, a bailing tank (a large iron chest) was repeatedly lowered into the shaft to be filled, raised to the surface and emptied.

While the above operations were continued on Sunday 14th, a crowd of four or five thousand, which all but filled the roads, railway tracks and paths leading across the moor to Stanrigg, gathered near the pithead for a special service of remembrance at 3.30 p.m. But such was the throng that the service was delayed until sometime after 4.00 p.m. The Rev. Jack, who conducted the service, chose as his lesson Matthew 24.39 – 'And knew not till the flood came, and took them all away'. To the background drone of pumps and the distant clatter of hutches carrying blaes along the twin tracks hurriedly laid from the bing to the hole, a collection was taken on behalf of the wives and dependants.

On Monday 15th another borehole was begun, reaching the Humph workings the following day when it was found that the water and moss appeared to have largely cleared from the seam. From this it was decided that operations to pump out No. 3 shaft should be continued with a view to clearing the moss from the pit bottom and the surrounding passages. When this was done a search for the victims could begin.

Work continued over the next few days on two major fronts, the new shaft being driven towards the Humph workings and the pumping operations to clear No. 3 shaft. A certain amount of water was pumped down the shaft to mix with the mossy sludge and this enabled the pumps to carry the moss to the surface more quickly. Thomas Thomson, manager of Whiterigg Colliery, reckoned that 38,700 cubic yards of moss had entered the Stanrigg workings through the breach.

Operations were brought to a brief halt the following week when moss once again came flooding into No. 3 shaft. However, as the new flood quickly began to ease off again, work was restarted. It was believed that this new inundation had been caused, not by a fresh inrush from the surface, but by obstructions – perhaps dams of wood and rubble in the passageways – giving way and releasing the accumulated moss pent-up behind them.

In Parliament on Thursday 25th July, local MP Duncan Millar asked if an inquiry would be held into the circumstances surrounding the accident and the Under Home Secretary, Mr Brace, assured him that such an inquiry was planned. He added that the Home Office Inspector was urging Messrs McCracken, the colliery owners, to expedite the work with a view to recovering the bodies of the victims.

On Wednesday 14th August, while operations continued to clear the moss from the passages via No. 3 shaft, the new shaft being driven from the surface finally broke through into the Humph workings. It was found that, to a large extent, the section was still filled with moss. The following day W. Walker, HM Chief Inspector of Mines, arrived at Stanrigg for consultations with officials. As a result of the meeting pumps were set up and moss was also drawn out through the new shaft until the roads from the shaft to the top of the drift mine leading to the Virgin Seam were clear. Before search operations could begin, and for the safety of the rescuers, barricades were then erected in three places to isolate the area of the inrush.

On Tuesday 27th, the body of William Marshall was the first to be found. Although his belongings had been found earlier in the day, it was late evening when one of the rescuers noticed a pair of heels protruding from a hole in the wall. The hole was cleared out and Marshall's body found. In a tragic twist of fate, the rescuer who found him was his own brother, Thomas, who had slept in for work on the morning of the disaster.

On the following Friday (the 30th), the body of John Queen was found. The grim search continued with the days now turning to weeks. On Thursday 19th September, the body of fourteen-year-old Bernard McAdams was discovered, jammed among hutches and badly mutilated. On the following Saturday (the 21st) George Templeton was found, and the next day the bodies of David McNiven (17), Neil Lindsay (16), Leslie Gilchrist (15) and James Sneddon (14) were recovered.

With roads from the new shaft to No. 3 pit bottom now cleared and no further bodies recovered, it was assumed that the remaining eleven who were yet missing were lying somewhere on the far side of the three barricades. One of the barricades was removed and the roads immediately beyond it were searched as far as the rescuers felt it was safe to proceed, and again, although the coalface itself was reached in three places, no more bodies were found. As the missing men were almost certain to be behind the remaining two barricades, and the rescuers thought it impossible to penetrate beyond them without risking further loss of life, recovery efforts were halted. All concerned in the rescue efforts agreed with this decision.

*

On Wednesday, 18th December 1918, the official inquiry into the Stanrigg disaster was begun in the County Buildings in Airdrie. Acting Chief Inspector W. Walker presided and was assisted by A.D.

Lindsay, Procurator Fiscal. McCracken Brothers Ltd, the colliery owners, were represented by solicitor James Bell of Airdrie and the relatives of the victims by G. Craig McIntyre of Hamilton.

First to give evidence was George Johnston, who had been manager of the colliery for the past three and a half years. He said that in his time at Stanrigg, he never felt that the mine was unsafe – despite having knowledge of falls of material from the roofs prior to the disaster. Johnston accepted full responsibility for the changes of extraction methods from stoop-and-room to longwall, and back again, and when asked if he would do the same again, he said that he would not. As he had been working on his own judgement, the court felt that Johnston had not been guilty of malpractice as such. However, as Larry O'Hare points out in his book *The Stanrigg Pit Disaster*, '. . . it seems difficult to condone the fact that there was no qualified mining engineer about the colliery available for consultation.'

All the witnesses called to give evidence were of the opinion that the entombed men could not have survived for more than two hours after the moss broke through into the workings. While two hours was the longest estimate given, others thought half an hour to one hour at maximum. Most of them agreed that the roof of the Humph seam was good – despite the reported falls of material.

Edward Quinn, a checkweighman at Ballochney No. 9 pit, organised the first volunteer search party to go below. Giving evidence, it was his opinion that there had been 'an unnecessary delay' in sending assistance below. This delay was occasioned by 'a lack of deliberate consultation among the officials' as to the best method of approaching the rescue.

Among several witnesses called to give expert testimony on working conditions in collieries as regards to moss, James Crawford, manager of Darngavil Colliery, put forward the following suggestions:

Surface Precautions:

1. A proper system of shallow surface drains to run off the water as it fell and prevent it accumulating on the top of the underlying clay until the whole moss was in a liquid condition.

2. All old sits or subsidence to be drained dry.

3. A careful system of boring, so that the various thicknesses of moss and metals were known.

4. Where any doubt still existed as to the condition of the moss, a small shaft or hole should be put down throughout the moss to the clay.

Underground Precautions:

1. Drawing roads to be no wider than necessary and to be well secured with timber at all branches or junctions, also where necessary along the roads.

2. Waste to be properly packed throughout, supporting the roof.

3. All hitches and dislocations of metals to be carefully noted and the roof at such parts secured by a proper system of pillaring.

When called to the stand, R.W. Dron, a mining engineer, had this suggestion of his own: 'In the event of coal or other minerals being worked underneath a deposit of peat moss or other soft material containing water, intimation shall be given to the Mines Inspector before such working approaches nearer to the bottom of the peat or moss than 50 feet, or ten times the thickness of the seam which is being worked, whichever the greater. The system of working above the 50 feet limit should be determined after consultation with experts, and for this purpose the proposed Ministry of Mines might form an Advisory Committee with local knowledge.'

Although he had been called to the stand relatively early in the proceedings, it was to be the fifteen-year-old drawer, John McCabe, who produced the most graphic and memorable recollections of that day. To a hushed court he recounted that he had been drawing hutches from about seven that morning until about ten-thirty, at which time he arrived at No. 3 pit bottom with a full hutch. Miners Matthew Penman and James Bennett arrived there at the same time and told the bottomer that the moss had broken into the workings. On hearing this, young McCabe turned and ran back to warn his workmates at the coalface a quarter of a mile away.

Asked by Mr Walker if he could have gone to the surface if he had wanted to, the boy said 'Yes,' then added, '. . . but I thought it better to go to the face to fetch the men out.' Mr Walker – no doubt with a smile of admiration – commented, 'That was very good of you,' at which the courtroom burst into spontaneous applause. McCabe's quick and selfless action had given 62 miners precious time to reach safety.

When the fatal accident inquiry opened the following week before Sheriff Lee, manager George Johnston told the court that he thought the men would have been suffocated within half an hour to an hour of the moss breaking in. Dr Kirkland – who had been present at the colliery and had examined the bodies of the eight victims recovered from the workings – told the court that they had all died from suffocation. It was also his opinion that the eleven men who as yet remained entombed had more than likely died from the same cause.

A formal verdict was returned and the young drawer, John McCabe, was commended for heroism. Dubbed 'The Brave Drawer' by the newspapers, he received a citation to appear before King George V and was presented with the Edward Medal which, many years later, after his retirement, would be replaced by the George Medal. In 1919 the Carnegie Hero Fund presented him with a silver watch bearing the inscription: 'Presented by the Trustees of the Carnegie Hero Fund to John McCabe, Airdrie, for heroism in saving human life, 9th July 1918'.

*

On Wednesday, 12th March 1919, Mr W. Walker, HM Acting Chief Inspector of Mines, completed his report into the Stanrigg disaster and it was presented to Parliament a week later by the Home Secretary. Having first described the colliery and detailed the narrative of the accident, Mr Walker turned to the thickness of the strata lying above the Humph seam between the workings and the moss. Boreholes put down before and after the inrush had indicated there had been a certain thinning of the till below the moss in the neighbourhood of the sit.

On the earlier reported falls of roof near Pollock's platform and in Williamson's place he said that if they did not actually go right up to the blue clay, they went close enough to leave little reliable support for the weight of the moss above. There had been three separate falls reported to the manager on the inside of Pollock's platform, the first just inside the platform and the second some eight feet further inbye, while the third happened at the point where the one-foot upthrow fault crossed the road. It was Mr Walker's opinion that this fault and the stopping of the longwall face had had a very important bearing on the cause of the accident.

He explained: 'Owing to the natural subsidence of the strata over the longwall workings, as soon as the stoop-and-room method was [re-]commenced, a break-off would necessarily occur in the roof over the longwall waste, and the fracture would probably go up at an angle of about 45 degrees until it met the listing of the one-foot fault referred to, when a triangular piece would be formed probably reaching up to the blue clay. The weakest point would be, of course, the roadway, and all the more, because of the recent falls that had taken place there, and that was, in point of fact, the place where the inrush of moss occurred.'

Coming to the stoop-and-room versus longwall debate, Mr Walker said there had been a diversity of opinion as to whether the seam should have been worked by the longwall method or by stoop-and-room. However, it was generally agreed that it was dangerous practice to change from one to the other and then to revert back to the first method employed – in this case stoop-and-room. The method adopted at the outset should have been continued.

Most of the expert witnesses at the inquiry, he said, had come to the conclusion that it would have been more desirable, under the circumstances that existed in Stanrigg, to leave some 30 to 40 per cent of the coal in as a support, and to have done this it follows that the longwall method of working should not have been employed at all.

At the inquiry colliery manager George Johnston had accepted full responsibility for the change from stoop-and-room to longwall, but it has to be remembered that the decision to bring in an expensive longwall coal-cutting machine would not have been his alone. His superiors, more than likely the McCracken brothers themselves, had to have had some say in the matter – after all it was they who would be footing the bill. But why was there no qualified engineer available at Stanrigg for consultation on such an important change of working practice?

It also has to be said that, while manager Johnston may have promoted the idea of changing from stoop-and-room to longwall extraction on his own initiative, in doing so he was simply promoting the main principle of the company – indeed *every* private coal company – that increased output led to increased profit. No one appears to have challenged the suggested change and, had the change to longwall proved cost effective, all he could have hoped to gain from it would have been greater job security. All else (i.e. profit) would have gone to McCracken Bros. Ltd.

Mr Walker ended his report with these conclusions:

1. There had been no contraventions of the Coal Mines Act, 1911, or of the General Regulations in connection with the accident.

2. There had been considerable avoidable delay in the work of exploration after it had been ascertained by boreholes that the whole area in which the deceased men were entombed was under water.

3. The accident was caused by an inrush of moss into the Humph seam due to (1) the small thickness of strata between that seam and the bottom of the moss, (2) the nature of that cover, (3) the probable thinning of the blue clay underlying the moss, (4) the presence of faults near to the line of the longwall face when it was stopped, and (5) the stoop-and-room by which the seam was extracted when it was first opened having been changed.

4. The manager, in changing the system of working, committed an error of judgement.

5. In the circumstances which existed the safest method of working to adopt and adhere to was the stoop-and-room, with rooms of a maximum width of eight feet and stoops left for support of the clay of such a size that not more than 50 per cent of coal was extracted.

He also concluded that it was not possible – considering the wide variation in the thickness of clay and depth of moss, etc. from mine to mine – to have a regulation which would cover all the precautions necessary for safe working in all circumstances. It was his opinion that a regulation should be established requiring, where coal or any other mineral was being worked under moss, quicksand, etc., that steps should be taken by boring or otherwise to ascertain the depth of the moss and the thickness and composition of the strata lying between the moss and the workings. To this he added that, where the strata between the moss and the workings is found to be less than ten fathoms (60 feet) or ten times the thickness of the seam being worked – whichever the greater – all working should be stopped and notification be sent to the mines inspector for that area.

The second of the inspector's conclusions made reference to the 'considerable avoidable delay in the work of exploration'. This delay commenced on the discovery that the area where the eleven men were yet trapped was still flooded by moss. The owners and management realised that, to reach these men (who were probably dead anyway), great care would have to be taken not to endanger the lives of the rescuers. They also realised, however, that such care would involve considerable time and *expense*. This last brought them up short as they agonised over what to do. In the end they decided that it would be more economical to close the section off permanently, leaving them there, than to venture an unknowable amount of time and money rescuing dead men. It was simple fiscal policy – cut your losses. It was private mine owning at work.

As a result of the inquiries and report into the Stanrigg disaster, the Moss Regulation Act of 1920 came into force. Regulation 29 laid down in law the precautions to be taken when working under liquid or other unstable matter as suggested by Mr Walker.

*

From the tragedy of Stanrigg two divergent yet evocative pictures emerged to trouble the conscience of the nation. That of a fifteen-year-old boy running alone through the darkness of a rapidly flooding mine, bent not on escape, but on warning his brothers and their comrades of danger. And that of owner Leslie McCracken and a huddled group of company officials arriving at the cold-hearted decision to abandon eleven miners in their watery grave – and deny them a Christian burial – because they considered it unprofitable to attempt a recovery.

In 1987, when Larry O'Hare wrote about the Stanrigg disaster, he said: 'Today, seven decades later, a tongue of land, protected from the opencast excavations which cover much of the area, marks the miners' desolate grave.' Fairly recently, however, that tongue of land came under threat from those same opencast operations. In 2004 relatives' concerns were voiced when the Scottish Executive gave permission for a new landfill site at nearby Dalmacoulter. Seventy-five-year-old Jean Blades, whose three uncles were buried alive in the disaster, said: 'After all this time it should be left as it is. It's consecrated ground and the bodies should be left in peace.'

G.M. Mining, owned by ex-Glasgow Rangers chairman Sir David Murray, gave assurances that '. . . the proposed mining will not disturb the bodies buried as a result of the Stanrigg mining disaster.' But relatives remained unconvinced. Eighty-year-old May Davies, who also lost uncles in the tragedy, said: 'On no account should anyone be allowed to go anywhere near the graveyard.' However, Jim Marshall, who also lost an uncle, was in two minds. If the proposed extension went ahead, something positive might come of it. 'It would be a good idea,' he said, 'if they looked for the men and gave them a proper Christian burial.'

The opencast operation did not interfere with the disaster site.

Chapter 7
Cardowan Colliery, Stepps:
Wednesday, 16th November 1932

Owned by coalmasters James Dunlop & Co., Cardowan Colliery was located beside the old Garnkirk and Glasgow railway near the village of Stepps on the northeastern outskirts of Glasgow. Cardowan was a particularly gassy pit, so much so that the gas was used to fire the boilers for the steam-driven pithead winding engines. Later, some was piped to Buchanan's whisky bottling plant at Stepps and 50 million cubic feet to the Provan Gas Works in Glasgow.

In late 1932 the colliery agent and manager was John Macdonald Williamson and James Peacock was his under-manager. The colliery surveyor (part of whose duties were to collect dust samples from the roof, sides and floor of the individual roads and to test for firedamp in the return airways) was George Ernest Sleight.

Cardowan had two shafts, No. 1 being the downcast and, just over 30 yards to the east, No. 2 serving as the upcast. While both shafts were sunk to the Kilsyth Coking Coal Seam at a depth of 342 fathoms, they passed through two other seams – the Main coal at 237 fathoms and the Wee coal at 242 fathoms. Since production began, the Main coal and Coking coal seams had been extensively worked, but the Wee coal had been discontinued after a time when it proved to be uneconomic. Output from the Main coal seam was wound via the No. 1 shaft while that from the Coking coal seam was wound via No. 2.

The workings were ventilated by means of a double inlet Sirocco fan sited at the top of No. 2 upcast shaft. At the time of the accident a total volume of 220,000 cubic feet of air per minute was being passed through the mine, and of this quantity, around 100,000 cubic feet were circulating round the Main coal seam. The seam was considered to be very gassy, but with the coal being hard and particularly brittle, the seam was not dusty. Notwithstanding the absence of coal dust, limestone dust was used for dusting the roof, floor and sides of the roads. The dust was stored in bags on the main intake road from where it was taken to the various roadheads as and when required.

In the Main coal seam the workings were divided into three districts – the East, the South heading, and the West. In all districts the method of extraction was longwall advancing employing coal-cutting machines, conveyors and gate-end loaders driven by compressed air. At the face in the West District two chain coal-cutting machines were used to undercut the coal to an average depth of four feet.

In the West District the longwall face, some 760 feet in length, dipped at a rate of 1 in 6 to the northeast. The face was divided into two parts by the main intake airway and the haulage road, that part to the rise being 480 feet long and that to the dip 280 feet. The seam to the dip side of the haulage road, where the accident happened, was some three feet thick with a blaes roof and a fireclay floor. The current ventilating this part of the face, having split from the main intake, was directed down the face, which had two return airways. Halfway down was the first return, the 7 x 7 road, and at the bottom of the dip was the second return, the Downset road.

Cardowan operated on 24-hour production with three shifts being employed – the night shift (11.00 p.m. to 6.30 a.m.), comprising 35 men, the day shift (7.00 a.m. to 2.30 p.m.) with 47 men, and the back shift (3.00 p.m. to 10.30 p.m.) with 30 men. Each shift was supervised by a fireman who, on the night and back shifts, was responsible for firing the shots. While all work on the West District face was carried out by contractor Robert Kirkland, it was the day shift fireman, William Horn, assisted by two shotfirers, who fired the shots. Firemen and shotfirers at Cardowan were provided with two flame safety lamps and an electric cap lamp, the latter also being used by the greater majority of the miners.

Shot holes were three and a half to four feet deep and four to five feet apart, bored into the top six to nine inches of the seam where the coal was hard. Evidence was later given at the inquiry that this six to nine inches of hard coal stuck to the roof and that every day, on some part of the face, the remainder of the seam, in lengths of up to 40 feet, broke away from the top portion. This happened in particular when all the 'gum' (cuttings from the machine) had been cleared out of the cut, leaving a clean gap of about two inches between the two parts of the seam.

Alexander Beaton, the day shift shotfirer working on the rise side of the West face, told the inquiry that, on occasion, he had waited until the gum had been cleaned out from underneath the place where he intended to fire a shot. This was done, he said, to allow the bottom coal to drop.

*

At about 8.45 a.m. on Wednesday, 16th November 1932, putter Patrick Johnson – with the conveyors and gate-end loader having been idle for several minutes due to a lack of empty hutches – decided he would have something to eat. He walked outbye on the haulage road the fifteen or so yards to where he left his piece box and was bending down to open it when he heard 'a loud report, a sort of dull report'. He was blown forward onto his hands, and when he looked round in the direction of the face, he saw 'a flame practically in the full head of the working, in the roof. After that the coal dust came, and you could hardly see your hand . . .'.

At the same time Robert Kirkland, the contractor, was standing a little farther up the haulage road, about 30 to 40 feet from the gate-end loader, with his back towards the face. He remembered having heard no noise but felt 'a slight heat' on the back of his neck, then a blast of air that raised a thick cloud of dust. Turning towards the face he saw loader attendant Michael Flynn with his shirt on fire. He and Johnson tore Flynn's burning shirt off and Johnson took him outbye on the haulage road.

Others then came staggering from the face – conveyor engine attendant Andrew Murphy and miners William Rae, John Sharp, William Bradley and John Watt Jnr. Miner Peter Lusty, who had been standing on the rise side of – and no more than seven feet from – the gate-end loader, came out next, followed by shotfirer John Whiteford. Of those who came out from the face only Lusty was uninjured, the others having been burned. Kirkland asked Whiteford what had happened and the shotfirer, probably in shock, replied absently, 'I was firing my shot.'

At the time of the explosion fireman William Horn was standing near the top of the rise side face. Shotfirer Alexander Beaton and seventeen other miners were also working on the face. On hearing the explosion they at first thought that one of the compressed air hoses feeding the machines had burst, but when the cloud of smoke and dust came up from the dip side they made their way out by way of the return airway. Some of them, having reached the air crossing doors leading into the West main intake and haulage road, returned inbye to give assistance.

These men, when they arrived at the end of the intake road, were met by Robert Kirkland who led them onto the dip side face. They found George Mullen about 30 to 40 feet down the face and Peter Fratti close to the corner of the 7 x 7 road. Both men were helped out to the haulage road. Beyond the 7 x 7 road Kirkland, who did not have a flame safety lamp with him, felt the air ahead might be contaminated so he waited until fireman William Horn arrived. When Horn arrived he carried out tests and, finding no firedamp, both men moved on.

At the edge of the open waste below the 7 x 7 road they came across the body of John McNab, and farther down the face the body of James Reynolds. Horn stepped over the conveyor and, using his flame safety lamp, tested for firedamp. 'Steady,' he warned Kirkland, 'I think there's some gas here.' Kirkland, unimpressed, ignored him and carried on down the face to the end of the conveyor where they found the bodies of William McAllister and Richard Maroney. Like McNab and Reynolds, McAllister and Maroney had been severely burned, but the immediate cause of death would prove to be carbon monoxide poisoning.

An official statement was issued by the management of Dunlop & Co. stating that the explosion had happened shortly before 9.00 a.m. in No. 1 pit in the Main coal seam in the Main West level. It was believed, they said, to have been caused by a pocket of gas being ignited by shot firing. There had been no fire after the explosion, and company officials had been able to enter the affected area and tend to the injured before bringing them to the surface. Doctors and adequate ambulance facilities had been available and the injured were immediately sent to the Royal Infirmary in Glasgow. All the victims had been recovered before the rescue brigade arrived from Hamilton. Seventy men had been working in the section where the explosion occurred, some of them having had remarkable escapes.

While four men had been killed by the blast and its after effects, the tragedy was not to end there. Five of those who had been taken out from the face – George Mullen, William Bradley, Peter Fratti, John Watt Jnr and James McVey – succumbed to their injuries the following day, shotfirer John Whiteford died on Friday 18th, and Michael Flynn on Saturday 19th. Leaving three victims alive but suffering from burns, the death toll stopped at eleven.

As usual, the press were early on the scene. According to *The Times* of 11th July, 'Cardowan Colliery, Stepps, was the scene of a terrible pit explosion yesterday morning, when four men were killed and ten others injured. A feature of the disaster was the heroism shown by many of the miners in attempting to rescue their comrades. Some of the survivors had to crawl through dense smoke clouds to safety, but the work of rescue was carried through with remarkable expedition.'

The survivors told their stories. Peter Lusty, who had been working at the coalface, said that there was a single big explosion, and that it was over in a few seconds. The explosion was so violent that he was hurled against the coalface and completely dazed. When he recovered he crawled into a manhole and found a jacket containing a flask of tea or water. A swallow of the contents helped to revive him, and then he saw John Whiteford, one of the injured, staggered blindly through the smoke towards him. Lusty caught hold of him and remained with him until rescuers arrived.

Eighteen-year-old Andrew Murphy, who was injured, told how the explosion had lifted him right off his feet, and that for a moment everything went dark. When he came round he saw a light in the distance, and on moving towards it came across one of his friends. Neither of them knew what had happened, but they managed to help each other to the pit bottom where they were found by the rescuers. Before they reached the bottom they met some of the others who had crawled in the same direction. They had somehow escaped the full force of the explosion, and when they met they formed themselves into a rescue squad and went back to help the others.

One man, whose injuries were of a serious nature, displayed remarkable fortitude while he was being carried on an improvised stretcher to the pit bottom. 'Tell my father about this, but don't tell my mother,' he told his bearers before he lapsed into unconsciousness. Another man, who escaped unhurt, told a reporter that the vibration of the explosion shook the ground beneath their feet. His squad volunteered to take part in the rescue operations, but as they did not have gas masks they were not allowed to enter the west section. Fortunately, no roof collapse occurred during or after the explosion.

Cardowan Colliery

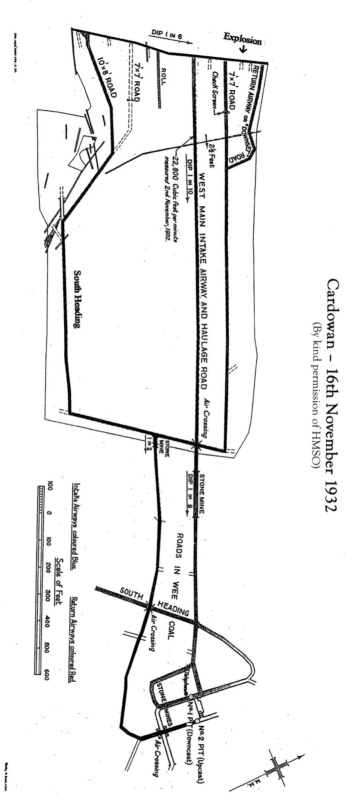

Cardowan – 16th November 1932
(By kind permission of HMSO)

72

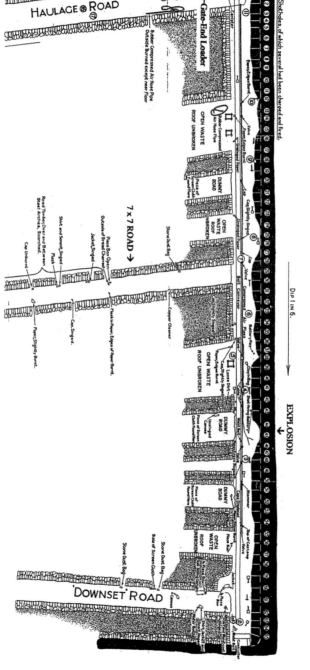

Plan of the location of the explosion.

WEST DISTRICT WORKING FACE

Cardowan – 16th November 1932
(By kind permission of HMSO)

With many anxious relatives and workmates visiting the injured, according to the *Scotsman* of 17th November, '. . . pathetic scenes have been witnessed at Glasgow Royal Infirmary since the injured men were admitted, relatives keeping constant vigil at their bedsides, and some collapsing under the strain and anxiety.'

*

On the morning of Tuesday, 10th January 1933, in the Justiciary Buildings, Jail Square, Glasgow, an inquiry was begun into the disaster at Cardowan Colliery. Presided over by Sir Henry Walker, Chief Inspector of Mines, 34 witnesses were called to give evidence. Over the seven days of gathering evidence certain topics were gone into in great detail, for example ventilation in the mine, shotfiring procedure, and stonedusting.

John MacDonald Williamson, the colliery agent and manager, was questioned on the practice of firing shots in the top coal when it was, on average, only six to nine inches thick. From his answers it was established that, in everyday practice, the shot holes (which were about one and a half inches in diameter) were generally bored about one inch from the roof, but not into the roof itself. The drill may have touched the roof, but did not go *into* it. Adding together one and a half inches for the hole and one inch to the roof would leave – in the case of the top coal at that point being only six inches – three and a half inches of coal to be blown down. If that were the case, he told the court, only a very light shot would be used.

While examining the dip side face after the explosion, a party consisting of Arthur Stoker, Senior Mines Inspector, and John Masterton, Divisional Mines Inspector, along with P.G. Dominy and H.R. Houston, Junior Mines Inspectors, had found '. . . a shotfiring cable in two parts, with the leads of a detonator attached to the end near to the shots numbered 44 and 45 on the plan; these shots had evidently been fired.' The shotfiring battery itself was not seen at that time but was seen close to the cable earlier in the day by miners John Ford and Thomas Timlin as they accompanied Kirkland and Horn in their search of the face.

A total of fourteen electric and two flame safety lamps were collected from the workings and sent to Captain C.B. Platt of the Mines Department Testing Station at Sheffield for examination. 'None of them,' he reported, 'was capable of igniting firedamp in the condition in which it was received.' However, miner Thomas Timlin had earlier found a flame safety lamp near to the shotfiring battery and handed it in at the lamp cabin without making any report on it.

In addition, another flame safety lamp – found ten yards below the 7 x 7 road between the conveyor and the coalface – was brought to the surface by miner John Kane who, like Timlin, made no report on it. It was eventually found to have been issued to William McAllister who had been working at the return end of the dip face. As the lampman had no particular information on the lamp (therefore did not know it had been found in the area covered by the explosion) he cleaned and filled it and issued it for use each day following the explosion. The two lamps found by Timlin and Kane were never submitted to Captain Platt for examination.

The cause of the explosion produced general agreement among the witnesses. A shot had been fired in either No. 44 or No. 45 shothole, opposite the first dummy road below the 7 x 7 road. Contractor Robert Kirkland – who, while standing on the intake road, had felt the heat of the blast – had no doubts that firedamp was lighted by that shot.

Unfortunately, there would be no consensus of agreement on the means by which the explosion was extended. All they had to go on by way of first-hand evidence was the statement made to

Kirkland by shotfirer John Whiteford when he emerged from the face to the intake road following the explosion: 'I was firing my shot.' Unfortunately, John Whiteford had died of his injuries two days after the accident.

James Peacock, the under-manager, was of the opinion that the first shot fired had been No. 45, followed by No. 44. The first shot, he believed, did more work than was expected, taking out coal from either side including that covered by No. 44. When No. 44 was fired, firedamp in the cut and amongst the broken coal from the first shot was ignited. The flame passed across to the dummy road lying opposite and ignited further firedamp in the brushing of that road. As far as dust was concerned, he did not believe there was enough to ignite and carry the explosion.

Colliery manager John Williamson told the inquiry he thought there had been 'a considerable volume of firedamp in the dummy road opposite where the two shots had been fired.' Firedamp, he added, had probably been in all the dummy roads as well as the waste, and that firedamp had been ignited either by flame, or by a piece of undetonated but burning explosive projected into the dummy road from one or other of the two shots. He was also of the opinion that dust had nothing to do with the explosion, and if he had believed dust was responsible, he 'never would have looked in the waste for gas'.

Mr Houston contended that the two shots (Nos. 44 and 45) had been fired one after the other, as a result of which the first shot had blown down a considerable amount of the softer bottom coal beyond the position of the second shot. This left the second shot much less work to do than the first. It was also possible the first shot had opened breaks into the second and that, when the second shot was fired, flame ignited firedamp in the undercut or amongst the coal brought down by the first shot. The resulting explosion then raised dust, which carried flame out to the main intake road.

Mr Dominy agreed with his colleague, but he added that it was also possible the explosive in the second shot had burned and not exploded, thus igniting firedamp amongst the broken coal brought down by the first shot. There was an explosion of firedamp, he suggested, followed by an inflammation, or a 'flashing' of dust.

*

On Friday, 24th March 1933, the report on the Cardowan Colliery disaster was completed and in April was presented to Parliament by Ernest Brown MP, Secretary for Mines. The author of the report, Sir Henry Walker – who had overseen the inquiry – remarked on several points raised during questioning.

Regarding examinations made for firedamp prior to a shot being fired, Clause 6, paragraph *f* (i) of the Explosives in Coal Mines Order ruled that no shot could be fired until the shotfirer had first examined, with a locked flame safety lamp, all accessible places within a radius of 20 yards from the place where the shot was to be fired and found them clear of inflammable gas. The inspector stated, 'I do not think the requirements of this clause were fulfilled. I think such examination as was made was restricted to the near vicinity of each shot; it did not extend to all contiguous accessible places within a radius of 20 yards and was not made immediately before firing.'

He was also in grave doubt whether, in view of the condition which frequently existed in the West District – namely, a gap left between the top six to nine inches and the remainder of the seam – that the firing of a shot in the top portion was legal. He had no doubt that such condition added materially to the risk.

As to the subject of stonedusting before firing shots, shotfirer Beaton and fireman Horn had given evidence that before firing shots they always applied stone dust where they thought it was required.

The normal method of application was simply to throw handfuls of dust into the ventilation current, which carried it along the face. Again, Inspector Walker did not think this practice fully complied with the regulations (Clause 6, paragraph *f* (ii)): 'As the firing of the shots proceeded, stonedust spread in this way would become covered with [fresh] coal dust; to comply with the spirit of the clause, stonedust should have been applied separately for each shot.'

Following an examination of the records detailing the amount of shots normally fired in a day by firemen and shotfirers at Cardowan, there was much debate on whether or not so many shots could be fired while still maintaining the essential elements of safety, i.e. checking for gas and stonedusting before the firing of shots. Firemen and shotfirers were timed during the procedure and examples from other collieries were quoted. The inspector, however, was not impressed. Having regard to the conditions, he said, he did not think it was possible for the shotfirers to have fired as many shots per shift as the records show they were firing, and at the same time to fulfil all the statutory requirements.

The firing of more than one shot in the same place at the same time was forbidden by paragraph *g* (i) of Clause 6: 'Two or more shots shall not be fired in the same place simultaneously . . .'. However, paragraph *g* (iv) gives this: 'The requirements of this paragraph shall not apply to stone drifts or in sinking pits . . .'. In evidence fireman Robert Wilson spoke freely of firing two shots simultaneously in the brushings.

The inspector recalled that Wilson, when asked if he had any particular reason for firing two shots together, replied that '. . . he thought it was the safest method of firing in brushing because when firing one shot it might take away too much of the material from the other hole and so, by leaving the second shot too little work to do, make it dangerous to fire that second shot.' Wilson also understood that brushing was in the same category as stone drifts.

Inspector Walker studied the history of the dip side in the West District with regard to shotfiring practice, the results of firedamp tests both before and after the accident, and the condition of the workings in the immediate area of the explosion. He concluded that the view advanced to account for the spread of the explosion – namely, that there had been a sudden outburst of firedamp from the wastes, of the precise quantity and at the precise moment at which the shot was fired – seemed quite untenable.

He continued: '. . . attention had not been paid to the evidence given during the inquiry. For example, it was stated that the evidences generally of heat and scorching in and about the roadhead in the main intake, were confined to the roof and therefore indicated a burning of firedamp and not of coal dust; whereas, evidence was given during the inquiry that the shirt of one of the men (Flynn) and the trousers pocket of the other (McVey), both of whom were standing next [to] the loader in the roadhead, which was ten feet high, were set on fire. There was evidence of heat even nearer the floor level in this roadhead, in that the upper surface of the compressed air hose pipes was partially melted. The four men who were found dead in the face were poisoned by carbon monoxide; that fact alone is strong evidence that coal dust was inflamed.

'I have no hesitation in reporting that the explosion was caused by the firing of a shot in coal which had been loosened and broken by a shot fired shortly before; that the firedamp thus ignited had been contained in the undercut and amongst the coal already brought down by the previous shot, and that flame was extended throughout the face and into the intake roadhead by coal dust.'

By the time the report was published, the firing of shots in the coal at Cardowan had been discontinued.

Chapter 8
No. 2 pit, Auchengeich Colliery, Chryston: Friday, 18th September 1959

In operation by 1914, Auchengeich Colliery stood close by the village of Chryston, about seven miles northeast of Glasgow. Known to be a gassy pit, it was situated in the No. 3 (Central West) Area of the National Coal Board's Scottish Division and had two shafts, both reaching down to the No. 2 pit level at 180 fathoms. In the downcast No. 1 shaft, two hinged gratings known as 'the needles' marked the No. 1 pit level at about 75 fathoms, where the cages stopped. No. 1 pit worked the Meiklehill Wee seam only.

From the bottom of No. 1 shaft the ventilation current travelled inbye for over a mile before splitting at No. 6 bench; the lesser part to ventilate the Kilsyth Coking coal sections, and the greater part continuing on to ventilate the Meiklehill Main coal workings. The return air from both sections came together about a mile from the pit bottom, the air from the Coking coal joining that from the Main coal to pass through a booster fan built into the return airway. From there it travelled to No. 2 pit bottom and was vented by an exhaust fan at the top of the shaft.

While the tragic events of the morning of Friday, 18th September 1959, would centre on problems caused by the booster fan in the return airway, the fan – or more accurately the transmission belt driving the fan – already had a history. Originally installed in 1946 close to the bottom of the No. 2 shaft, its intended purpose was to balance the flow of air between the Coking coal sections and the more distant workings at the Meiklehill Main coal. Set up and running, the fan appeared to work to the satisfaction of the engineers. However, after a time it was noticed that, operating so close to the intake, it was causing a considerable amount of air leakage between the intake and return airways. To obviate the problem the fan was moved the following year a distance of one mile inbye on the return airway to its junction with a crosscut road leading to No. 5 bench on the intake road.

With the return now effectively blocked for travelling, a bypass road was cut around the fan house and three air-separation doors installed to ensure that the maximum amount of return air would be drawn through the fan. The doors were also designed to open automatically by a change in ventilating pressure in the event the fan should stop. In its new position the booster fan could now operate without hindrance.

In the following years the fan operated more or less to the satisfaction of the engineers with only an occasional problem being reported. These reports usually concerned the fan belt slipping. On one occasion in 1951 two deputies found the belt to be smouldering, and about three feet of belt burned through at the motor pulley. Using two extinguishers they put the fire out.

In May of 1959, with the prospect of further underground developments in the foreseeable future, the colliery manager, James F. Smellie, decided to investigate the possibility of speeding up the fan. This, he reasoned, would provide the additional ventilation that would be needed for these developments, and in the meantime improve present ventilation in the mine. Having discussed the idea with his superiors and the area engineer, an approach was made to the manufacturers who confirmed that the fan could safely operate at the increased speed of 540 rpm – with the sole reservation that the fan was in sound mechanical condition. This agreement was made by phone and, despite the manufacturer's reservation, no attempt was made to assess the condition of the fan by means of a thorough inspection.

On Friday 19th June, safety officer Robert Harvey, along with James Dickson, day shift assistant oversman, saw sparks flying from the fan outlet. Having notified Alexander Pettigrew, the under-manager, the fan was stopped and a mechanic sent for. M. Barr, the engineer, found that the thrust collars on the shaft had moved. He adjusted them to centralise the fan and left it working satisfactorily. On the 20th the speed of the fan was increased from 490 to 540 rpm – but it was noted by assistant oversman Dickson in his report of the night of the 23rd/24th that the results of the increase were falling far short of expectations.

On Saturday 11th July, G. Neilson, a deputy, having been called to the fan, found that the belt had left the pulleys and was wrapped around the motor pulley shaft. He said later there was some smoke but no signs of burning or smouldering. A new belt was brought down and fitted later that day by mechanic Daniel O'Connor and would remain in use until Wednesday 16th September. Although the mechanics who subsequently checked the fan said that they found it 'to be slipping rather more frequently than the previous belt', they made no such criticisms in their reports.

On Monday 7th September the belt came off the fan pulley and was damaged by coming into contact with the pedestal of the fan, one of the fasteners having been pulled out. J. Steel, the workshop mechanic sent to repair it, found that the belt was in a very poor condition. He repaired it as best he could and took measurements for a new belt, which would be prepared in the engineer's shop and sent down the pit. On Wednesday 9th, engineer M. Barr, having inspected Steel's repaired belt and deciding that a new one should be fitted, made a written report to that effect – but no immediate action was taken (and Barr was unaware that Steel had already ordered a new belt).

The belt recommended by the manufacturers for use with the fan was seven-ply and twelve inches wide. This type of belt was known as balata belting and was constructed of a folded high-tensile cotton duck and balata gum. The contract required that all such belting supplied to National Coal Board collieries should be made in accordance with 'British Standard No. 2066: 1953 Balata Belting'. This requirement added that, unless otherwise stated on the order, the belting should be made with 33½ oz. duck. The roll of new belting in the colliery store, delivered on 7th September, did not carry the manufacturer's name, nor was it stamped with the British Standard number as required by B.S. 2066. Moreover, it was constructed with *31 oz.* duck, not the required 33½ oz.

On Wednesday 16th September – with the pit idle due to a strike – assistant oversman Dickson told D. McAuley, the day shift mechanic, to attend to the fan because the belt was slipping. Having examined the belt McAuley decided to replace it with the new one, which had been delivered to the site of the fan shortly after being ordered by Steel the workshop mechanic on the 7th. With the assistance of two others, he replaced the belt and watched it running for about half an hour. The belt began to slip. Stopping the motor, he cut six inches out of the belt, tensioned it, and re-started the motor, again watching for slippage. This time the belt ran satisfactorily and he eventually left the scene to get on with his other duties.

Some time later that day, James Bell, the back shift oversman, checked the fan and found the ammeter reading 65 amperes, a clear indication there was a great deal of slippage on the belt. He tried to tension the motor back but could not tighten it enough to stop the belt from slipping. He sent for Thomas Bone, the back shift mechanic. Assisted by Bell and two others, Bone cut a further seven inches out of the belt. An electrical fault in the rotor starter was then found and an electrician was called to fix it. With the fan now re-started and running smoothly, they left for other duties.

The next morning, Thursday 17th, the pit was still idle. Day shift oversman Robert Boyd told McAuley that the drive belt on the fan was slipping again. When McAuley arrived at the fan, about 7.45 a.m., he saw that the ammeter was reading somewhere between 60 and 70 amperes so, assisted by three other men, he cut a further four inches from the belt. During the work the fan rotor was pushed out of alignment, but no one having noticed this, they started the motor. The belt immediately moved to the side, drifting partially off the fan pulley, and one of the fasteners was ripped out when it caught on the fan pedestal.

McAuley again trimmed the belt, repositioned the fastener and centred the fan rotor. He left about 1.30 p.m., satisfied that the fan was running properly. Before he left he noticed that there was oil spilled on the blades and the apron of the fan. There was also oil spilled on the pavement on the outbye side of the fan and on the walls of the airway.

In the meantime the strike had been resolved and it was agreed that the men should return to work on Friday 18th September.

*

Early on that morning night shift oversman James Love was underground arranging work for the night shift. At 1.20 a.m. he looked in on the fan, examined it and was satisfied that it was working properly. The ammeter was reading 90 amperes and he considered that this would be normal – although the previous day McAuley had considered a reading of 90 as an indication of belt slippage. At 3.40 a.m. Love once again checked the fan, but this time he found that part of the ply of the belt had become separated and was flapping loose. The ammeter reading had also dropped to 60 amperes. He called the surface from the nearest telephone, situated in the Coking coal return, and asked for an electrician and an engineer to be sent down. He also told them to inform the No. 1 pit oversman that the fan would have to be stopped. He then rung off, went back to the fan and switched it off.

Love cut three feet of loose ply from the belt, trimmed some other loose ends and restarted the fan. At about 4.15 a.m., when Daniel O'Connor, the night shift mechanic, and electrician William Murray Black arrived at the fan they found that the ammeter was still reading 60 amperes and they stopped the motor. They saw that the balata had exuded from a length of about twelve inches. Both the belt and the motor pulley were very warm to the touch. Love and two others cooled these down using water. Moving the motor back about three inches to tension the belt, O'Connor restarted it just after 5.00 a.m. The ammeter reading reached 100 amperes where it remained while they kept watch. At 5.30 a.m. the three men returned to the surface.

At the pithead Love met Boyd, the day shift oversman, and told him what had been happening with the fan and advised that a new belt would be needed. Love then saw Alexander Pettigrew, the under-manager, and told him about the behaviour of the fan during the night, showing him the length of ply he had cut from the belt. In the meantime O'Connor had written a report in which he stated that the belt was 'ruined' and he told David McKinnon, the colliery's chief engineer, that a new one was required immediately. In the two-day life of the belt, the mechanics had been obliged to cut a total of seventeen inches from it in an effort to stop it from slipping. This unsatisfactory performance seems not to have attracted the urgent attention it warranted. No evidence was found to indicate that anyone else went near the fan between 5.30 a.m., when Love left it, and 7.00 a.m., when a fire was discovered.

At 6.25 a.m., Alexander Paton, the night shift engineman in charge of the man-riding haulage, sat in his engine house near the upcast pit bottom. With most of the night shift having already gone to the surface and the day shift expected down shortly, he had almost reached the end

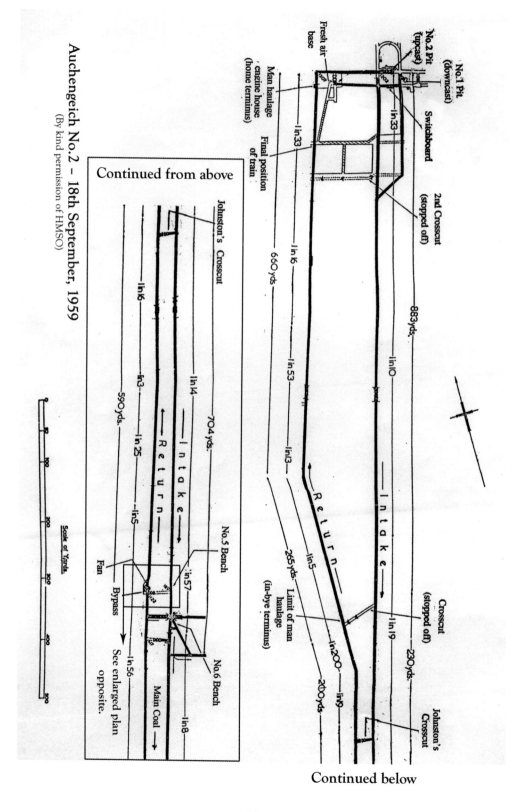

Auchengeich No.2 – 18th September, 1959
(By kind permission of HMSO)

Continued from above

Continued below

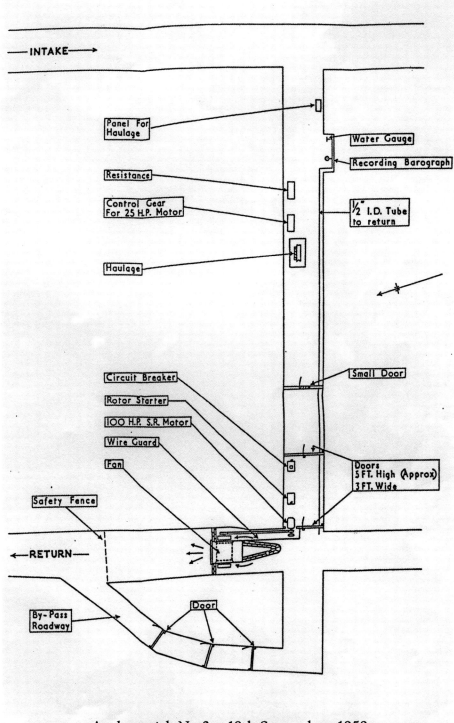

INTAKE →

Panel For Haulage

Water Gauge

Recording Barograph

Resistance

Control Gear For 25 H.P. Motor

½" I.D. Tube to return

Haulage

Circuit Breaker

Small Door

Rotor Starter

100 H.P. S.R. Motor

Wire Guard

Fan

Doors 5 FT. High (Approx) 3 FT. Wide

Safety Fence

← RETURN →

By-Pass Roadway

Door

Auchengeich No.2 – 18th September, 1959
(By kind permission of HMSO)

of his working night. He awaited only the arrival of engineman Thomas Campbell with the day shift to relieve him.

As he waited he noticed 'a slight haze and the very slight smell of something burning'. He was not worried by this and, a little after 6.30 a.m., went to the pit bottom to meet the first cage of day shift miners descending. One of those who arrived with the cage was James Dickson, assistant oversman for the day shift, and Paton drew Dickson's attention to the haze and the smell. Unfortunately, Dickson was at that time suffering from a heavy cold and could smell nothing. But he would state later that he sensed signs of 'a kind of heat' in the air. He decided to investigate and, having left word with an oncost worker that Robert Boyd, the day shift oversman, be informed of his movements, he boarded the man-riding train with about seventeen other men. Arriving back in his engine house, Paton sent the first train down the man-haulage road along the main return airway. The time was about 6.40 a.m.

Although there were only seventeen passengers, the train comprised four bogies, each with seating for twelve men in three compartments. The endless under-rope system pulling the bogies was powered by an electrical motor at the outbye end of the return, the home terminus. This motor was provided with protection against over-running at either end of the haulage road and also against excessive speed. In his engine house, Paton could monitor the position of the bogies in the return by way of an indicator and, at each end, by a warning stop light.

The man-haulage extended a little over half a mile down the return airway before reaching its limit at a stopped-off crosscut road a little under half a mile away from the booster fan. About 200 yards inbye of the man-riding limit another road, Johnston's Crosscut, led through to the intake road and fresh air. With the train journey normally taking about eight minutes to complete, Dickson and his companions arrived at the inbye terminus between 6.45 and 6.50 a.m.

Having climbed from the train, it was the usual practice for some of the men to continue along the return airway to reach their work places. That morning Dickson, with safety in mind, gave instructions that all of them should follow him through Johnston's Crosscut to the intake airway and instructions were passed to that effect. Leaving the train, they signalled the engineman to take it back to the home terminus. With the men following, Dickson reached the intake and travelled inbye, stopping at No. 5 bench, the crosscut nearest to the fan. The time was about 7.00 a.m.

In the engine house, Paton, having received the appropriate return signal from the first group of miners, began to bring the empty train back to the home terminus. The time was now a little before 6.50 a.m. and it was about then he was relieved by Thomas Campbell, the day shift engineman. He told Campbell that the haze of smoke had not long started and, his shift over, he walked the short distance to No. 2 cage and went to the surface. At the pithead he went directly to the engineers' shop and told David McKinnon, the chief engineer, and Alexander Pettigrew, the under-manager, about the haze of smoke in the return airway. In the meantime, the empty train had reached the home terminus and was immediately boarded by the 48 men who had been awaiting its arrival. Shortly after 6.55 a.m. these men began their journey.

Shotfirer Thomas McMonagle, stepping out of the cage on his way to the home terminus to travel inbye, stopped to help a young lad who had started work only the day before and had managed to soak his boots, which had dried hard overnight. While McMonagle took time to help the lad soften them, he missed the first two trains. This act of kindness would save his life. Miner Paddy McKeown was another who missed the second train. When he arrived at the home terminus he found he was too late to get a seat beside his mate, Pat Harvey, so he stood back with a dozen or so others to wait for the third run. Two days earlier he and Pat had been on their way to a strike meeting and stopped for a quick pint. Paddy had been a little short of cash and Pat pressed half a crown into his hand. Today he would repay his friend's thoughtfulness.

At the pithead Alexander Pettigrew, knowing that it had been causing trouble during the night, suspected that the haze might well be coming from the fan belt. He and McKinnon went to the lamp room and Pettigrew telephoned a warning to the oversman in No. 1 pit that the booster fan might not be working. As soon as he rang off a call came in from Dickson, who had by this time arrived at the fan house to find the belt ablaze. He said that a fire had broken out at the fan and extinguishers and hoses were urgently needed. The time was a few minutes past 7.00 a.m.

In the meantime, having arrived below, Boyd received Dickson's message that he had gone inbye to investigate the haze. Boyd went immediately to the main switches near the downcast shaft. It was his intention, for safety's sake, to cut off the electric current. However, being unsure of the switching arrangements, he asked David Kirkpatrick, a pump maintenance man who was familiar with the switchgear, to cut the current. To make certain that the No. 1 pit workings would not be affected by this action, Boyd telephoned an electrician at the surface for advice. While on the phone he overheard Dickson's call to report that the fan was on fire.

Having come across the fire, Dickson had immediately stopped the motor and ran to No. 5 haulage house, a distance of about 50 yards, to collect a fire extinguisher. He returned to the fire but found that the extinguisher would not work. He told the deputy, Alexander Cunningham, and others present to try to smother the fire with sand and stone dust while he telephoned the surface from No. 6 bench, about a hundred yards from the fan, requesting extinguishers and hoses to be sent down. He then collected a second extinguisher from No. 6 transformer house and returned to the fire – but found this extinguisher was also not working. Giving up on the extinguishers, he telephoned the surface for the third time and asked for the rescue brigade to be sent for. The time was then around ten or fifteen minutes past seven.

When the second train arrived at the terminus, somewhere between five and ten past seven, the men climbed out of the bogies but did not walk inbye. According to stone worker Thomas Green, the sole survivor from the train, the haze had thickened very slightly on the journey. However, on their arrival at the inbye terminus, a blanket of thick smoke came up the return towards them. It was obvious that they could travel no farther in the face of this smoke, so they reboarded the bogies and gave the signal to return to the home terminus.

In the engine house, Thomas Campbell acted on the signal and began to draw the train home. Shortly after, he received signals to stop and start the train three times in quick succession. This rash of signals made him think that something had gone wrong on the train. The last signal had been to haul outbye and this he did. Some men who were standing near the engine house witnessed the series of confused signals received by Campbell. Sitting on the train, Thomas Green knew nothing of these signals and could recall they stopped the train only once on its journey from the inbye terminus. This was done at the top of the 1 in 5 gradient to assist a passenger who, unconscious, was slumped in his seat and in danger of falling off. The train was then signalled away again after a delay, which Green later said was no more than a few moments.

The train was about halfway out when the haze at the engine house suddenly turned to heavy smoke. As a result of this, Campbell could no longer see his train position indicator as conditions became rapidly worse. He felt he would have to get out soon or be overcome himself, and he was faced with the difficult decision of whether or not he should stop the train. He did not know how many men were or were not travelling on the bogies, and it occurred to him that before he left he could simply leave the train running. In that case, when the train reached the home terminus, it would come to a halt itself as the engine cut out automatically.

He began to slow the engine down but, on hearing a voice coming from the smoke, decided to stop the train altogether for fear of running down any men who might be trying to escape on foot. The train eventually came to a halt about a hundred yards short of the home terminus. The time was now around 7.15 and Campbell, almost overcome, finally left the engine house and made his way out through the separation doors leading to the intake airway. From there he later took the cage in No. 1 shaft to the surface.

With his jacket covering his mouth and nose, Thomas Green was sitting at the outbye end of the train – nearest the home terminus – when it slowed down and finally came to a halt. He later described the smoke at this point as being 'very thick indeed'. Feeling that it would be unwise to sit in thick smoke on a stationary train, he got off and staggered along the return towards the pit bottom.

In the intake, following his call to McKinnon at the surface, Dickson travelled the short distance to No. 5 bench to prepare the hydrant there for the fire hoses when they arrived, but he discovered that the water range had been blanked off. He knew there was another hydrant some 300 yards away in No. 6 roadway, but thought this was too far from the fire. With the help of others he brought the hydrant from No. 6 and fixed it onto the water range at No. 5 bench so that it would be ready for the hoses. Around 7.15 a.m. he called the surface again and spoke to David Gray, a general duties man who was in the lamp room, and asked that the Coatbridge Rescue Brigade be sent for.

Two deputies, F. Lynch and Joseph Roe, had walked down the return airway after the first train had left and, going through Johnston's Crosscut and along the intake, had arrived at the fan house shortly after Dickson. They had seen the fan casing and oil from the bearings burning and had helped to throw stone dust on the blaze. A little later Roe went through the three bypass doors towards the return. Lynch, who had had some experience with the local fire service, tested the extinguishers brought by Dickson and also found them to be unworkable. He then followed Roe through the doors and, standing at the junction of the bypass with the return airway, they saw flames coming from the fan outlet. The flames, they later said in evidence, were touching both the roof and the right hand side of the road between the fan house and the safety fence.

F. MacDonald, a brusher who had reached at the scene around 7.15, said that by that time the fan belt had been reduced to ashes and the fan casing was on fire. He also went through the bypass doors and saw fire at the roof of the return outbye of the fan. Robert Boyd, the day shift oversman, arrived shortly before 7.30 and saw the fan still burning. When he went through the doors to the return he now saw only smouldering on the roadway between the fan and the safety fence, but the return airway was ablaze outbye of the bypass junction. When Alexander Pettigrew, the under-manager, went through the three doors a few minutes later he found fire and a fall of roof at the junction.

Near the home terminus, the group of men who were waiting for the returning train to take them inbye watched the haze warily. When the haze abruptly turned to a thick cloud of smoke, they quickly retired into fresh air leaking through the separation doors a short distance away. Again they waited and a short time later heard noises that told them someone was moving about in the smoke-filled return. Some of them went back into the smoke to find who was making the noise and, groping around in the dark, they eventually found Thomas Green lying face down and on the point of being overcome.

Bringing him out of the return, he was escorted by one of his rescuers to the No. 2 upcast shaft and from there to the surface where he was taken to the first aid room. Gordon Brown, the bottomer at the upcast shaft, then collapsed and was himself rescued but, because of the thickening smoke, he was taken to the surface via the No. 1 downcast shaft.

Meanwhile, David Kirkpatrick had learned about the fire from electrician John Thornton at the pit bottom. Knowing that fire-fighting equipment would be required at the scene he immediately went to the surface with James White, a rope splicer, and began to organise the assembly of fire hoses and extinguishers for transportation below. In this, however, he would experience more difficulty than he ever imagined. James Smellie, the manager, who had learned of the fire from Pettigrew, also prepared to go below. Like Pettigrew and McKinnon, he was not aware at that point that there were lives in danger.

Shortly after 7.20 a.m., on his way to the lamp room, he saw Green being brought out of No. 2 pit unconscious and realised that something was seriously wrong below. He could see by the volume of smoke reaching the surface that it was no longer safe to use the upcast shaft, so he immediately ordered that winding in it be stopped. He sent White to the banksman at No. 1 downcast shaft to tell him that the needles were to be lifted at once to allow the cage to reach the No. 2 pit level below, and told White that he, personally, should go down in order to make sure that the lifting operation was carried out properly, but with speed. The fire-fighting equipment collected by Kirkpatrick and White was, in the meantime, taken to the downcast shaft to await the lifting of the needles.

At about 7.35 a.m., a little earlier than usual, telephonist Myra Loney took her place at the switchboard in the telephone exchange at Stepps. Within minutes she received a call from James Smellie, manager of Auchengeich, to alert the Coatbridge Central Rescue Station. Dialling 'Coatbridge 10', she made the connection before also contacting the police, fire brigade and ambulance services. In a very short time the Stepps Road would become busy with traffic coming from and going to Auchengeich.

At No. 1 pit the banksman, Thomas Montgomery, timed White's descent at a little after 7.35 a.m. and said that, a few minutes before eight, the needles had been raised and the length of the cables adjusted to allow the cages in No. 1 to travel down to the No. 2 pit level. The manager later gave this time as 7.55 a.m., calculated by his movements following the call made to the rescue brigade. He gave as the reason for this order of priority the fact that No. 2 pit workings could not be reached until the needles in No. 1 shaft had been raised. This operation, he said, would take about 20 minutes.

At Coatbridge Rescue Station, having logged the alarm call from Auchengeich at 7.40 a.m., the first team scrambled and left five minutes later, arriving at the colliery, seven and a half miles away, at 8.00 a.m. The second team followed about ten minutes later. Having been briefed on the situation by the manager, the first team, consisting of five men, went below just before ten past eight and set up a fresh air base behind the air separation doors nearest the man-haulage home terminus. It was from behind these doors that Thomas Green had been rescued earlier.

Wearing Proto Mark 4 self-contained breathing apparatus, they made a preliminary inspection of the return airway near the terminus, returning a short time later. They reported that the atmosphere was very bad and they had been unable to see anything – but they had stumbled across a body. Leaving the fresh air base once again, they went into the smoke and brought the body out. Using artificial respiration they worked on the victim for over half an hour, but without success.

While this was going on, the second team went into the return airway, but came back within fifteen minutes to report that conditions were no better. When they emerged from the smoke the members of the team were in a distressed state, due mainly to the excessive heat they had encountered. Mr K.W. Dyer, the rescue superintendent, having looked at the return for himself, decided that conditions were so bad he could not justify risking the lives of team members by instigating a full-scale search. At this point the tragic conclusion had been reached by all concerned that there could be no hope of survival for those who were trapped.

In the meantime, the fight to defeat the fire had got under way. Between 8.20 and 8.30 a.m., fire hoses and extinguishers had reached the scene of the fire and were put into use by men under the supervision of under-manager Pettigrew. Initially they began by using only one hose, but when the rescue brigade arrived below, two more were brought into play. Sometime later in the morning Pettigrew learned that there were men still trapped in the return airway and he told Robert Harvey, safety officer, to carry out a thorough check on all the men presently underground. Harvey did this before going to the surface, where he found that a similar check had been carried out by James Smellie, the colliery manager, around 8.00 a.m. When they put their results together, it became apparent that a total of 47 men were still unaccounted for.

From about 9.30 a.m. onwards, from their base behind the air separation doors, members of the rescue brigade made regular examinations of the air quality a short distance into the return airway. The task of fighting the fire in the return airway continued throughout the day, and for several hours the fire-fighters – assisted by men from the rescue squads – were able to keep up with the blaze. However, after a time they began to find themselves hampered by falls from the roof as the wooden lagging behind the steel girders was burned away.

When man-haulage signal bells were heard around 4.30 p.m. miners, with men from the rescue brigade standing by, began at once to open a path to the return through the stopped-off crosscut road leading from the intake to a few yards beyond the end of the inbye terminus. Two men eventually broke through into the return, but they found the atmosphere so bad as to confirm the opinion, voiced earlier in the day, that no one could possibly have survived in such conditions. It was later discovered that the signals from the man-haulage bell had been caused by falls of rubble from the burning roof fouling the haulage signal pull wire in the return airway.

All through the afternoon and early evening the methane content of the air passing over the fire was closely monitored. The flow of air was regulated by varying the openings in certain doorways and by erecting brattice screens at strategic points. Using this method of regulation, they had managed to keep the methane content to below two per cent. Around 9.00 p.m. the volume of smoke coming out of the return began to diminish, leading the fire-fighters to believe that they were at last beginning to get the fire under control. But looking into the return at Johnston's Crosscut, however, they found the smoke to be still very dense; disappointed, they had to admit they were wrong in thinking they were overtaking the fire.

Just before 9.30 p.m., Richard John Evans, District Inspector of Mines and Quarries, who had been underground at the fire for three hours, noticed that a methanometer was recording two and a half per cent of methane just outbye the junction of the two return airways. With almost four and a half per cent being recorded in the return from the Coking coal sections, he advised that all the men below be withdrawn to the intake airway. By 10.15 p.m. the methane content had risen in some places to five per cent, posing a real risk of explosion. After agreement was reached with all parties concerned – including Dr Henry Hyde, Divisional Inspector of Mines and Quarries, who had arrived at the pithead – the workings were abandoned, with everyone withdrawing to the surface.

Before leaving, water seals were placed at both ends of Johnston's Crosscut, and fire hoses – brought down and left lying at No. 1 pit bottom for such an eventuality – were connected to the hydrants. The water was then turned on and left running to flood the valleys in the intake and return airways near Johnston's Crosscut in an effort to seal off and extinguish the fire.

At 11.00 p.m. on Friday night a statement was read out to the waiting press by Raymond W. Parker, NCB Chairman, Scottish Division: 'The Board regret to announce that after every possible effort has been made to reach the area of the accident, it is now our considered opinion that there is practically no hope of there being any survivors. An accumulation of firedamp has made it necessary to withdraw the men engaged in fighting the underground fire and arrangements are in hand to flood a part of the roadway (below the level where the 47 men are) and so put out the fire. This decision has had to be taken to avoid the risk of further loss of life. It was taken after consultation with all interested parties and with the approval of Her Majesty's Divisional Inspector of Mines.

'In these circumstances, it will not be possible to restart rescue operations until the area is flooded, and, along with other safety precautions necessary, this will take approximately twelve hours. Renewed steps to reach the area where the men are will thereafter be made as soon as possible. In addition to the safety measures at Auchengeich, men will be withdrawn for the time being from the adjoining and connecting colliery of Wester Auchengeich. In these very distressing circumstances, the Board and the National Union of Mineworkers wish to express their deepest sympathy to the relatives of the men involved in this very tragic accident.'

Illuminated by the full moon, by the pithead lighting, and by the brighter floodlights of television vans, a crowd of several hundred had stood waiting all evening, holding on to hope yet knowing there was no hope. With that grim statement any possible rescue had now turned to mere recovery and the last flicker of hope was extinguished.

In a statement issued on Sunday, David Lang, Area General Manager, said the area to be flooded lay between a half a mile inbye from the bogie train and half a mile outbye of the booster fan at which the fire had started. To complete the seal the water had to fill not only the roadway, but the waste area on either side. 'There was,' he added, 'sufficient water in the burn at the side of the colliery to complete the seal. It was being pumped in at the rate of 200 gallons a minute. When the water reached the roof of the roadway, the fire and the poisonous gas would be isolated, and after a suitable interval had elapsed the rescue teams would be able to go down in safety.'

By Sunday there was little activity at the pithead, the hundreds of bystanders who had arrived on Friday having melted away. Those who still remained gradually dispersed after 3.00 p.m. when the fine drizzle turned to heavy rain. On Tuesday afternoon, with news having filtered round the area that the victims had at last been found, a crowd once more converged on the scene. Many of them women, they stood motionless in the high wind and driving rain watching the rescuers as they gathered at the pithead buildings. Shortly after 2.00 p.m. a coal board official issued the following statement: 'After the restoration of ventilation in the pit bottom, rescue men have travelled to the top part of the return airway and located the position of 44 of the bodies. Arrangements are now being made to bring the bodies to the surface and continue the search for the two bodies not yet located.'

By Thursday 24th September – six days after the disaster – the fire had been put out and all the victims recovered from the return airway. Of the victims, one had been found near the home terminus and recovered earlier, two were found close to another stopped-off crosscut about 150 yards inbye, and the fourth just over 400 yards inbye. The remaining 43 men were found less than a hundred yards inbye of the home terminus – untouched by the fire and still seated on the train. All had died from carbon monoxide poisoning.

*

On Monday, 4th January 1960, the fatal accident inquiry into the disaster at Auchengeich opened in the Justiciary Court, Glasgow, presided over by Mr T. A. Rogers, C.B.E., Chief Inspector of Mines and Quarries. The proceedings lasted ten days, closing on Friday 15th, and a total of 85 witnesses were called to give evidence. While the inquiry followed the familiar pattern of many such investigations which had gone before, to a certain extent the proceedings of the Auchengeich disaster would be noted for the incisive questioning of the witnesses by Mr Abe Moffat, President of the National Union of Mineworkers, on behalf of the relatives of the victims.

As the witnesses came and went several facts came to light. Although it was well known that the fan belt had been causing problems for some time, no one had been delegated to police it on a full-time basis. Oversman James Love and a man called Johnny Anderson had shared responsibility for the fan up until Anderson retired a few weeks previously. From that point on Love had taken it upon himself to keep an eye on it.

Questioned by Abe Moffat, R. Murray, the storekeeper, informed the court that the roll of new belt, delivered to the store on 7th September, did not come from the usual supplier but from a different source. Also, the new belt was not stamped with the supplier's name or the British Standard number (B.S. 2066) as required by regulations. The storekeeper was not able to say why the supplier was changed or who made the change – but he could quote the arithmetic. The original supplier (R. & J. Dick, who stamped the belt with their name and the B.S. number) charged a little over £1 per foot for the belt. The new supplier (H. A. Cole, whose belt was unmarked) charged 12s 3d. per foot – a saving of around eight shillings per foot.

Pumpman David Kirkpatrick told the court of going to the surface with James White and of his attempts to organise fire-fighting equipment and the lifting of the needles in No. 1 shaft. Unable to find anyone to assist him he appealed to James Love, the night shift oversman, whom he saw coming from the lamp cabin. When asked by Dr Henry Hyde, Divisional Inspector of Mines, if he managed to get the material taken down, his feelings at the general lack of urgency emerged. 'No, sir,' he said. 'There was nobody to carry them that I could get. I saw the oversman crossing from the cabin. I ran after him. I felt a sort of frustration things were going as they were. So I ran after Jimmy [Love]. I said, "For God's sake, Jimmy, come and use your authority and lift the needles".'

When asked if anyone started to lift the needles after that, Kirkpatrick replied: 'No. I said, "For God's sake use your authority to lift the needles and [get] fire-fighting apparatus." Love said, "Have you taken leave of your senses, have you gone mad?" I said to him, "Be your age. Look at the fan". He then said [having presumably seen the smoke pouring from the upcast shaft] he would have to go and change his pit clothes and I did not give him a nice answer.' While giving his own evidence to the court three days earlier, Love did not mention this exchange.

Rescue superintendent W.K. Dyer was questioned on a subject that had been argued over for some time in the mining industry. Abe Moffat asked him, 'Mr Dyer, what is your opinion regarding the use of self-rescue apparatus?' The superintendent replied, 'I honestly believe that most of these men, if not all these men, would have got out if they had been carrying self-rescue apparatus.'

On the closing day of the inquiry Abe Moffat, in his summing up, detailed the history of the fan and, in particular, the transmission belt that drove it. He highlighted the strange circumstance of colliery engineers and electricians who, despite seemingly never-ending repairs, admitted they had never entered reports concerning the fan in the daily statutory report book as required by the regulations. Entries *were* made, but it was someone else who initialled those entries in their names. The delay in both reporting the fire and getting water to the scene also came in for much criticism – along with the inexplicable delay in sending for the rescue services. In their defence the colliery officials maintained they were unaware that men were in danger.

Although there had undoubtedly been other rescuers at the pit bottom who remained nameless, those named by Mr Moffat were Edward Savage, Tom McMonagle, Thomas Halpin, Thomas Quinn, Edward Docherty, Albert Coyle and J. McConnachie. In going into the smoke-filled return airway to save the life of Tom Green and later George Brown, their selfless bravery was recognised by all at the hearing.

Paddy McKeown, who was one of those who missed the fateful second train, also took part in the rescue of Tom Green and carried hoses and fire-fighting equipment to the scene of the fire. Later, he took part in the recovery of the victims.

*

On Wednesday, 27th April 1960, the report into the Auchengeich disaster was completed and passed to the Rt. Hon. Richard Wood, MP, Minister of Power, who presented it to Parliament the following month. The author, T.A. Rogers, C.B.E, H.M. Chief Inspector of Mines and Quarries, related events leading up to and including the disastrous fire at the booster fan and the rescue of Thomas Green and Gordon Brown by those whom the *Scottish Miner* had referred to as 'the Unassuming Heroes'.

Concerning the inexplicable delay in raising the alarm with outside agencies, Rogers made this telling observation: 'It became apparent quite early in the inquiry that there was a period of an hour or so during which every minute was potentially significant in considering whether or not, once the fire had started, anything could have been done to avert the loss of life.' Also coming in for close scrutiny were the stuttering attempts to organise fire-fighting equipment, the fighting of the fire itself, and the ultimate failure to defeat the blaze.

On the provision of fire-fighting equipment underground the inspector said there had been no means of fighting the fire in the airway until hoses were brought from the surface. The hoses did not arrive underground until between 8.20 and 8.30 a.m. In the one and a half hours that elapsed between the discovery of the fire and the water being turned on, the fire had taken a substantial hold on the timber in the return airway, so much so that the fire fighters were faced with an impossible task.

The colliery officials maintained that the underground fire extinguishers and hydrants had been 'tampered with on frequent occasions' and the failed fire extinguishers were a result of this 'tampering'. As for the fire hoses being stored on the surface, this was as a result of the brass fittings having been cut off (presumably for scrap) by a person or persons unknown some years before. The hoses had been removed to the surface for safekeeping. While the inspector did not believe that the delay in delivering water to the fire directly caused the deaths of the miners on the train, he believed that, in other circumstances, such delay could have put lives in jeopardy.

On the rescue efforts, he thought the outcome of the accident might have been less tragic if the men had been carrying self-rescue apparatus. Sir Andrew Bryan, he said, had '. . . included in his report on the underground fire in 1950 at Cresswell Colliery . . . a recommendation that underground trials of improved forms of self-rescue apparatus should be expedited.' Extensive trials on rescue apparatus had been carried out over a long period but, after careful consideration of the results, all parties had agreed to discontinue the trials. Mr Rogers said, 'In view of the circumstances in which the men at Auchengeich Colliery met their death, I recommend that the whole question should again be reviewed by the industry.'

In general discussion he had this to say: 'In the light of subsequent knowledge it is difficult to understand why the haze observed at the pit bottom, and also inbye by the men on the first train, was not recognised as a symptom of an outbreak of fire. But it was not so recognised by anybody. It had no effect on the eyes, or on the breathing and, although some of the men mentioned a smell, this was not sufficiently distinctive to be identified. Many of the men who saw the haze were experienced underground workers, but none was alarmed in any way.'

He ended by making several recommendations, including:

1. That all transmission belts used in collieries should be made from fire resistant materials.

2. That all managers should carry out thorough reviews of their fire-fighting arrangements, and make certain that all fire-fighting equipment is in proper working order.

3. That any places of unusually high fire risk be identified and measures taken to minimise that risk.

4. That the attention of all officials should be drawn to their obligation under Regulation 11 (1) of the Coal and Other Mines (Fire and Rescue) Regulations, 1956, that men must be withdrawn as soon as there is any indication that fire has, *or may have*, broken out below ground.

5. The industry should reconsider its decision to discontinue the trials of self-rescuers.

In addition, he also recommended that, 'There should be a suitably constituted standing committee of experts . . . charged with the task of keeping under close and constant review the prevention of explosions and fires in mines, with particular reference to the lessons of actual fires and explosions in this country and abroad . . .'.

*

While there is no art in hindsight, a study of the evidence suggests that the tragedy of Auchengeich appeared to have hinged on two main points: inaction and timing. In looking at these points, we will begin with the subject of inaction.

If we leave aside its earlier teething problems, from June 1959 (when the fan was speeded up) until the time of the disaster – a period of some three months – problems with the fan belt steadily mounted. They began the day before the speed was increased, when sparks were seen in the fan outlet, and from that point on the situation grew steadily worse.

As far as anyone was aware at that time, the type of belt driving the booster fan was that recommended by the manufacturer. It would later transpire that it was not. However, what was assumed to have been the 'recommended' belt had lasted less than ten weeks – far short of the usual life of such a belt. As for the length of new belting fitted only two days before the disaster, in that short time the mechanics, collectively, had been obliged to cut a total of seventeen inches from its length in an effort to stop it from slipping. Surely this dire performance should have raised some doubts in the minds of those concerned that the capacity of the belt being used – whether recommended or not – fell far short of that required to carry the load?

Despite its woeful history, management and officials had consistently failed to act to resolve the seemingly never-ending problems caused by the belt. The fan *and* the belt should have been investigated as a matter of urgency long before the situation reached a point of crisis. Unfortunately they were not, and 47 men paid for that omission with their lives.

There was also inaction when Dickson reported the fire shortly after 7.00 a.m. Having made abortive attempts to fight the blaze, he called again for extinguishers and hoses to be sent down. About 7.15 a.m., realising they could not defeat the fire, Dickson called again to request that the Coatbridge Mines Rescue Brigade be sent for. The call to the rescue station was eventually logged at 7.40 a.m. With the request having initially come from someone at the scene of the fire, the call for the rescue service should have been made *immediately*, not 25 minutes later. Although painful, it has to be recognised that, as events transpired, even if the rescue service had been at the scene underground when the fire was first discovered, they still could have done nothing to save those unfortunate souls on the second train.

With the fire having been reported to the surface by Dickson shortly after 7.00 a.m., there again followed an inexplicable delay, this time in getting the requested hoses and other fire-fighting appliances to the scene of the fire. They eventually arrived and went into service somewhere between 8.20 and 8.30 a.m., almost *one and a half hours* after the alarm was raised.

On the subject of timing, it would seem as though circumstances had conspired against the victims. When Boyd, the day shift oversman, went to the switches at the downcast shaft he decided to phone the surface for advice. Before he made the call he asked oncost worker Pat Keirnan to tell Thomas Campbell at the engine house not to send any men down the man-haulage until he received further instructions. It was Boyd's intention that any men in the haulage road were to be withdrawn, and in giving this instruction he was satisfied that anyone else coming in would be stopped.

The message that passed between Boyd and Keirnan produced a conflict of evidence at the inquiry. Boyd maintained that his message had been that no men should travel down the return airway. On the other hand Keirnan swore in court that he received no such message, his own recollection of Boyd's instruction having been either 'Stop the bogies' or 'Hold the bogies'. Edward Docherty, who had met Keirnan at the pit bottom, stated that Keirnan's message had simply been to stop the man-riding haulage. When he eventually produced his report, the mines inspector would accept Boyd's version of events. However, regardless of the exact wording of the message, by the time it was given it was shortly after 7.00 a.m. and the second train was already on its way outbye.

Was there any point at which the men could have been saved? Many of those who had travelled on the first train later gave evidence concerning the haze seen around No. 2 pit bottom and down the return. While there were those among them who sensed that something might be wrong somewhere inbye, not one of them felt in any way alarmed. Some, including Dickson, stated that the haze had been 'very slightly thicker' at the inbye end of the haulage road than it had been at the pit bottom. The smoke was thicker – yet they still did not sense danger.

It would appear that only one of three things could have saved the men on the second train. Firstly – and perhaps most obviously – if the men on both trains, in particular the first, had recognised that 'the haze of smoke' seen at the pit bottom constituted a possible source of danger. Had that been the case, it is unlikely that any of them would have boarded the train in the first place. Smoke, light or heavy, coming out from underground workings would – or *should* – have set alarm bells ringing in the minds of experienced miners.

Secondly, if assistant oversman Dickson and the men in the first train had raised the alarm *immediately* they reached the intake (there being a telephone at the intake side of Johnston's Crosscut), the second train could have been stopped. The timing of events had them arriving at the intake just before 6.50 a.m. and, with the second train leaving the home terminus shortly after six-fifty-five, a period of some five minutes elapsed when a phone call to the pit bottom could have stopped the second train. There was a telephone near No. 2 pit bottom, 130 yards from the haulage engine room, and a runner would have carried the alarm in seconds.

Failing that, deputies Lynch (who had some fire service experience) and Roe – having walked down the return in the wake of the first train and been passed by the empty train returning to the home terminus to collect more men – could also have raised the alarm from the telephone at Johnston's Crosscut. But Lynch and Roe, like Dickson before them, had passed through the smoke and passed by the telephone without a thought for the men who would be coming behind them.

Thirdly, if the stopped-off crosscut close to the end of the man-haulage had been left open and fitted with air crossing doors, the men in the second train would have undoubtedly used it to reach the safety of the intake airway before the heavy smoke caught up with them. As it was, with the only available exit road a hundred yards farther on through the incoming cloud of thick smoke, they took the only option open to them, re-boarding the train and signalling to be hauled back to the home terminus. Unfortunately, the smoke was travelling faster than the train, and in the end only Thomas Green survived the journey.

In June of 1960 the return airway was cleared of water and the recovery of the victims was begun. Miner Paddy McKeown was one of those who volunteered to work with the rescue teams and, tragically, one of the first bodies he helped to carry out was that of ex-NCB boxing champ Pat Harvey, his friend.

According to *Reports of HM Inspectors of Mines and Quarries for 1960*: 'Following the Public Inquiry and Report by H.M. Chief Inspector of Mines and Quarries, Mr T.A. Rogers, C.B.E., in regard to the underground fire at Auchengeich Colliery, Lanarkshire, on 18th September, 1959, legal proceedings were taken by the Crown against the manager and under-manager. Nine charges were laid against the manager. He was joined in two of them by the under-manager, who faced one other charge alone. After a trial lasting eight days, the manager was found guilty on two counts, being fined £100 on one and admonished on the other, and not guilty on two others, the remainder receiving 'non-proven' verdicts. The under-manager came with the manager under two 'non-proven' verdicts and was found not guilty on the other.'

Following the recovery of the victims Auchengeich never reopened.

Appendix 1: Mining Accidents in Lanarkshire

Prior to the introduction of the *Act for the Inspection of Coal Mines* in 1850 (and the appointment of only four inspectors to cover the whole of Great Britain), a great many mining accidents, in particular those involving single or a small number of fatalities, went unrecorded. The following list (by no means complete) has been drawn from many sources – inspectors' reports, contemporary newspapers, magazines, etc., some of them being at variance with others – therefore 100 percent accuracy of information cannot be guaranteed. Note: although Cardowan (195) involved no loss of life, but for an accident of fate the death toll could have been considerable. Where recorded, the owning company is named. An asterisk (*) indicates an entry (or entries if followed by a number in parenthesis) in the Index of Victims if the name of the victim is known.

1. Govan Colliery, Glasgow – operated by William Dixon & Co. On Saturday, 20th December 1788, one man was killed and another injured when a bucket, being lowered 100 feet down the shaft, overturned.

2. Lead Mine, Leadhills – owned by Horner, Hurst & Co. On the morning of Saturday, 1st March 1817, exhaust smoke from an underground engine found its way into the workings, resulting in the deaths of five miners from asphyxiation. Two other miners who went below to attempt a rescue also perished. Some of the victims left wives and large families, some eight to ten in number. *(6)

3. Whiteflat Colliery, Coatbridge. Early on the morning of Saturday, 20th February 1830, four miners on their way to their working places uncovered their safety lamps to light their pipes. A body of gas ignited at the lamps and a tremendous explosion followed, killing a total of five men.

4. Keppisbyre Colliery, Airdrie – operated by Frew & Co. About six o'clock on the morning of Wednesday, 8th June 1831, an explosion of firedamp killed one young miner and badly injured three others. The explosion was heard upwards of a mile away, its violence demonstrated by the fact that the headgear and surrounding structure were totally destroyed. *

5. Wishaw Colliery – operated by John Wilson & Co. On the morning of Thursday, 8th September 1836, a father and son were descending the shaft to their work in a bucket when a link in the chain holding the bucket snapped. The son fell to the bottom of the shaft and was killed. The father, who had a hold of the rope when the chain snapped, managed to hold on for about a minute, but when the crash was heard above and the engine stopped, he lost his hold and followed his son to the bottom.

6. Polmadie Colliery, Govan, Glasgow – operated by William Dixon & Co. About five o'clock on the afternoon of Saturday, 13th October 1838, five miners climbed into a bucket to ascend the shaft. As it began to move they noticed that one side of the crossbar had come loose from the chains and that the bucket was being raised by one side only. Two of the men jumped out when it was still near to the bottom while the others stayed on board. When they were within a few feet of the surface the final rivet holding the bucket sprung loose and the men fell, along with the bucket, to the pit bottom some 100 fathoms below. The shaft had a stair which was supposed to be used to ascend the shaft, but it was common practice to use the bucket which was quicker. *(3)

7. Quarter Colliery, Hamilton – owned by the Duke of Hamilton. About eight o'clock on the morning of Tuesday, 16th March 1841, the sudden release of gas from a pocket trapped in the solid coal resulted in an explosion that killed six men and a boy who were at work underground. Seven men at the mouth of the mine ran to their assistance and were immediately overcome by carbon monoxide. When they failed to reappear the one man left outside entered the mine and dragged the seven out. Four of the rescuers died and three survived. Seven of the eleven victims were married men and left a total of 60 dependants. *(10)

8. Stevenston Colliery, Holytown. On the morning of Wednesday, 24th July 1844, an oversman was killed when he was caught by blasting operations while in the process of examining the workings. Two others were 'dreadfully' burned. *

9. Carfin Colliery, Holytown. On Saturday, 30th November 1844, while two miners were cutting through a dyke, an oversman went to check the opposite side. Just as he reached the spot the miners lit a shot that blew through on the oversman to his serious injury. He died a few hours later. *

10. Mossend Colliery, Bellshill. On Tuesday, 30th June 1846, a young miner lost his life when the roof collapsed, burying him. *

11. Dalzell Colliery, Hamilton. On Saturday, 23rd September 1848, an explosion of firedamp occurred, severely burning six miners, one of whom later died. *

12. No. 6 pit, Wishaw Colliery – operated by John Wilson & Co. About five-thirty on the morning of Monday, 13th August 1849, while about 30 men were still waiting at the pithead to descend, an explosion took place near the bottom of the shaft. Of the nine men who had

already gone down, one was reportedly blown up the shaft into the headgear, with 'fragments of human flesh and bone' found up to 400 yards from the shaft. Immediately following the blast, a boy was heard calling out from below, but by the time rescuers could reach him it was too late. All nine who had gone down perished. *(9)

13. Chapelhall Colliery, Airdrie – operated by the Monkland Iron & Steel Co. On Tuesday, 1st July 1856, four men were killed when the winding machinery for the cage became detached from the engine, sending the cage to the pit bottom. While the engineman was acquitted of culpable homicide at the Glasgow Autumn Circuit, the investigating inspector remained convinced the accident was caused solely by the engineman's neglect. *(4)

14. Espieside Colliery, Coatbridge. On Wednesday, 23rd July 1856, while working from a hanging scaffold in the shaft, two workmen called for a pick to be sent down. As the pithead man sent it down on the end of a rope, the fastening came loose and the pick either fell onto the men, or hit them, and one of them fell to the bottom of the shaft. *

15. Wishaw Colliery – operated by James Anderson & Co. On Wednesday, 15th October 1856, two boys were killed by an explosion of firedamp as they were standing on the cage waiting to go to the surface. *(2)

16. No. 6 pit, Palace Craig Colliery, Airdrie – operated by William Baird & Co. On Thursday, 15th January 1857, a worker was killed when he was struck by runaway hutches on an incline. *

17. Coathill Colliery, Coatbridge. On Wednesday, 1st July 1857, a drawer, described as a 'boy', approached the shaft pushing a full hutch. A bottomer was normally in attendance, but had left his post temporarily. The boy, seeing a light ahead of him, trusted that the bottomer was there and pushed the hutch onto the cage, which was not there. The hutch pulled him into the shaft and both fell to the bottom. *

18. Gartgill Colliery, Coatbridge. On Monday, 13th July 1857, an oversman and a labourer were working in the shaft when a crowbar, which had been about the pithead, fell down the shaft and passed right through the oversman's body. Although there were two men near the mouth of the shaft, they could throw no light on the matter. *

19. Chapel Colliery, Newmains – operated by the Coltness Iron Co. On Saturday, 21st November 1857, a miner carrying a naked lamp entered a place that had been stopped off due to the presence of firedamp. A small quantity of gas exploded at the lamp and he was burned so severely that he died a week later. *

20. Parkhead Colliery, Motherwell – operated by King & Henderson Ltd. On Wednesday, 20th January 1858, an explosion of firedamp occurred in this new, partially opened colliery. The explosion was relatively small, but the blackdamp created by the blast took the lives of three miners. One man who had encountered the gas died before he reached the surface. Another, who reached the pit bottom to find his son had not arrived, went back into the workings to find him. Both father and son were found dead the next day. Parkhead closed in 1928. *(3)

21. Stanrigg Colliery, Airdrie – operated by William Black & Sons Ltd. On Thursday, 4th February 1858, a woman pithead worker died when she fell down the shaft with an empty hutch. *

22. Millfield Colliery, Airdrie – operated by John Hendrie & Co. On Monday, 9th May 1859, a miner was killed when, carrying a naked flame lamp, he went into a discontinued part of the workings and a body of firedamp ignited at his lamp. As a result he was severely burned and died the next day. There had been no adequate fence or signal put up to warn the workman of danger. *

23. Rosehall Colliery, Coatbridge – operated by Robert Addie & Sons Ltd. On Wednesday, 31st August 1859, a bottomer put a hutch onto the cage preparatory to sending it up the shaft when the cage was raised unexpectedly and he was crushed between the hutch and the side of the shaft. Drawers who were close to the pit bottom testified that no signal to raise the cage had been given by the bottomer, and the bell handle was so positioned that it could not be signalled by mistake. *

24. No. 3 pit, Stevenston Colliery, Holytown. On Saturday, 24th December 1859, a section of roof weighing several tons came down, burying a young miner and killing him instantly. Only a moment before the accident, eight men were gathered at the very spot where the roof came down. *

25. Crowwoods Colliery, Airdrie. On Thursday, 10th May 1860, a labourer, who normally worked about the boats transporting the coal from the colliery, went in an idle period to the pithead. There, in the absence of the pithead man, he tried to put an empty hutch onto the cage to be returned to the bottom. Unfortunately, he pushed it into the wrong side and fell with it to the bottom of the shaft, a distance of 49 fathoms. *

26. Auchenheath Colliery, Kirkmuirhill – operated by James Ferguson & Co. On Thursday,

9th August 1860, four men were widening a road in the workings when the face collapsed on them, killing one man instantly. *

27. Rosehall Colliery, Coatbridge – operated by Robert Addie & Sons Ltd. Shortly after 6.00 p.m. on Saturday, 29th September 1860, while preparing to carry out his check of the workings, the fireman warned a particular brusher not to go to his working place as firedamp was known to be there. As soon as the fireman had gone the brusher left for his working place with an unprotected light and there ignited the firedamp, as a result of which he died of severe burns. *

28. Gartsherrie Colliery, Coatbridge – operated by William Baird & Co. Although the colliery fireman carried out safety checks before each shift descended, one contractor was working outwith the normal shift pattern and his two-man squad were allowed to go to their work before the fireman arrived. On the morning of Monday, 24th December 1860, they were approaching their workplace without using the safety lamp provided and their naked lights ignited a body of firedamp. The explosion swept the mine, killing the two men, destroying the brattice-work and disrupting the ventilation flow. *(2)

29. Stanrigg Colliery, Airdrie – operated by William Black & Sons. On Saturday, 2nd February 1861, a miner was killed in an explosion of firedamp. *

30. Gartgill Colliery, Coatbridge. On Monday, 4th February 1861, having completed a througher between his own heading and another three or four days previously, a miner was in the process of widening the passage in the stoop-and-room workings when an explosion occurred and he was killed. It transpired that, the througher having been cut, the overman and fireman took out the brattice that had carried air to the heading,

wrongly assuming the draught in the througher would remove any firedamp. *

31. No. 2 pit, Palace Craig Colliery, Airdrie – operated by William Baird & Co. On the morning of Tuesday, 30th April 1861, a fireman and overman, conducting a check of the working places, found a body of firedamp and attempted to dislodge it into the return air current. Their efforts were unsuccessful and they put it down to some kind of interruption to the flow. Being able to travel only a short distance forward with the safety lamp, they abandoned it and attempted to go forward a few yards in the dark to find the interruption. When rescuers went in after them they found the fireman had died and the overman was dragged out unconscious. *

32. Stanrigg Colliery, Airdrie – operated by William Black & Sons. On Saturday, 11th May 1861, a miner was killed when the roof collapsed on him. *

33. Dykehead (Summerlee) Colliery, Shotts – operated by John Wilson & Co. On Wednesday, 7th August 1861, twelve miners were suffocated when woodwork at the bottom of the 40-fathom shaft caught fire, deranging the ventilation flow. It was thought that the woodwork had been too close to the ventilating furnace. Another miner died later. *(13)

34. Faskine Colliery, Airdrie – operated by William Baird & Co. On Thursday, 31st October 1861, a bottomer pushed a loaded hutch onto the cage and signalled to have it drawn up. A little later he pushed forward another full hutch without realising that the cage had yet to return. He fell with the hutch to the bottom of the shaft. *

35. Coal pit, Newmains. On Tuesday, 31st December 1861, a young miner was killed instantly when the roof collapsed. *

36. Auchenheath Colliery, Kirkmuirhill – operated by James Ferguson & Co. At about two o'clock on the morning of Tuesday, 14th January 1862, while engaged in sinking a new shaft, two men were caught in a fall of stone. One of them was struck on the head by a large stone that had fallen some five to six fathoms. He later died. *

37. No. 2 ironstone pit, Carluke. About two o'clock on the afternoon of Monday, 20th January 1862, two miners reached the pithead and made to step from the cage. The first cleared the gate but, just as the other was about to follow him, a bolt in the machinery snapped and the man, along with the gearing, fell to the bottom of the shaft 30 fathoms below. Despite his injuries, he clung to life for over a week. *

38. No. 2 pit, Polmadie Colliery, Govan, Glasgow – operated by William Dixon & Co. On Thursday, 6th February 1862, two miners were killed when one of them illegally entered the underground powder magazine. It was assumed that the powder had somehow been ignited by one of their lamps. *(2)

39. Draffan Colliery, Kirkmuirhill – owned by the Duke of Hamilton. On Monday, 3rd March 1862, a miner was caught by a fall of roof from which he sustained a broken leg. Having been taken home and attended by the doctor, his condition grew worse and he died two days later. *

40. Kilcadzow opencast mine, Carluke – operated by Hastie & Waddell for the Coltness Iron Co. On Wednesday, 5th March 1862, a young worker was killed when a large piece of material, dislodged in a previous fall, came down on him. A native of Ireland, he had been in the country only a few days. *

41. Quarry Colliery, Calder, Coatbridge. The machinery (winding engine, rope and pit bottom pumps) had been standing idle for over a year when, due to a breakage at another colliery, the pumps were started. Five or six days later, on Monday, 17th March 1862, it was found that the pumps required some maintenance and the cage was lowered with a weight on it to test the guides, etc. Having proved satisfactory, the oversman and an assistant descended, carried out the work and were coming back up the shaft when, within a few feet of the surface, the winding rope snapped. The cage plunged to the pit bottom and the men were killed. *(2)

42. Milton Colliery, Carluke – operated by the Coltness Iron Co. On Wednesday, 19th March 1862, a young boy was severely injured when, working at the foot of an incline, he was caught unawares and struck by a runaway hutch. He died four hours later. *

43. Merryton Colliery, Hamilton. On the morning of Tuesday, 13th May 1862, a fireman – with a naked tally lamp on his cap and a Davy lamp in his hand – was making his examination of the workings. He passed two roadsmen at the pit bottom and about ten minutes later an explosion took place. The roadsmen were knocked down by the blast, one of them receiving fatal injuries. The fireman's body was found eight days later. It was subsequently found that the ventilating furnace had not been fired regularly the previous day. *(2)

44. Clydesdale pit, Sunnyside Colliery, Wishaw – operated by Archibald Russell & Co. On Tuesday, 27th May 1862, a fireman and two companions were employed clearing a fall of stone. Unbeknown to them, firedamp had accumulated in the overhead cavity and the gas ignited at the fireman's lamp, severely burning one of the men. He later died. *

45. No. 5 pit, Rosehall Colliery, Coatbridge – operated by Robert Addie & Sons Ltd. On Tuesday, 15th July 1862, two oversmen, having made an examination of the shaft for loose material, gave the signal to be raised to the surface while still in the cage. Just as it began to move, some loose material fell onto the roof of the cage and one of the men, alarmed, attempted to get off. He died when he was crushed between the cage and the side of the shaft. *

46. Pather Colliery, Wishaw – operated by Boyd & Spencer Ltd. Worked by the stoop-and-room method, firedamp was known to gather in the rooms. Unfortunately, these places were not bratticed to carry the gas out; instead the fireman wafted the gas out with a fan every morning. On Monday, 1st September 1862, a workman entered by mistake a room that had been imperfectly fenced off and the gas exploded at his lamp. *

47. Morningside Colliery, Wishaw – operated by the Shotts Iron Co. On Sunday, 16th November 1862, the pithead man was off work and an improper signal was made from the pithead to the bottom just as a pumper was about to ascend. Following a misunderstanding, the man was carried up before he was properly inside the cage and he was crushed at the door-heads. *

48. Sunnyside Colliery, Wishaw – operated by Archibald Russell & Co. On Saturday, 20th December 1862, a workman was sending hutches of dross up to a higher scaffold using the cage. He ran a loaded hutch into the pit when the cage was not there and the hutch fell down the shaft, taking him with it. *

49. Quarry Colliery, Calder, Coatbridge. On the morning of Thursday, 19th February 1863, two pony drivers were descending the shaft when, passing a mid-working, one of them attempted to step off the cage as though at the pit bottom. He fell to the bottom of the shaft and was killed. Strangely, his companion did not notice his absence until the cage reached the pit bottom. *

50. Greenhill Colliery, Holytown – operated by Robert Young & Co. On Wednesday, 16th December 1863, a worker was killed when the winding engineman failed to secure the engine in proper winding gear. *

51. Greenhill Colliery, Holytown – operated by Robert Young & Co. In January 1864, one month after the above, a similar accident happened at the same pit, also resulting in loss of life. The inspector concluded that, as the machinery was in good working order, the machineman was at fault.

52. No. 3 pit, Coats Colliery, Coatbridge – operated by Coats of Paisley. On Friday, 29th July 1864, having been employed at his working place for some three hours, a miner was killed when his naked light came in contact with a previously undetected body of firedamp. The inspector was of the opinion that the gas had been released and forced towards his naked light by a fall of roof in some part of the waste. *

53. Britton Colliery, Coatbridge. While the colliery fireman carried out an examination of the workings every morning, an arrangement existed between him and the men contracted to push the headings towards a rise pit – namely, that he examined the workings for gas and they examined the headings for the same. On the morning of Monday, 1st August 1864, after the fireman had carried out his examination and left, the contractors arrived and one of them went into the west heading carrying an open light, which ignited a quantity of firedamp resulting in the deaths of three miners. *(3)

54. No. 6 pit, Cambusnethan Colliery, Wishaw – operated by James Sneddon Ltd. On Friday, 31st March 1865, two miners were killed when the rope of the bucket they were travelling in snapped, sending them to the bottom of the shaft. *(2)

55. Victoria Colliery, Wishaw – operated by the Wishaw Iron Co. On Friday, 26th May 1865, a miner was killed when an explosion of firedamp occurred in the Splint seam. *

56. Victoria Colliery, Wishaw – operated by the Wishaw Iron Co. Since the previous accident the Splint workings had stood idle until pumps were installed to draw water. On Thursday, 14th September 1865, one of the workmen involved in putting the pumps in the shaft went down to the Splint coal level with a naked light and was killed when he ignited a body of firedamp. *

57. Drumpark Colliery, Bargeddie. On Tuesday, 26th November 1867, three miners were descending in the cage when one lost his grip on the frame and fell out, plunging to the bottom of the shaft. *

58. No. 4 Coal pit, Rutherglen. On the morning of Wednesday, 14th April 1869, a miner was fatally injured when a block of coal fell from the face. He died a few hours later. *

59. No. 1 pit, Motherwell Colliery – operated by John Watson Ltd. On the morning of Sunday, 24th April 1870, a young boy was killed when, in the process of being lowered to the pit bottom along with two pony drivers, the winding engine was suddenly reversed and the cage was sent up the shaft and over the pulley wheel. While the pony drivers were thrown clear but injured, the boy fell down the shaft and was killed. It transpired that the dead boy's older brother was at the time operating the machinery. *

60. Climpy Colliery, Forth – operated by Gray & Paul Ltd. On the afternoon of Sunday, 3rd July 1870, while the engineman, Walter Annan, was at church, his twelve-year-old son went to the engine house to pump some water. His mother and three of the family also took a walk to the pit and while they were there the boiler (20 feet long and 4 feet in diameter) 'exploded with tremendous force', killing one child instantly and severely injuring the others. Another child died later that evening from injuries received. Such was the force of the explosion that the boiler was thrown a distance of 160 yards from its former position and the blast was heard almost two miles away. Having lost two children, another child of the family died of illness fifteen days after the tragedy. *(2)

61. Ferniegair Colliery, Hamilton – operated by Archibald Russell & Co. On the morning of Tuesday, 19th July 1870, a drawer was taking an empty hutch from the pit bottom to the coalface when it went off the rails. With help, he was attempting to get the hutch back on the rails when it hit him on the neck, under the chin, and he died soon after. *

62. No. 14 ironstone pit, Cadder, Bishopbriggs, Glasgow – operated by the Carron Iron Co. On the afternoon of Thursday, 13th July 1871, while connecting pump rods 30 fathoms down the shaft, three men were killed when the scaffold they were working from collapsed. Along with the wreckage of the scaffold, the men fell 30 fathoms to the bottom of the shaft, which was flooded to a depth of 30 fathoms. *(3)

63. Allanton Colliery, Hamilton – operated by Austine & Co. On Thursday, 11th January 1872, a young miner lost his life during a roof fall. *

64. Priestfield Colliery, Blantyre – operated by William Dixon & Co. On Monday, 2nd March

1874, two miners were killed by an explosion of firedamp. *(2)

65. Greenfield Colliery, Hamilton – operated by the Hamilton Coal Co. On the evening of Thursday, 16th April 1874, a surface boiler exploded without warning, seriously injuring an engineer (who died the following day) and killing John Hailes, one of two young brothers who were warming themselves at the furnace room door. The egg-ends of the boiler, one of six, flew in opposite directions. One of the boiler ends travelled 300 feet, taking down telegraph wires, destroying wagons and tearing up railway lines. Had the explosion happened five minutes later, a crowded train could have been added to the carnage. It was only the quick thinking of pointsman George Wilson that averted a catastrophe. On hearing the explosion, he threw the block signals to warn the driver and prevent the train from reaching the damaged lines. The other boiler end, the largest, destroyed walls and tore the roofs off a nearby miners' row before crashing through the roof of the local schoolhouse in which a prayer meeting had just begun. The explosion claimed four victims, two at the pithead and two in the schoolhouse, and 28 men, women and children were seriously injured. Mines Inspector Ralph Moore concluded that the boilers, having been heavily corroded (therefore weakened) at the water line, were no longer able to take the pressure. *(4)

66. No. 2 pit, Stonecraig Colliery, Wishaw – operated by the Coltness Iron Co. On the afternoon of Wednesday, 2nd December 1874, a young miner was working at the face when a roof fall broke both his legs. His companions immediately began work to free him until another fall threatened, and they had to run for their lives. When they returned they found that the second fall had killed the trapped man. *

67. No. 1 pit, Haughhead Colliery, Uddingston – operated by Merry & Cunninghame Ltd. Just before eleven o'clock on the evening of Monday, 14th February 1876, two roadsmen were employed repairing and strengthening the roof in the main road by replacing old props with new ones. As they worked a piece of roof, about nine tons in weight, fell and killed them instantly. *(2)

68. Ashgill Colliery, Dalserf, Larkhall – operated by Andrew Spencer Ltd. About noon on Tuesday, 15th February 1876, a miner was taking out stoops in the Splint seam when the supports collapsed and the roof fell on him. *

69. No. 1 pit, Blantyre Colliery – operated by William Dixon & Co. About two o'clock on the afternoon of Tuesday, 15th February 1876, a worker was instantly killed when, in the process of coupling two moving wagons together, his head was jammed between the buffers. *

70. No. 5 pit, Braehead Colliery, Forth – operated by Dunn Bros. Ltd. On the afternoon of Wednesday, 16th February 1876, two miners were erecting props at the face to support the roof when a large section of coal fell and buried them. They were killed and a pony driver who was nearby had his leg broken. *(2)

71. Cadder Colliery, Bishopbriggs, Glasgow – operated by the Carron Iron Co. On the afternoon of Saturday, 19th February 1876, when the shift had ended and the men away, two miners remained to carry out some blasting for Monday's day shift. About four o'clock, wondering why they had not come up, the brother of one of them descended and found a body in the darkness. With the alarm raised, a party went down and found both miners dead. It was assumed that the men, impatient at the slowness of the fuse, went forward to investigate and were caught by the blast. *(2)

72. Allanshaw Colliery, Hamilton – operated by James & David Sneddon Ltd. On Wednesday, 29th March 1876, while four men were sinking a new shaft, the spring clip attaching the kettle to the winding rope snapped. The kettle, filled with about three-quarters of a ton of rubble, was only feet from the top of the shaft when it happened and the four men below had no warning and no chance to escape. One man died and the others were injured. *

73. Mainhill Colliery, Bargeddie – operated by William Baird & Co. On Wednesday, 30th August 1876, while measuring the work done for the month with a contractor, a mining engineer was killed when their naked flame lamps ignited a body of firedamp. The engineer was found under a mass of stone from the roof, having died from the effects of afterdamp. *

74. No. 1 pit, Greenfield Colliery, Hamilton – operated by the Hamilton Coal Co. On Monday, 8th January 1877, while blasting at the coalface, a miner set a charge of powder and retired to safety. Having waited for a time, and thinking the fuse had gone out, he approached the face just as it exploded. He was killed instantly. *

75. Home Farm Colliery, Larkhall – operated by Hamilton, McCulloch & Co. for the Duke of Hamilton. Eight days before the accident a fall of roof in the extreme rise workings of the Ell coal seam weakened the 108-foot barrier between the surface and the pit. About six o'clock on the morning of Tuesday, 23rd January 1877, four miners were drowned when a large volume of slurry broke through into the workings. *(4)

76. No. 1 pit, Allanton Colliery, Hamilton – operated by Austine & Co. Shortly after 6.30 on the morning of Friday, 13th April 1877, when the day shift were preparing to start work, a miner was travelling to work along the Ell coal

workings. Carrying a naked flame lamp, he passed through an opening into a disused working in which a small quantity of firedamp had accumulated. The gas ignited, burning the man and starting a fire among the dry timber. He survived, but one miner was suffocated by the smoke. *

77. No. 1 pit, Allanshaw Colliery, Hamilton – operated by James & David Sneddon Ltd. About two o'clock on the morning of Tuesday, 24th July 1877, while disassembling pipes for removal from the shaft, a workman lost his balance and fell to the pit bottom 60 fathoms below. *

78. Blantyre Colliery – operated by William Dixon & Co. On Monday, 20th August 1877, three brothers, working alone, were caught in an explosion of firedamp. While one was unhurt the other two were badly burned, one of them later dying of his injuries. *

79. Blantyre Colliery – operated by William Dixon & Co. On Tuesday, 11th September 1877, two miners were killed by an explosion of firedamp. *(2)

80. Larkhall Colliery – operated by William Black & Sons. In 1877 an inrush of mud drowned four miners.

81. No. 3 pit, Blantyre Colliery – operated by William Dixon & Co. On Tuesday, 5th March 1878, as a result of an overwinding accident, six miners fell to their deaths down the shaft. At the inquiry it was established that the indicator, which showed the position of the cage, was faulty and tended to slip due to vibration. It also transpired that a simple (and inexpensive) device, called Walker's Detaching Hook, was available and had proved to be ideal in preventing the loss of life due to overwinding. Although some other collieries in the Blantyre area had already

installed the device, William Dixon & Co. had refused to spend the money. *(6)

82. No. 4 Pit, Blantyre Colliery – operated by William Dixon & Co. On Sunday, 14th March 1880, a young pony driver died when fire broke out in the workings. He was last been seen running to the stables on the other side of the fire and was never heard of again. Ten months later, on 11th January 1881, while clearing a fall of roof about 300 yards from the location of the fire, workmen came across his body. The watch in his pocket had stopped at nine minutes to six, about the time he was last seen. *

83. Shawfield Colliery, Carluke. On the afternoon of Monday, 11th April 1881, a pithead labourer, having been warned to keep clear by the engineman, was killed when he stepped between two wagons and was crushed by the buffers. *

84. No. 4 pit, Motherwell Colliery – operated by John Watson Ltd. On the afternoon of Wednesday, 13th April 1881, a young miner was engaged in taking away the supports when he was buried under a fall of roof. *

85. Carfin Colliery, Bellshill. On the evening of Tuesday, 3rd May 1881, three men were working on the cage at the entrance to the Splint seam when the bell was accidentally touched. As the cage was hoisted to the surface one of the men fell to the bottom of the shaft. *

86. No. 2 pit, Ferniegair Colliery, Hamilton – operated by Archibald Russell & Co. On the evening of Friday, 27th May 1881, a fireman was withdrawing props when a large stone fell from the roof and killed him instantly. *

87. Upper Flemington Colliery, Cambuslang. On Tuesday, 12th July 1881, a miner was seriously injured when he was caught by a fall of roof. He died in Glasgow Royal Infirmary the following day. *

88. No. 1 pit, Auchinraith Colliery, Blantyre – operated by Merry & Cunninghame Ltd. On Saturday, 16th July 1881, while preparing a shot in the Ell coal seam, an acting fireman was killed when the shot went off prematurely. *

89. No. 3 ironstone pit, Muirhead Colliery, West Benhar, Harthill – operated by the Coltness Iron Co. On the afternoon of Saturday, 8th October 1881, an oversman was working on a scaffold in the shaft when the rope of a bucket being lowered snapped. The bucket, weighing about half a ton, fell down carrying the scaffold, and the oversman, to the bottom of the shaft 22 fathoms below. *

90. No. 1 pit, Bent Colliery, Hamilton – operated by the Bent Coal Co. On Thursday, 29th December 1881, a miner, working at the face with his son, complained of feeling unwell and left to go home. Shortly afterwards his body was found lying in the main road having been run over by hutches. His doctor had previously treated him for epilepsy and it was his opinion that the man had taken a fit and had fallen in the way of the hutches, which were propelled by an endless rope. *

91. No. 2 pit, Eddlewood Colliery, Hamilton – operated by John Watson Ltd. On Thursday, 26th January 1882, four men were sinking a shaft when a mass of fireclay, weighing about a ton, fell on them from a height of fourteen feet. While three of them had a narrow escape, one of them was crushed to death. *

92. No. 1 pit, Bartonshill Colliery, Old Monkland, Coatbridge. On Tuesday, 7th March 1882, while the cage was descending the shaft, the winding rope began to jerk. Realising something was wrong, the engineman stopped his engine. The bottomer, wondering what was wrong, shouted up but got no answer, so he began to climb the shaft. When he reached the cage he found the single occupant lying unconscious and the cage was wound to the surface, but the injured man died some 20 minutes later. Examination revealed his ribs to be crushed and his arm to be broken among other injuries, and it was assumed that, for some reason, he must have leaned out of the cage and been caught between the cage and the side of the shaft. *

93. Camp Colliery, Motherwell – operated by Williams & Co. On Thursday, 16th March 1882, the cage arrived at the surface carrying three men. Due to an error by the banksman who operated the engine, the cage travelled several feet above the landing stage and the men, fearing that they would be carried into the head frame, leapt out. Two of them landed safely, but the third either slipped or was caught by something and fell down the shaft. *

94. Udston Colliery, Hamilton – operated by the Udston Coal Co. About 4.30 on the afternoon of Monday, 15th May 1882, an explosion of firedamp occurred when a miner and his son were driving through to a back drift in the Main coal seam. The colliery manager and an overseer, who were carrying out an examination of the workings at the time, happened to be there and only the overseer, John Bolton, survived the blast. *(3)

95. No. 1 pit, Netherhouse Colliery, Baillieston. On Wednesday, 23rd August 1882, a miner was killed when a mass of stone weighing about two tons fell from the roof and buried him. *

96. No. 1 pit, Ferniegair Colliery, Hamilton – operated by Archibald Russell & Co. On Friday,

17th November 1882, a fireman was working in the shaft repairing the wooden slides. As he was sawing one of them it gave way and he fell with it twelve fathoms to the bottom of the shaft. *

97. Bog Colliery, Larkhall – operated by James Hamilton & Co. On the afternoon of Tuesday, 21st November 1882, two miners were being taken up the shaft in the cage. The winding rope was of steel, strongly riveted to an iron clasp, to which the cage was attached. When the cage was halfway up the shaft the rope suddenly overlapped on the revolving drum, slipping from the drum and causing the cage to drop a distance of 36 feet. When the loose rope reached its end, the jerk was so violent that it drew the rope from the clasp through nearly a dozen rivets. The cage plunged 40 fathoms to the bottom of the shaft and the two men died. *(2)

98. Lochhill ironstone pit, Airdrie – operated by the Monkland Iron & Steel Co. In early December 1882 a brusher was boring near to the face when a stone, weighing about half-a-ton, fell from the side wall and crushed the lower half of his body. He held out until 4th December when he died. *

99. Clydesdale Colliery, Wishaw – operated by Archibald Russell & Co. On the evening of Wednesday, 31st January 1883, a father and son were taking out stoops when a large quantity of stone fell from the roof, trapping them. The father was got out with a broken leg, but his son was found to be dead. *

100. No. 1 pit, Earnock Colliery, Hamilton – operated by John Watson Ltd. About 10.30 a.m. on Friday, 16th March 1883, a contractor and five brushers were replacing wood propping put up a few days previously in the wrong place. While they were working several tons of stone fell from the roof and injured four of them. One of the men died thirteen hours later. *

101. No. 1 pit, Gilbertfield Colliery, Cambuslang – operated by the Cambuslang Coal Co. On the night of Wednesday, 1st August 1883, having left the cage at an upper level to get something he needed, a miner returned to the cage. He had no light and as he reached the shaft he went to the wrong side and stepped into the open shaft, falling to the bottom. *

102. No. 2 ironstone pit, Muirhead Colliery, West Benhar, Harthill – operated by the Coltness Iron Co. On Monday, 4th February 1884, a miner, working in the dook section, was killed when a stone weighing between five and six cubic weight fell from the roof onto his back, pinning him to the ground. He was released and taken to the surface but died shortly after. *

103. Cadzow Colliery, Hamilton. On Saturday, 12th April 1884, a miner was working in the Soft coal seam when the roof collapsed, completely burying him. *

104. Earnock Colliery, Hamilton – operated by John Watson Ltd. On the morning of Tuesday, 6th May 1884, two brothers were working at the stoops in the Ell coal seam when a piece of coal fell from the roof and struck one of them. *

105. Allanshaw Colliery, Hamilton – operated by James & David Sneddon Ltd. On Friday, 22nd August 1884, while repairing a line of rails, a miner was killed when a stone weighing two cubic weight came away from the roof, breaking his left leg and injuring his spine. He later died of his injuries. *

106. Home Farm Colliery, Larkhall – operated by Hamilton, McCulloch & Co. for the Duke of Hamilton. On the morning of Friday, 12th September 1884, a young pithead worker was in the act of snibbling wagons coming down an incline when he was knocked in front of the wheels. The wagons passed over both his legs, causing such injury that they had to be amputated above the knee. However, he died within an hour of the operation. *

107. No. 2 pit, Tannochside Colliery, Bellshill. On the evening of Sunday, 5th October 1884, a miner was severely cut on the forehead by a piece of coal. He died of his injury three days later. *

108. Overtown Station Colliery, Wishaw – operated by Brand & Co. On the afternoon of Tuesday, 11th August 1885, while helping to fill a hutch at the face of the Main coal seam, a miner was killed when a large stone, weighing about four cubic weight, fell on him. *

109. Stanrigg Colliery, Airdrie – operated by William Black & Sons. On Tuesday, 25th August 1885, a miner was run over and killed by a hutch. *

110. Bothwell Castle Colliery, Bothwell – operated by William Baird & Co. On Monday, 21st December 1885, as the cage was being lowered down the shaft, the rope gave a jerk and a miner fell from the cage to the bottom of the shaft, 100 fathoms below. It was stated that the cause of the jerk was the rope slipping on the drum. *

111. Fence Pit, Hamilton area. On the afternoon of Monday, 29th March 1886, four men were being raised to the surface when the cage partially overturned and became stuck in mid shaft. While two men managed to hold on inside the cage, the other two fell to the bottom of the shaft and were killed. *(2)

112. Hallcraig ironstone pit, Carluke – operated by the Coltness Iron Co. On Thursday, 22nd April 1886, a young lad was killed when (it was assumed) he attempted to jump onto a hutch to get a ride and fell under it, where he received fatal injuries. *

113. No. 2 pit, Bothwell Castle Colliery, Bothwell – operated by William Baird & Co. On Friday, 28th June 1889, while five men were descending No. 2 shaft, the engineman failed to shut off the steam in time and the cage smashed into the pit bottom killing them all. *(5)

114. Stanrigg Colliery, Airdrie, Lanarkshire – operated by William Black & Sons. On Sunday, 5th January 1890, a miner jumped down the shaft. *

115. Haughhead Colliery, Uddingston – operated by William Dixon & Co. On Saturday, 4th June 1892, a young girl was killed when her clothes were caught in a revolving shaft at the pithead. Having been carried round the shaft at least 20 times, she died from strangulation and multiple injuries. *

116. Hamilton Palace Colliery, Bothwell – operated by the Bent Coal Co. On the morning of Monday, 20th March 1893, a screening plant worker overbalanced and fell between coal wagons that were in the process of being shunted into place. He died of his injuries two hours later. *

117. No. 2 pit, Orbiston Colliery, Bellshill – operated by Robert Addie & Sons Ltd. On the morning of Saturday, 27th May 1893, a fire broke out in the workings and three men, engaged in fighting the fire, were suffocated by afterdamp.

118. Blantyre Colliery – operated by William Dixon & Co. On Thursday, 5th April 1894, a pithead worker was killed when he was crushed between wagon buffers. *

119. Hamilton Palace Colliery, Bothwell – operated by the Bent Coal Co. On the morning of Monday, 14th October 1895, a female screening

plant worker was killed when, having occasion to step over an exposed revolving shaft, her petticoats became entangled and she was drawn into the machinery. With a broken back and head injuries, she died soon after. *

120. Blantyre Colliery – operated by William Dixon & Co. On Tuesday, 22nd October 1895, two men engaged in sinking a new shaft were killed when the kettle they were travelling in was struck by a fall of rock. *(2)

121. Eddlewood Colliery, Hamilton – operated by John Watson Ltd. On Wednesday, 19th February 1896, a miner was injured by a fall of roof. He was removed to Glasgow Royal Infirmary but died five days later. *

122. No. 11 pit, Drumpellier Colliery, Coatbridge – operated by the Summerlee Iron Co. On Friday, 28th January 1898, three miners were killed in an explosion caused by a shot igniting coal dust. A member of the rescue party also lost his life. *(4)

123. Hamilton Palace Colliery, Bothwell – operated by the Bent Coal Co. On Tuesday, 6th December 1898, a workman was fatally injured in the pumping engine house when he fell between part of the gearing and the brick wall and was crushed to death. *

124. Blantyre Colliery – operated by William Dixon & Co. On Saturday, 1st April 1899, two men were killed when they were run over by a locomotive. *(2)

125. Ferniegair Colliery, Hamilton – operated by Archibald Russell & Co. On the afternoon of Sunday, 9th April 1899, the son of the colliery oversman was descending the shaft with the ostler to feed the pit ponies when he toppled out of the cage, falling to the pit bottom. *

126. Hattonrigg Colliery, Bellshill – operated by the Summerlee Iron & Steel Co. On Tuesday, 16th January 1900, while driving a horse yoked to two hutches, a young pony driver died when he was run over and crushed to death. *

127. Stanrigg Colliery, Airdrie – operated by William Black & Sons. On Wednesday, 24th January 1900, a miner died when he was overcome by blackdamp. *

128. No. 4 pit, Hattonrigg Colliery, Bellshill – operated by the Summerlee Iron & Steel Co. On the night of Wednesday, 7th November 1900, three bricklayers, who had been working on the shaft of No. 4 pit, stepped into the kettle to be raised to the surface. On the way up the kettle struck a board on one side of the shaft then a beam on the other. As a result, one of them fell to the bottom of the shaft while the others managed to cling on. *

129. Monkland Colliery, Coatbridge – operated by James Dunlop & Co. On Monday, 6th May 1901, a miner was killed in a fall of roof at the face in the upper Drumgray seam. The fall, which was about 20 feet long, three feet wide and one foot thick, threw out some timber which hit the miner and caused his death. *

130. No. 4 pit, Hattonrigg Colliery, Bellshill – operated by the Summerlee Iron & Steel Co. Late on the evening of Thursday, 11th July 1901, a miner attempted to leave the cage at a mid-working and was caught between the cage and the side of the shaft. He died almost immediately. *

131. No. 3 pit, Blantyre Colliery – operated by William Dixon & Co. On Monday, 22nd July 1901, a workman was killed when he (illegally) used a pit prop to slow down a wagon (by pushing it between the spokes). Catching in the wheel, the prop struck him and threw him in front of the wagon, which ran over him. *

132. No. 1 pit, Auchinraith Colliery, Hamilton – operated by Merry & Cunninghame Ltd. On Wednesday, 24th July 1901, the cage was descending with eight men when, for some unknown reason, it left the slides and two of them fell to the bottom of the shaft. *(2)

133. Hamilton Palace Colliery, Bothwell – operated by the Bent Coal Co. On Monday, 23rd December 1901, a miner was killed by a fall of roof. *

134. No. 3 pit, Bellefield Colliery, Coalburn – operated by Barr & Son Ltd. On Thursday, 3rd April 1902, while working at the face, a miner was killed when a fall of coal partially buried him. *

135. Hamilton Palace Colliery, Bothwell – operated by the Bent Coal Co. On Saturday, 12th April 1902, a miner stumbled and fell in front of a hutch. The hutch ran over him and he died a few hours later. *

136. No. 3 pit, Eddlewood Colliery, Hamilton – operated by John Watson Ltd. On the morning of Monday, 12th May 1902, a workman was putting a hutch onto the cage when the engineman lowered it before the hutch was properly aboard. The workman was carried down the shaft with the cage, a depth of 100 fathoms, and killed. *

137. No. 2 pit, Stanrigg Colliery, Airdrie – operated by William Black & Sons. On Saturday, 24th May 1902, a pithead worker went down in the cage to adjust a water tap in the shaft. When he stepped out onto a ledge he missed his footing and fell down the shaft into the sump 500 feet below. *

138. Victor Emmanuel Colliery, Whiterigg - operated by United Collieries Ltd. Early on Monday, 9th February 1903, two brothers were employed moving hutches when one of their naked (tally) lamps ignited an accumulation of firedamp resulting in an explosion which killed one brother and badly burned the other. *

139. No. 1 pit, Earnock Colliery, Hamilton - operated by John Watson Ltd. On Tuesday, 10th February 1903, a fireman was travelling towards the pit bottom when he met a rake of hutches which, leaving the rails, knocked out a prop and caused a large mass of stone to fall on him. *

140. No. 13 pit, Rosehall Colliery, Bellshill - operated by Robert Addie & Sons Ltd. On Thursday, 9th April 1903, as a miner was propping the workings, a mass of stone weighing many hundredweights fell from the roof, killing him instantly. *

141. No. 12 pit, Holytown Colliery, Motherwell - operated by James Nimmo & Co. On Tuesday, 28th April 1903, two miners were putting Bellite into a blasting hole when it exploded prematurely to their severe injury. One of the men died the next day. *

142. No. 7 pit, Carfin Colliery, Newarthill - operated by William Dixon & Co. On Thursday, 30th April 1903, a young miner was standing on some loose coal to reach the top coal when he slipped and fell. A heavy fall of roof landed on him, crushing him so severely that he died after being taken home. *

143. No. 1 pit, Woodhall Colliery – operated by Barr & Higgins Ltd. On Thursday, 7th May 1903, a miner was killed in the Main dook of the lower Drumgray seam when a stone weighing half a ton fell on him, crushing him to death. *

144. No. 2 pit, Bothwell Park Colliery, Bellshill – operated by William Baird & Co. Early on the morning of Thursday, 28th May 1903, while engaged in blasting operations, a miner was killed when a charge exploded prematurely. *

145. Nos. 3 & 4 pits, Bothwell Castle (Priory) Colliery, Bothwell – operated by William Baird & Co. On the morning of Thursday, 4th June 1903, a workman was killed when, travelling in a wagon as it ran below the moving tables of the screening plant, his head was caught between the end of the wagon and the bottom of the tables, death being instantaneous. *

146. Hamilton Palace Colliery, Bothwell - operated by the Bent Coal Co. On Tuesday, 9th June 1903, a pony driver was driving a horse pulling an empty hutch, in which he was seated, when a large stone fell from the roof and pinned his neck against the edge of the hutch, strangling him. *

147. Bothwell Park Colliery, Bellshill – operated by William Baird & Co. On Friday, 19th June 1903, a fireman was killed when the shot he was loading went off prematurely. *

148. No. 1 pit, Hamilton Palace Colliery, Bothwell - operated by the Bent Coal Co. In the early hours of Saturday, 20th June 1903, while two miners were drawing wood in the Soft coal seam, a stone weighing over eight cubic weight suddenly fell from the roof. One of the men sustained only a few bruises, but his companion was pinned to the ground and killed. *

149. Eddlewood Colliery, Hamilton – operated by John Watson Ltd. On Friday, 26th August 1904, a pony driver set out to take a rake of hutches from the face to the pit bottom. About 20 minutes later he was found dead, jammed between the last hutch and the roof of the roadway. *

150. No. 2 pit, Hamilton Palace Colliery, Bothwell – operated by the Bent Coal Co. On Thursday, 20th October 1904, one man was killed and three others severely injured when the wooden supports in the brick arch they were building gave way. The arch collapsed, burying the men underneath. *

151. No. 2 pit, Hamilton Palace Colliery, Bothwell – operated by the Bent Coal Co. On Saturday, 19th September 1908, while employed in the screening plant, a workman had his arm drawn into the machinery. Before the engine could be stopped, however, his arm had been broken in several places and his chest so severely crushed that he died almost immediately. *

152. No. 1 pit, Ferniegair Colliery, Hamilton – operated by Archibald Russell Ltd. About 1.45 p.m. on Sunday, 27th June 1909, three miners were at work operating a coal-cutting machine in the Virtuewell seam when an explosion occurred. One man died at the scene and two others crawled to the pit bottom to raise the alarm. They were taken to Glasgow Royal Infirmary where they later died. *(3)

153. Star Mine, Glenboig – operated by the Union Fireclay Co. On the afternoon of Thursday, 5th August 1909, as they were stooping out following firing a round of shots, four miners died when a section of roof weighing about 20 tons fell on them. The wife of one of the victims had given birth the previous day. *(4)

154. No. 1 pit, Hamilton Palace Colliery, Bothwell – operated by the Bent Coal Co. About four o'clock on the morning of Monday, 18th October 1909, a miner was killed when he was buried by a fall of roof. *

155. No. 4 pit, Hattonrigg Colliery, Bellshill – operated by the Summerlee Iron & Steel Co.

About three o'clock on Wednesday, 19th January 1910, when the day shift miners were being raised to the surface on their way home, the engineman misjudged where the cage should have stopped. The result of his mistake was that the cage was overwound, crashed into the beams of the headgear and snapped the steel cable at the 'hose' where the four chains supporting the cage converged. The cage, weighing over two and a half tons, plummeted 192 fathoms (1,152 feet) into the sump at the bottom of the shaft, killing eight men. At the time of the accident the rest of the shift was waiting at the pit bottom to ascend and, hearing the noise from the shaft, they realised what had happened and retreated out of danger. Six of the eight victims were Lithuanians. *(8)

156. Hunter's Hill Sandstone Mine, Lanark – operated by Thomas Gibb & Sons. On Tuesday, 13th September 1910, an unsupported block of sandstone 40 feet thick detached itself from the roof and fell, killing five men. *(5)

157. Loanhead Colliery, Cambuslang. On Friday, 21st April 1911, while attempting to remove a screen at the top of an incline to disperse an accumulation of firedamp, an under-manager was overcome. Miner Thomas Macfarlane went up to help but was himself overcome. Sixty-year-old miner Walter Cullen then made two attempts to rescue the under-manager and, failing, was helped back by Macfarlane who had by then recovered. The under-manager's body was recovered later. Both Cullen and Macfarlane were awarded the Edward Medal, Second Class, for their bravery. *

158. No. 2 pit, Udston Colliery, Hamilton – operated by the Udston Coal Co. On Tuesday, 16th January 1912, a roadsman was driving a rake of six loaded hutches along the level horse road in the Pyotshaw seam when, on reaching the engine haulage way, he noticed that two of them had become detached. He went back with his pony and hitched them up and, as he was walking ahead of them going down an incline on the way back, he was knocked down and killed by the hutches he was pulling.*

159. Blantyre Colliery – operated by William Dixon & Co. On Monday, 15th April 1912, two miners were killed when a haulage wheel they were setting up fell on them. *(2)

160. No. 12 pit, Garriongill Colliery, Overtown – operated by the Coltness Iron Co. On Monday, 22nd December 1913, a miner had his left arm almost severed at the shoulder when a large stone fell from the roof and jammed him against a hutch. He died on the way to the infirmary. *

161. Bothwell Park Colliery, Bellshill – operated by William Baird & Co. On the night of Friday, 15th May 1914, a workman was killed when a number of large pine beams, which he had been moving, fell on him. *

162. Hamilton Palace Colliery, Bothwell – operated by the Bent Coal Co. On the afternoon of Friday, 2nd October 1914, the communication signal wire between the pit bottom and the engine house became jammed and two workmen were sent down to free it. When freed the bell rang and the cage began to move, throwing one of them to the bottom of the shaft. *

163. Bedlay Colliery, Stepps – operated by William Baird & Co. On Saturday, 27th November 1915, when three miners were cut off by a roof collapse, rescue workers fought to re-establish the airflow to them. When they were eventually reached, however, one of them had died from the effects of blackdamp. *

164. Dykehead Colliery, Shotts. On Monday, 24th April 1916, three men were killed by a large fall of roof. *(3)

165. No. 1 pit, Neilsland Colliery, Hamilton – operated by John Watson Ltd. Over the years the abandoned Eddlewood No. 3 shaft, adjacent to Neilsland, had been gradually filling with sludge from a coal washer. On Wednesday, 26th April 1916, the barrier at the bottom of the shaft collapsed and the black sludge flooded into the Neilsland workings, drowning five men. Four of the victims were never recovered. *(5)

166. Blantyre Colliery – operated by William Dixon & Co. On Sunday, 9th July 1916, a miner was killed when a fully loaded hutch ran out of control. *

167. Blantyre Colliery, Hamilton – operated by William Dixon & Co. On Monday, 18th July 1921, three miners were killed in a blasting accident at the coalface. *(3)

168. Wilsontown Colliery, Forth – operated by William Dixon & Co. On Monday, 23rd February 1925, a woman (who had possibly been collecting coal-spillage on the tracks from passing trains) was struck down and run over by two wagons of a mineral train. She survived for 20 minutes before dying from shock. *

169. No. 2 pit, Brownlee Colliery, Law – operated by the Wilson's & Clyde Coal Co. About seven o'clock on the morning of Tuesday, 5th May 1925, four miners entered the cage to descend at the start of their shift. The pithead man signalled to the engine house, but instead of going down the cage began to move upwards. Below the winding gear safety catches were fitted to prevent overwinding and, in this event, to prevent the cage from falling down the shaft. The catches had been renewed a week earlier and were checked every morning. However, when the rope was released and the cage fell back, the catches failed to operate and the cage carrying the four men plunged 160 fathoms down the shaft. *(4)

170. No. 2 pit, Cardowan Colliery, Stepps – operated by James Dunlop & Co. At about 3.50 p.m. on Monday, 1st August 1927, when No. 2 shaft was being sunk, a gas explosion occurred 241 fathoms below at the bottom of the shaft, resulting in three deaths. A round of shots had been fired at the end of the day shift (2.00 p.m.) and ten back shift workers were clearing away the rubble when the explosion took place. The bottom of the shaft had not been checked for gas emissions. The Coatbridge Rescue Brigade was quickly on the scene and, with the help of volunteers, one body and eight injured men were taken to the surface. The inspector's report concluded that, with the atmosphere untested for gas, one of the men had struck a match to smoke and ignited the gas. Three men – John Burt, William Boyd and Roderick McKinnon – were commended for their heroism during the rescue efforts. *(3)

171. Parkhead Colliery, Hamilton – operated by the Wilson's & Clyde Coal Co. On Tuesday, 6th August 1929, a miner was killed when he was buried by a fall of roof. *

172. Auchinraith Colliery, Blantyre – operated by Merry & Cunninghame Ltd. About 8.15 a.m. on Saturday, 30th August 1930, an explosion of firedamp at one of the working places in the Black Band seam killed six men and injured nine others. Survivors said that the explosion 'resembled a brilliant flash of lightning passing along the workings' and 'the men were hurled about like ninepins'. Those who were slightly injured immediately helped those less fortunate to the pit bottom before the Coatbridge Rescue Brigade arrived. *(6)

173. No. 2 (round) pit, Auchengeich Colliery, Chryston – operated by James Nimmo & Co. About four o'clock on the morning of Thursday, 22nd January 1931, an explosion of firedamp –

caused, it was thought, by unauthorised shot firing – killed five miners. Within 25 minutes a rescue team from Coatbridge was underground and, despite being hampered by heavy blackdamp, brought out the victims. Another miner died in hospital the following day. *(6)

174. No. 2 (round) pit, Auchengeich Colliery, Chryston – operated by James Nimmo & Co. On Wednesday, 1st April 1931, as the fatal accident inquiry into the previous accident (173) was opened, two miners were killed in a roof collapse at the colliery.

175. No. 2 pit, Tannochside Colliery, Bellshill. On Tuesday, 3rd November 1931, two miners were attending an underground pump when they were buried by a fall of roof. When the debris was cleared they were found to be dead. *(2)

176. No. 1 pit, Cadzow Colliery, Hamilton. On the afternoon of Thursday, 14th September 1933, while repairing the main roadway in the Kiltongue section, the roof collapsed burying two miners, one of whom died. *

177. Branchal Colliery, Cambusnethan – operated by the Coltness Iron Co. On the morning of Friday, 29th September 1933, a workman was buried by a large fall of stone from the roof. When he was extricated an hour later he was found to be dead. *

178. Quarter Colliery, Hamilton – operated by Colin Dunlop & Co. On the evening of Tuesday, 20th March 1934, a worker was killed and another seriously injured when a large stone fell from the roof and crushed them. *

179. No. 10 pit, Rosehall Colliery, Coatbridge – operated by Robert Addie & Sons Ltd. About two o'clock on the morning of Tuesday, 14th August 1934, six miners were injured in an

explosion of firedamp at a working face in the Main coal seam. According to *The Times* of 15 August, 'Great heroism was shown by the uninjured miners, who carried their comrades half a mile along the underground roadways to the bottom of the shaft, which is 150 fathoms deep. The rescuers risked their lives by crawling through dense choking fumes in which they found the injured men trying to crawl to safety.' The injured men were taken to the surface by the Coatbridge Rescue Brigade, but five would die in hospital. *(5)

180. Ferniegair Colliery, Hamilton – operated by Archibald Russell & Co. On the evening of Sunday, 17th March 1935, three miners were at work in the Main coal seam. A sudden fall of stone from the roof crushed one man against the coal-cutting machine, inflicting head injuries from which he died almost immediately, and the other two were trapped under the rubble. Rescue parties worked for two hours to free them and they survived. *

181. Hamilton Palace Colliery, Bothwell – operated by the Bent Coal Co. On Monday, 17th June 1935, a miner was killed when he was struck by a rake of hutches that ran out of control down an incline on the main road. *

182. Bardykes Colliery, Blantyre – operated by Merry & Cunninghame Ltd. About 7.30 p.m. on Saturday, 21st March 1936, a seven-man squad of brushers was preparing the section for the next day's production when the roof collapsed, killing five of them. The first victim was recovered almost immediately, but because of the threat of further falls, the last victim was not recovered until just before noon the following day. When she heard of her loss Mrs Dawson, pregnant wife of one of the victims, said, 'It's just the life of a miner's wife. You see them go out in the morning in their pit clothes, and you never know if they will come back alive.' (*The Times*, 23 March 1936.) *(5)

183. No. 2 pit, Viewpark Colliery, Uddingston – operated by Robert Addie & Sons Ltd. On Tuesday, 15th February 1938, while repairing a mine in the upper Ell seam, a miner was killed when a rake of hutches broke away and crushed him against the building. *

184. Newton Colliery, Cambuslang. On Friday, 11th March 1938, while drawing pans of coal, a miner was electrocuted by a faulty wire. Hearing his cry, another ran to his assistance but also collapsed. Two other miners who tried to help were injured. The stepfather of one of the injured men eventually knocked the power switch off with a piece of wood. Dr Anne Mitchell went below to attempt resuscitation but two of the men could not be revived. *(2)

185. Hamilton Palace Colliery, Bothwell – operated by the Bent Coal Co. On Thursday, 31st March 1938, a young lad was killed when he became entangled in a belt and wheel operating the screening plant. *

186. Auchengeich Colliery, Chryston – operated by James Nimmo & Co. On Wednesday, 16th November 1938, while travelling on a hutch on No. 7 haulage road from the pit bottom to No. 7 bench, a miner received injuries from which he later died. *

187. No. 14 pit, Rosehall Colliery, Coatbridge – operated by Robert Addie & Sons Ltd. A little before seven o'clock on the morning of Sunday, 14th May 1939, four miners were injured when a haulage chain snapped and struck them. One man, thrown by the lash of the chain onto a loaded hutch standing nearby, died later that night. *

188. No. 1 pit, Auchengeich Colliery, Chryston – operated by James Nimmo & Co. On Wednesday, 31 May 1939, seconds after he had shouted a warning to his mate, a young clipper was killed when he was struck by a runaway train of eight hutches. *

189. Mosside Mine, Airdrie – owned and operated by Francis McLean Ltd. About noon on Friday, 22nd September 1939, the mine was flooded when exploratory drilling operations broke through into the abandoned Keppisbyre No. 6 workings nearby. Five miners had a narrow escape, running for their lives as the water level in the passage rose higher until, by the time they reached the shaft, it had reached their necks. In a lower section three men were trapped by the rising water and, with the pumps flooded out and unworkable, there was no way they could be reached. A mines rescue brigade from Coatbridge was quickly on the scene but, with the water still draining from Keppisbyre into the Mosside workings, they could do nothing. Although pumps were brought in and pumping operations were continued for some time, the mine had to be abandoned and was never reopened. The bodies of the three victims were never recovered. *(3)

190. Swinhill Colliery, Larkhall. On the afternoon of Thursday, 26th October 1939, two miners were killed by a gas explosion in the Drumgray section of the workings. Seven men working in the section who were not affected rushed to help. Covering their mouths and noses with handkerchiefs and cloth, they made five attempts to reach the victims. *(2)

191. Blantyre Colliery, Hamilton – operated by William Dixon & Co. On Sunday, 23rd February 1941, two miners were killed when they fell down the shaft from the cage. *(2)

192. Blantyre Colliery – operated by William Dixon & Co. On Saturday, 2nd May 1942, two men were killed by a runaway hutch. *(2)

193. Kennox Colliery, Glespin. On Sunday, 30th May 1943, three miners were trapped in the workings by an inrush of water. Having fought to within a few yards of the trapped men, a rescue party were almost killed when the roof suddenly came down in front of them. They then waded chin-deep through water to reach higher ground. When the miners were reached three weeks later it was found they had been overcome by blackdamp. *(3)

194. Nos. 1 & 2 pits, Cardowan Colliery, Stepps – operated by the National Coal Board. On Monday, 25th July 1960, an explosion followed the reopening of the North Side Coking Coal Districts, which had been sealed off six months previously after an outbreak of fire. Having cleared a fall of roof, a party of men were employed in examining the workings when the explosion occurred, killing three of them outright and injuring another seven, one of whom died six days later from his injuries. District Inspector F. Tootle, who had been a member of the party, was seriously injured. The investigating inspector concluded that, with air now passing through the workings, it came into contact with carbonised material, which began to reheat due to oxidisation. Spontaneous combustion eventually took place, igniting a body of firedamp. *(4)

195. Cardowan Colliery, Stepps – operated by the National Coal Board. In January 1982 an explosion of firedamp injured 41 miners. If it hadn't been for the fact that coal dust present in the workings failed to ignite, the results could have been devastating.

Appendix 2: Index of Victims

As with Appendix One, and for the same reasons, 100 percent accuracy of information cannot be guaranteed. The age, occupation and address of the victims, if known, appear after their names, followed by the relevant chapter if they are individually named in the text. Numbers in *italic* type refer to entries in Appendix One. Abbreviations: B (buried), B/o (brother of), ch (child / children), C/o (cousin of), D (died), F/o (father of), G-f/o (grandfather of), G-s/o (grandson of), N/o (nephew of), Pr (pregnant), S/o (son of), Ss/o (stepson of), U/o (uncle of), W (widow).

A

Adams, James, 14, pony driver, King's Land, Mossend, *126*
Adams, John, 26, machineman, 46 Union St., Hamilton, *152*. (W, Penelope McMillan, & 3 ch. D: Glasgow Royal Infirmary)
Aitken, Alexander, fireman, *96*
Aitken, Robert, miner, Crawford Dyke St., Carluke, *37*. (W & 4 ch. D: Tue, 28th Jan 1862)
Allan, James, 22, bottomer, Auchinraith, Blantyre, **ch. 2**. (B: Blantyre)
Allan, Michael, miner, *113*
Allan, Robert, miner, *12*
Allan, William, 34, miner, 19 Main St., Coatbridge, *153*. (W)
Allison, James, 44, chainman, Udston Rows, Hamilton, **ch. 4**. (W & 5 ch)
Alston, James, miner, *2*
Anderson, Hugh, bencher, Lambhill House, **ch. 5**. (B: Wed, 6th Aug 1913)
Anderson, Joseph, 35, miner, 6 Ashbank, Glenboig, *153*. (W)
Anderson, Peter, 15, pony driver, Hunthill, Blantyre, **ch. 2**
Anderson, Robert, 36, miner, 27 Bank St, *191*
Annan, Agnes, 2, *60*. (Sister of Archibald)
Annan, Archibald, 10, *60*. (B/o Agnes)
Archibald, William, 52, manager, Udston Rows, Hamilton, *94*
Armstrong, Charles, miner, Flemington St., Garscube Rd., Glasgow, **ch. 5**. (B: Wed, 6th Aug 1913)
Armstrong, Patrick, 41, quarryman, *156*
Armstrong, Thomas, 20, shunter, *131*
Atkinson, W, miner, *111*
Auchterlonie, Hugh, 41, miner, Kirkton, Blantyre, **ch. 4**. (W & 3 ch. Stepfather of James & John Nelson)
Austin, William, miner, *2*

B

Bailie, John, oversman, *8*. (W & ch)
Baillie, William, a boy, drawer, *15*
Bain, John, miner, *2*
Banks, Archibald, miner, Millheugh, *164*. (F/o Archibald)
Banks, Archibald, miner, Millheugh, *164*. (S/o Archibald)
Barkey, Patrick, 49, miner, 24 Caldervale Rows, *167*
Barton, Robert, fireman, *43*

Campbell, Robert, 30, miner, Low Meadow Head, Airdrie, **ch. 6**. (W, Margaret Barclay)

Campbell, William, 35, miner, Kirkton, Blantyre, **ch. 2**. (Widower of Janet Park. F/o William [14]. B: Wed, 24th Oct 1877, Blantyre)

Campbell, William, 14, miner, Kirkton, Blantyre, **ch. 2**. (S/o William [35]. B: Blantyre)

Campbell, William, miner, Govan Colliery, *38*

Campbell, William, 48, miner, Ford Bridge Cottage, Barblues, Airdrie, **ch. 6**. (W, Annie Reay Murray)

Canavan, Patrick, 17, miner, 10 Chapelbank, Glenboig, *153*

Cannon, Matthew McIlwain, 38, coal stripper, 3 Queenslie St., Glasgow, **ch. 8**

Carlin, Peter, 34, miner, 2 Hall St., Blantyre, **ch. 2**. (W, Ann More. B: Sat, 3rd Nov 1877, Dalbeth)

Carmichael, Peter, 17, miner, Auchinraith, Blantyre, **ch. 2**. (B: Blantyre)

Carroll, James, 53, shunter, Stonefield, Blantyre, *69*

Carson, Robert, pumper, *47*

Casey, Francis, 29, miner, *33*

Cavanagh, James, 16, miner, 5 Calder St., Dixon's Rows, Blantyre, **ch. 2**. (B/o John [19]. B: Blantyre)

Cavanagh, John, 19, miner, 5 Calder St., Dixon's Rows, Blantyre, **ch. 2**. (B/o James. B: Sat, 20th Oct, 1877, Dalbeth)

Cavanagh, John, 23, miner, 19 Miller St., Blantyre, **ch. 2**. (B: Wed, 31st Oct 1877, Dalbeth)

Chalmers, William, 50, brusher, Bargeddie, *122*

Chap, William, 30, drawer, Marshall's Land, 296 Main St., Bellshill, *155*. (B: Fri, 21st Jan 1910, Bothwell)

Cinnamond, James, miner, *113*

Clark, James, 19, miner, Pilot Acre, Blantyre, **ch. 2**. (B: Sat, 3rd Nov 1877, Dalbeth)

Clark, John, 16, miner, Birkenshaw, Larkhall, *190*

Clark, Victor, 23, miner, *193*. (S/o William)

Clark, Walter, 61, brusher, 3 Third Ave., Auchenloch, **ch. 8**

Clark, William, 60, miner, *193*. (F/o Victor)

Clayton, Henry, 62, train guard, 98 Monkland View Cres., Bargeddie, **ch. 8**

Cleghorn, Turnbull, 20, bottomer, Hart's Land, Blantyre, **ch. 2**. (B: Sat, 10th Nov 1877, Blantyre)

Clyde, James, 38, miner, 44 Dixon St., Blantyre, **ch. 2**. (W, Agnes Cornfield. F/o William & James. B: Sat, 3rd Nov 1877, Dalbeth)

Clyde, James, 12, miner, 44 Dixon St., Blantyre, **ch. 2**. (S/o James. B: Blantyre)

Clyde, William, 14, pony driver, 44 Dixon St., Blantyre, **ch. 2**. (S/o James. B/o James. B: Sat, 3rd Nov 1877, Dalbeth)

Conaghan, John, 20, miner, 5 Carfin St., Blantyre, **ch. 2**. (B: Sat, 3rd Nov 1877, Dalbeth)

Conlan, John, 14, pony driver, 57 Calder St., Dixon's Rows, Blantyre, **ch. 2**. (B: Sun, 28th Oct 1877, Dalbeth)

Conlin (or **Conlon**), James, miner, Glasgow Rd., Blantyre, *182*. (W & 4 ch)

Conn, Robert, 30, brusher, 27 Lanrigg Pl., Chryston, **ch. 8**

Connelly, John, 25, miner, **ch. 3**

Connelly, Thomas, pithead worker, *116*

Connerty, Peter, 55, brusher, Clarkston, *98*. (Died at home Mon, 4th Dec 1882)

Cook, James, 17, miner, Foundry Row, Greenfield, Hamilton, **ch. 4**. (S/o Richard. B/o Thomas)

Cook, Richard, 50, miner, Foundry Row, Greenfield, Hamilton, **ch. 4**. (W & 2 ch. F/o James & Thomas)

Cook, Thomas, 20, miner, Foundry Row, Greenfield, Hamilton, **ch. 4**. (S/o Richard. B/o Richard)

Corrigan, James, 50, miner, *87*. (D: Wed, 13th Jul 1881, Glasgow Royal Infirmary)

Cosgrove, Francis, 15, miner, 15 Carfin St., Blantyre, **ch. 2**. (B/o James. B: Blantyre)

Cosgrove, James, 14, miner, 15 Carfin St., Blantyre, **ch. 2**. (B/o Francis. B: Blantyre)

Coulter, Thomas, brusher, Bothwell St., Cambuslang, *182*. (W & 4 ch)

Cox, Andrew, 16, miner, 54 Hall St., Blantyre, **ch. 2**. (S/o John. B: Mon, 5th Nov 1877, Blantyre)

Cox, John, 46, miner, 54 Hall St., Blantyre, **ch. 2**. (W, Margaret Kirkwood. F/o Andrew. B: Mon, 5th Nov 1877, Blantyre)

Cox, Robert, 29, miner, 38 Broompark Rd, Blantyre, *159*

Coyle, Charles, 21, miner, Larkfield, Blantyre, **ch. 2**. (B: Blantyre)

Craig, Andrew, miner, Glebe St., Bellshill, *179*. (D: Wed, 15th Aug 1934, Glasgow Royal Infirmary)

Craig, Hugh, 15, miner, *33*. (B/o John)

Craig, John, 18, miner, *33*. (B/o Hugh)

Craig, Robertson, miner, *53*

Crawford, John, 24, miner, Stonefield, Blantyre, **ch. 2**. (W, Martha McCutcheon. B: Blantyre)

Crewe, John, 23, miner, Udston Rows, Hamilton, **ch. 4**. (B/o Washington)

Crewe, Washington, 25, miner, Udston Rows, Hamilton, **ch. 4**. (B/o John)

Crichton, David, 21, miner, Daisyknowe, Auchentibber, **ch. 4**. (B/o James)

Crichton, James, 31, miner, Daisyknowe, Auchentibber, **ch. 4**. (W & 5 ch. B/o David)

Crombie, Andrew, 42, oncost worker, 129 Clydesdale Ave., Hamilton, **ch. 8**

Crossan, Owen, miner, *13*

Crofield, James, miner, *113*

Cummings, Joseph, 28, miner, Loanfoot, Blantyre, **ch. 4**

Currie, Michael, 40, miner, Gardiner Pl., Blantyre, *81*. (W, Janet Campbell – who was blind – & 3 ch)

Currie, Thomas, 18, miner, *33*

D

Darroch, Patrick, brusher, Lochfauld Rd, **ch. 5**. (W & 1 ch. B: Wed, 6th Aug 1913)

Davidson, Adam, a boy, drawer, *15*

Davidson, George, redsman, Mavis Valley, **ch. 5**. (W & 2 ch. B: Wed, 6th Aug 1913)

Davidson, Moses, 61, miner, West Benhar Rows, *102*

Davies (or **Davis**), George, 32, miner, Udston Rows, Hamilton, **ch. 4**. (W & 1 ch)

Dawson, Robert, brusher, Church St., Cambuslang, *182*. (Pr W & 5 ch)

Denniston, Thomas, 17, miner, Turner's Buildings, Stonefield, Blantyre, **ch. 4**. (B/o William)

Denniston, William, 23, shotfirer, Turner's Buildings, Stonefield, Blantyre, **ch. 4**. (B/o Thomas)

Devine, James, 39, shotfirer, 80 Greenlea Rd., Chryston, **ch. 8**

Dewar, John, 40, engineer, *194*

Dickson, Robert, 22, miner, **ch. 1**. (W. B: New Monkland?)

Dingsdale, George, 23, miner, Udston Rows, Hamilton, **ch. 4**. (W & 1 ch)

Divers, Charles, 27, miner, 49 Calder St., Dixon's Rows, Blantyre, **ch. 2**. (W, Bridget Divers. B: Sat, 24th Nov 1877, Dalbeth)

Dobbie, John, 25, miner, Dixon's Rows, Stonefield, Blantyre, **ch. 2**. (B/o Thomas. B: Cambusnethan)

Dobbie, Thomas, 27, miner, Dixon's Rows, Stonefield, Blantyre, **ch. 2**. (W, Mary Jones. B/o John. B:

Cambusnethan)

Docherty, Andrew White, 43, coal-cutter operator, 5 Cairnview St., Waterside, **ch. 8**

Docherty, Thomas, 20, blaster, Burnbank, Hamilton, *74*

Dodds, John, 13, miner, 9 Watson St., Burnbank, Hamilton, **ch. 4**

Dolan, John, 19, miner, Dixon's Rows, Stonefield, Blantyre, **ch. 2**. (B/o Patrick. B: Fri, 30th Nov, 1877, Dalbeth)

Dolan, Patrick, 22, miner, 17 Dixon St., Blantyre, **ch. 2**. (B/o John. B: Blantyre)

Donald, Daniel, miner, native of Ireland, *6*

Donnelly, ?, 16, miner, *35*

Drain, William, 19, miner, Udston Rows, Hamilton, **ch. 4**. (W & 1 ch)

Drummond, Robert, 35, fireman, Drumpellier Colliery, *122*. (W & 8 ch)

Duffin, Patrick, brusher, Drummond St., Lambhill, **ch. 5**. (W & 2 ch. B: Wed, 6th Aug 1913)

Duffy, Henry, 35, brusher, 35 Calder St., Dixon's Rows, Blantyre, **ch. 3**

Duffie, James, miner, *7*

Duffie, John, miner, *7*

Duffy, John, 39, shotfirer, 5 Hazelwood Dr., Blantyre, **ch. 8**

Duffy, Joseph, machineman, Cleland, *177*. (W)

Dunbar, Andrew, redsman, Lambhill, **ch. 5**. (B: Wed, 6th Aug 1913)

Duncan, Robert, miner, *53*

Dunn, David, foreman sinker, 12 Beechlee St., Hamilton, *77*

Dunsmuir, Richard, 25, miner, 16 Small Cres., Blantyre, *172*. (D: Sun, 31st Aug 1930, Glasgow Royal Infirmary. B: Blantyre)

Dunstan, William Irons, 24, roadsman, Pilot Acre, Blantyre, **ch. 2**. (B: Sun, 28th Oct 1877, Blantyre)

E

Eadie, Robert, 50, fireman, Kirkton, Blantyre, **ch. 2**. (W, Margaret Drummond. B: Blantyre)

Edgar, Harry, 40, miner, *103*

Edgar, Robert, under-manager, *157*

Evans, James, miner, *59*

F

Ferguson, Duncan, labourer, *25*

Findlay, Elizabeth, 33, pithead worker, Cross Rows, Bothwell, *119*

Fisher, Francis Jones, 49, shotfirer, 138 Loch Rd., Kirkintilloch, **ch. 8**

Fisher, James, miner, *7*

Fleming, David, 27, miner, (native of Handleknowe, Strathaven) lodged at Udston Rows, Hamilton, **ch. 4**

Fleming, James, miner, *7*

Fleming, Martin, 51, coal stripper, Frankfield Rd., Stepps, **ch. 8**

Fleming, Michael, 47, shotfirer, 39 Bridgend, Chryston, **ch. 8**

Flynn, James, machineman, Drummond St., Lambhill, **ch. 5**. (W & 10 ch. B: Wed, 6th Aug 1913)

Index of Victims

B: Cambusnethan)

Gooldie, Patrick, brusher, *27*

Gordon, John, 42, fireman / rescuer, Cuilhill, *122*

Gracie, Thomas, 57, miner, Kirkton, Blantyre, **ch. 2**. (W, Jane Smellie. B: Thu, 25th Oct 1877, Blantyre)

Graham, William, 13, miner, 57 Hall St., Blantyre, **ch. 2**. (B: Sat, 3rd Nov 1877, Dalbeth)

Grahame, Peter, miner, *12*. (W. F/o William)

Grahame, William, miner, *12*. (W & 2 ch. S/o Peter)

Grant, Alexander, 11, miner, **ch. 1**. (S/o George [40]. B: New Monkland?)

Grant, George, 40, miner, **ch. 1**. (W. F/o Alexander. B: New Monkland?)

Grant, George, miner, *113*

Gray, Robert, 44, contractor, Mossvale, Chryston, *173*. (W & 2 ch. D: Fri, 23rd Jan 1931, Glasgow Royal Infirmary. B: Mon, 26th Jan 1931, Bedlay)

Gribben (or **McGribben**), Patrick, 38, brusher, 46 Dixon St., Blantyre, **ch. 3**. (W, Agnes McKeirnan, & 1 ch)

H

Hailes, John, 5, *65*. (B: Sat, 18th Apr 1874, Hamilton)

Hall, James, 64, pithead worker, 152 Bothwell Park, Bellshill, *161*

Hall, John, 40, miner, Blantyre Works, *120*

Halliday, David, miner, *19*

Halliday, Matthew, 48, miner, Stonefield, Blantyre, **ch. 2**. (W, Janet Johnston, & 6 ch. F/o Thomas [22]. B: Mon, 29th Oct 1877, Blantyre)

Halliday, Robert, 39, miner, 34 Hall St., Blantyre, **ch. 2**. (W, Agnes Strickland. F/o Thomas [19]. B: Mon, 29th Oct 1877, Blantyre)

Halliday, Thomas, 19 (a private in the 26th Cameronians), 34 Hall St., Blantyre, **ch. 2**. (S/o Robert. B: Mon, 29th Oct 1877, Blantyre)

Halliday, Thomas, 22, miner, Stonefield, Blantyre, **ch. 2**. (S/o Matthew. B: Mon, 29th Oct 1877, Blantyre)

Hamilton, Alexander, 16, miner, *33*. (B/o David)

Hamilton, Andrew, miner, *54*

Hamilton, David, 21, miner, *33*. (B/o Alexander)

Hamilton, Francis, miner, *53*

Hamilton, James, miner, *178*

Hamilton, John, 31, miner, Burnbank, Hamilton, **ch. 2**. (W, Elizabeth Nisbet, & 5 ch. B: Cambusnethan)

Hamilton, John, 43, miner, Ashgill Row, Dalserf, *108*

Hamilton, Richard, 48, coal stripper, 13 Lanrigg Rd., Chryston, **ch. 8**

Hamilton, Robert, miner, *2*

Hamilton, William, 58, deputy, *194*

Hanlon (or **Hanlin**), William, 23, miner, 31 Calder St., Dixon's Rows, Blantyre, **ch. 2**. (W, Jane Hanlon. B: Sat, 3rd Nov 1877, Dalbeth)

Hargey, Alexander, miner, 60 Woodrop St., Glasgow, *186*

Harkness, George, 30, shotfirer, 42 Gladstone St., Burnbank, Hamilton, **ch. 4**. (W. B/o John)

I

Irvine, Thomas, 60, bottomer / lamp-trimmer, 3 Dixon St., Blantyre, **ch. 3**. (W, Isabella English, & ch)

Izzat, Andrew, miner, **ch. 1**. (B: New Monkland?)

J

Jackson, George, sinker, 1117 Garngad Rd., Provanmill, Glasgow, *170*. (D: Sat, 6th Aug 1927, Glasgow Royal Infirmary)

Jackson, George, 21, coal stripper, 34 Fleming Ave., Muirhead, **ch. 8**

Jardine, Edward, 27, brusher, 53 Calder St., Dixon's Rows, Blantyre, **ch. 3**. (Widower of Mary Ann Finon)

Jarvis, James, 31, miner, Maxwelltown, East Kilbride, **ch. 4**

Jasmras, Hanisloas, 50, miner, 16 Stewart St., Mossend, *191*

Johnstone, John, miner, *114*

Jones, D, miner, Ferniegair, *176*

Jones, Edward, 15, miner, 15 Craig Row, Auchentibber, **ch. 4**

K

Kalinski, Andrew, 24, miner, 20 Merry's Rows, Blantyre, *172*. (B: Blantyre)

Kane (or **Kain**), James, 14, miner, 10 Udston Rows, Hamilton, **ch. 4**

Kelly, James, 33, miner, 18 Hall St., Blantyre, **ch. 2**. (W, Mary Ann Lachlan. B: Sat, 3rd Nov 1877, Dalbeth)

Kelly, James, 16, miner, 43 Calder St., Dixon's Rows, Blantyre, **ch. 2**. (B/o John [23]. B: Blantyre)

Kelly, John, 23, miner, Dixon's Rows, Stonefield, Blantyre, **ch. 2**. (B/o James [16]. B: Mon, 29th Oct 1877, Dalbeth)

Kelly, John, bencher, *138*. (W & 3 ch)

Kelly, Patrick, 27, miner, 7 Hall St., Blantyre, **ch. 2**. (W, Margaret Graham. B: Thu, 25th Oct 1877, Blantyre)

Kelly, Peter, 40, coal stripper, 4 Slakiewood Ave., Gartcosh, **ch. 8**

Kemp, James, 22, miner, 22 Merry's Rows, Blantyre, **ch. 2**. (B: Mount Zion, Coatbridge)

Kenny, John, 45, miner, 50 Hall St., Blantyre, **ch. 2**. (W, Margaret Kelly. B: Sun, 28th Oct 1877, Dalbeth)

Kerr, John, 30, miner, *64*. (B: Wanlockhead)

Kiernan, Francis, 26, beltman, 7 Lanrigg Pl., Chryston, **ch. 8**

Kilpatrick, John, sinker, 5 Kenmore St., Shettleston, Glasgow, *170*

Kilpatrick, Robert, 46, miner, Stonefield, Blantyre, *110*

King, Richard (or Robert), 56, miner, 182 High St., Blantyre, *172*. (W & 3 ch. B: Blantyre)

Kinnaird, Alexander, miner, 57 Davidson St., Airdrie, *189*. (W & 7 ch)

Kirk, George, brusher, Church (or Park) St., Cambuslang, *182*. (W & 4 ch)

Kirkland, Robert Orr, 20, miner, 41 Priestfield Terr., Blantyre, **ch. 2**. (B: Strathaven)

Kirkwood, Archibald, oversman, *9*. (Pr. W & 6 ch)

Kyle, Nicol, 35, miner, Kirkton, Blantyre, **ch. 2**. (W, Agnes Welsh. B: Wed, 24th Oct 1877, Blantyre)

L

M

McAnulty, Peter, 54, miner, 57 Hall St., Blantyre, **ch. 2**. (Widower of Catherine McSorley. F/o Joseph. B: Blantyre)

McArthur, Alexander, 55, brusher, 27 Calder St., Dixon's Rows, Blantyre, **ch. 3**. (W)

McAulay, John, 42, brusher, 30 Scarhill St., Kirkshaws, Coatbridge, **ch. 8**

McBride, Maurice, sinker, 1 South Stirling St., Glasgow, *170*

McCallum, Edward, 14, miner, 21 Hall St., Blantyre, **ch. 2**. (B: Fri, 2nd Nov 1877, Dalbeth)

McCart, Robert, 39, miner, *162*. (W & 5 ch)

McCartney, Hugh, 19, miner, Burnbank, Hamilton, *104*

McCoid, Robert, 55, coal stripper, 16 Kenmore St., Shettleston, **ch. 8**

McConville, Edward, 19, drawer, Reid's Land, Crossgates, *155*. (B: Fri, 21st Jan 1910, Bothwell)

McConville, Thomas, 35, boiler fireman, *137*

McCue, Miles, miner, Dukes Rd., Cambuslang, *184*

McCue, Patrick, 19, miner, 23 Dixon St., Blantyre, **ch. 2**. (B: Blantyre)

McCulloch, James, 40, miner, East Kilbride, **ch. 4**. (W & 5 ch. F/o James)

McCulloch, James, 14, miner, East Kilbride, **ch. 4**. (S/o James)

McCulloch, John, 44, miner, Auchinraith, Blantyre, **ch. 2**. (W, Allison Marshall, & 5 ch. F/o John. B: Tue, 30th Oct 1877, Blantyre)

McCulloch, John, 16, miner, Auchinraith, Blantyre, **ch. 2**. (S/o John. B: Fri, 2nd Nov 1877, Blantyre)

McCulloch, Thomas, 25, miner, Hart's Land, Blantyre, **ch. 2**. (W, Mary Cleghorn. B: Sat, 10th Nov 1877, Blantyre)

McCusker, Henry, 30, miner, 26 Calder St., Dixon's Rows, Blantyre, **ch. 2**. (W, Mary O'Neill. B/o James. B: Mon, 26th Nov 1877, Blantyre)

McCusker, James, 28, miner, Dixon St., Blantyre, **ch. 2**. (W, Ann Dolan. B/o Henry. B: Fri, 2nd Nov 1877, Dalbeth)

McDade, John, 21, miner, Auchentibber, **ch. 4**. (B/o Michael)

McDade, Michael, 32, miner, Auchentibber, **ch. 4**. (W & 4 ch. B/o John)

McDonald, Alexander, miner, *24*

McDonald, Alexander, 33, quarryman, *156*

McDonald, James, 23, miner, **ch. 1**. (W. B/o John. B: New Monkland?)

McDonald, John, 30, miner, **ch. 1**. (W. B/o James. B: New Monkland?)

McDonald, Joseph, 53, coal stripper, 14 East Springfield Terr., Bishopbriggs, **ch. 8**

McDonald, Thomas, 29, miner, 1 Gardiner Pl., Blantyre, **ch. 2**. (W, Jane Hall. D: Sat, 27th Oct 1877, Glasgow Royal Infirmary)

McDonald, Wilson, 19, miner, **ch. 1**. (B: New Monkland?)

McDougall, Allan Gibson, 38, oncost worker, *156*

McDuff (or **Duffy**), Thomas, 26, brusher, 19 Dixon St., Blantyre, **ch. 3**

McEachen, Thomas, 35, miner, 5 Muiredge St., Uddingston, *192*

McElhaney, Denis, 49, developer, 15 Holyknowe Rd., Lennoxtown, **ch. 8**

McEwan, George Thomas Thomson, 20, oncost worker, 94 Holyknowe Rd., Lennoxtown, **ch. 8**

McFadyen, James, 21, miner, Dixon's Rows, Stonefield, Blantyre, **ch. 2**. (W, Helen Buchanan. B/o John. B: Fri, 2nd Nov 1877, Blantyre)

McFadyen, John, 23, miner, 2 Carfin St., Blantyre, **ch. 2**. (B/o James. B: Mon, 29th Oct 1877, Blantyre)

McFarlane, John, 31, miner, Larkfield, Blantyre, **ch. 2**. (W, Sarah McCutcheon. B: Thu, 25th Oct 1877,

Blantyre)

McGarry, James, 35, miner, 62 Hall St., Blantyre, ch. 2. (W, Margaret Bennett. B: Sat, 3rd Nov 1877, Dalbeth)

McGarvie, Edward, 23, brusher, 16 Dixon St., Blantyre, ch. 3

McGarvie, Patrick, 50, brusher, 15 Miller St., Blantyre, ch. 3. (W, Mary Sweeney, & 6 ch)

McGeoch, Andrew, 52, miner, Tannochside, 107. (D: Wed, 8th Oct 1884)

McGeoch, Patrick, bottomer, 23

McGhee, Abraham, 18, miner, Larkfield, Blantyre, ch. 2. (B/o John & William. B: Fri, 9th Nov 1877, Blantyre)

McGhee, John, 16, miner, Larkfield, Blantyre, ch. 2. (B/o Abraham & William. B: Fri, 9th Nov 1877, Blantyre)

McGhee, William, 14, miner, Larkfield, Blantyre, ch. 2. (B/o Abraham & John. B: Fri, 9th Nov 1877, Blantyre)

McGibbon, Alexander, fireman, Cook's Land, Carfin Rd., New Stevenston, 141. (D: Wed, 29th Apr 1903, Glasgow Royal Infirmary)

McGill, Patrick, 37, miner, Spittal Hill, Cambuslang, 79

McGinnes, John, 16, miner, 47 Hill St., Blantyre, ch. 4. (B/o Peter)

McGinnes, Peter, 22, miner, 47 Hill St., Blantyre, ch. 4. (B/o John)

McGlinchy, Tobias, 17, pithead worker, Middle Row, 118

McGowan, James, 24, miner, Gardiner Pl., Blantyre, ch. 2. (W, Jessie Kerr. B: Blantyre)

McGregory, John, 50, miner, 75

McGuigan, David, 19, drawer, Peep O'Day, Calderbank, 143

McGuigan, John, 38, brusher, 67 Dixon St., Blantyre, ch. 3. (W, Margaret Monaghan, & 2 ch)

McGuire, Michael, 29, pony driver, 149

McGuire, Robert, roadsman, 105

McGurk, James, 37, bottomer, 54 Merry's Rows, Blantyre, 132

McGurty, Francis, 49, miner, Udston Rows, Hamilton, ch. 4. (W. F/o James)

McGurty, James, 17, bottomer, Udston Rows, Hamilton, ch. 4. (S/o Francis)

McHenry, William, 18, brusher, Lightburn, Cambuslang, 101

McIlvane, John, bottomer, 34

McIlwear, John, drainer, native of Ireland, 6

McIntosh, George Wilkie, 58, shotfirer, 2 Oxgang Pl., Kirkintilloch, ch. 8

McIntyre, Donald, 11, miner, ch. 1. (B: New Monkland?)

McIntyre, Gilbert, 47, miner, Kirkton, Blantyre, ch. 2. (W, Susan White. B: Fri, 2nd Nov 1877, Blantyre)

McIntyre, Robert, miner, Burke's Cottages, Law, 169. (W)

McKay, Hugh, 70, miner, 6 Calder St, Dixon's Rows, Blantyre, 166

McKay, William, 48, miner, 11 Miller St., Blantyre, ch. 2. (W, Elizabeth Arbuckle. B: Fri, 9th Nov 1877, Blantyre)

McKeever, John, 22, roadsman, Haughhead Colliery, Hamilton, 67

McKelvie, John, 19, miner, Burnbank, Hamilton, ch. 2. (B: Wed, 31st Oct 1877, Blantyre)

McKendrick, John, 49, fireman, Colliery Rows, Ferniegair, 86. (W & ch)

McKenna, Andrew, 42, deputy, 6 Lennox Rd., Lennoxtown, ch. 8

Mackie, Peter, 31, miner, Dixon's Rows, Stonefield, Blantyre, ch. 2. (W, Janet Drummond. B: Mon, 29th

Oct 1877, Blantyre)

McKillop, Archibald, 12, drawer, Windsor St., Burnbank, Hamilton, **ch. 2**. (B/o John. B: Tue, 30th Oct 1877, Blantyre)

McKillop, John, 14, miner, Windsor St., Burnbank, Hamilton, **ch. 2**. (B/o Archibald. B: Tue, 30th Oct 1877, Blantyre)

McKimmin, Alexander, miner, native of Tiree, *12*

McKinnon, James, 32, miner, Gladstone St., Burnbank, Hamilton, **ch. 2**. (W, Janet Hawthorn, & 3 ch. B: Cambusnethan)

McLachlan, Edward, 15, pony driver, 1 Jackson Pl., Stonefield, Blantyre, **ch. 2**. (B/o Moses & William. B: Sat, 3rd Nov 1877, Blantyre)

McLachlan, Moses, 23, roadsman, Commercial Pl., Blantyre, **ch. 2**. (W, Margaret Muir. B/o Edward & William. B: Blantyre)

McLachlan, William, 13, pony driver, 1 Jackson Pl., Stonefield, Blantyre, **ch. 2**. (B/o Edward & Moses. B: Thu, 25th Oct 1877, Blantyre)

McLauchlan, Edward, 18, miner, 17 Miller St., Blantyre, **ch. 2**. (B/o John. B: Mon, 29th Oct 1877, Dalbeth)

McLauchlan, John, 23, miner, 17 Miller St., Blantyre, **ch. 2**. (W, Mary O'Neill, & 2ch. B/o Edward. B: Mon, 29th Oct 1877, Dalbeth)

McLean, Alexander, 50, miner, Auchentibber, **ch. 4**. (W & 6 ch)

McLean, Andrew, 21, pony driver, Barnhill, Blantyre, *82*

McLean, George, roadsman, *43*

McLean, Hugh, miner, *7*

McLuckie, Colin, 19, miner, **ch. 1**. (B: New Monkland?)

McLuckie, miner, **ch. 1**. (B: New Monkland?)

McManus, John, miner, *76*

McMeechan, Thomas, 45, miner, 28 Calder St., Dixon's Rows, Blantyre, **ch. 2**. (W, Janet Stewart. B: Sat, 3rd Nov 1877, Blantyre)

MacMillan, Alexander, machineman, Jellyhill, Bishopbriggs, **ch. 5**. (W & 2 ch. B: Wed, 6th Aug 1913)

McMillan, Alexander, 48, miner, 21 Kenmore St., Glasgow, *167*

McMillan, Daniel, 42, miner, 13 Greenrigg St., Uddingston, *192*

McMillan, George, miner, *14*

McMillan, George, stripper, 3 Carbeth St., Possilpark, **ch. 5**. (W & 1 ch. B: Wed, 6th Aug 1913)

McMillan, James, 30, brakesman, Larkfield, Blantyre, **ch. 2**. (W, Sarah Jane McGhee. B: Thu, 25th Oct 1877, Blantyre)

McMillan, Peter, 55, shotfirer, 7 Drumsack Ave., Chryston, **ch. 8**

McNab, John, 30, miner, Blantyre, **ch. 7**. (W)

McNaught, George, 28, miner, **ch. 1**. (W. B: New Monkland?)

McNaught, Robert, 26, roadsman, Dixon's Rows, Stonefield, Blantyre, **ch. 2**. (W, Mary Russell. B: Mon, 29th Oct 1877, Blantyre)

McNeil, John, 36, miner, *75*

McNiven, David, 17, drawer, Brown's Building, Greengairs, **ch. 6**

McNiven, Robert, 25, miner, High Dykehead, **ch. 4**. (W & 1 ch)

McPhee, James, 54, shotfirer, 36 Raith Dr., Bellshill, **ch. 8**

Morgan, Elizabeth, pithead worker, *21*

Morgan, Hugh, 37, miner, 5 Calder St., Dixon's Rows, Blantyre, **ch. 2**. (W, Martha Crawford, & 6 ch. B: Mon, 29th Oct 1877, Dalbeth)

Morgan, James, miner, *52*

Morgan, John, drainer, native of Ireland, *6*

Morrison, Andrew, 48, miner, Dixon's Rows, Stonefield, Blantyre, **ch. 2**. (W, Elizabeth McFarlane. B: Tue, 6th Nov 1877, Blantyre)

Morrison, Charles, 35, miner, Windsor St., Burnbank, Hamilton, *94*. (F/o William)

Morrison, William, 12, miner, Windsor St., Burnbank, Hamilton, *94*. (S/o Charles)

Muir, John, 38, oncost worker, 18 Dalshannon Rd., Condorrat, **ch. 8**

Muir, William, 21, miner, Burnbank, Hamilton, **ch. 2**. (B: Mon, 29th Oct 1877, Blantyre)

Mulholland, John, 50, coal stripper, 72 Dalshannon Rd., Condorrat, **ch. 8**

Mullen, George, 28, miner, Glasgow, **ch. 7**. (W. D: Thu, 17th Nov 1932, Glasgow Royal Infirmary)

Mullen, Robert, 30, brusher, Pilot Acre, Blantyre, **ch. 3**

Murdoch, Robert, 20, miner, 1 Dixon St., Blantyre, *81*. (S/o Thomas, B/o Thomas)

Murdoch, Thomas, 17, miner, 1 Dixon St., Blantyre, **ch. 2**. (S/o Thomas, B/o Robert. B: Wed, 7th Nov 1877, Blantyre)

Murdoch, Thomas, 48, miner, 1 Dixon St., Blantyre, *81*. (W, Ann Burgess & ch. F/o Robert & Thomas)

Murdoch, William, 26, miner, Udston Rows, Hamilton, **ch. 4**. (W & 1 ch)

Murphy, Francis, 25, miner, Larkfield, Blantyre, **ch. 2**. (W, Ann McGhee, & 2 ch. B: Sun, 28th Oct 1877, Dalbeth)

Murphy, George, 13, drawer, 8 Carfin St., Blantyre, **ch. 2**. (B/o James. B: Blantyre)

Murphy, James, 20, miner, 8 Carfin St., Blantyre, **ch. 2**. (B/o George. B: Mon, 29th Oct 1877, Dalbeth)

Murphy, John, 25, brusher, 20 Miller St., Blantyre, **ch. 3**

Murphy, William, 54, deputy, *194*

Murray, Bernard, 21, miner, Larkfield, Blantyre, **ch. 2**. (B: Sat, 3rd Nov 1877, Dalbeth)

Murray, James, 50, bottomer, 3 Calder St., Dixon's Rows, Blantyre, **ch. 2**. (W, Elizabeth McSorley. B: Sat, 3rd Nov 1877, Dalbeth)

Mynes, Lawrence, 32, miner, 53 Merry's Rows, Blantyre, *159*

N

Neil, William John, 34, miner, *135*

Neilson, Hugh, 36, engineman, *123*

Nelson, Claude (or McLeod), 40, miner, *33*. (W & 6 ch)

Nelson, James, 16, miner, Kirkton, Blantyre, **ch. 4**. (B/o John. Ss/o Hugh **Auchterlonie**)

Nelson, John, 14, miner, Kirkton, Blantyre, **ch. 4**. (B/o James. Ss/o Hugh **Auchterlonie**)

Nelson, Joseph, 22, miner, Udston Rows, Hamilton, **ch. 4**

Nesbit, Robert, 19, miner, 65 Miller St., Larkhall, *97*

Newton, John, 50, roadsman, Jackson Pl., Stonefield, Blantyre, **ch. 3**. (W, Margaret Davidson?)

Nimmo, James, 32, oncost worker, 11 Roman Pl., Bothwellhaugh, **ch. 8**

Nisbett, George, 27, miner, Albert Pl., Larkfield, Blantyre, **ch. 2**. (W, Euphemia Fleming, & 5 ch. B: Blantyre. Euphemia died 6th Nov 1877 of phthisis [tuberculosis])

Noble (or **Navall**), John, 31, miner, Cemetery Walk, Blantyre, **ch. 4**. (Last to be brought out of the pit). (W & 5 ch)

Nugent, Catherine, 16, pithead worker, Braidwood's Land, Uddingston, *115*

O

O'Brian, John, 24, miner, 10 Calder St., Dixon's Rows, Blantyre, **ch. 2**. (W, Mary Tonner. B/o Peter. B: Sat, 3rd Nov 1877, Dalbeth)

O'Brian, Peter, 21, miner, 10 Calder St., Dixon's Rows, Blantyre, **ch. 2**. (B/o John. B: Mon, 29th Oct 1877, Dalbeth)

O'Brien, Bernard, 27, brusher, Stonefield, Blantyre, **ch. 3**. (W, Rosie McGovern, & 1 ch)

O'Donald, John, miner, *13*

O'Donald, Patrick, miner, *13*

O'Donnell, James, 24, brusher, 16 Salisbury St., Glasgow, *173*

O'Donnell, John, 26, miner, Larkfield, Blantyre, **ch. 2**. (W, Ann Hunter. B: Thu, 1st Nov 1877, Dalbeth)

O'Donnell, John, 23, miner, 14 Miller St., Blantyre, **ch. 2**. (B: Sat, 3rd Nov 1877, Dalbeth)

Ogilvie, Alexander, 21, miner, *133*

Olenskie, Joseph, 25, miner, 47 New Orbiston, Bellshill, *155*. (B: Fri, 21st Jan 1910, Bothwell)

Olenskies, George, 28, drawer, 9 Chapel Sq., Mossend, *155*. (B: Fri, 21st Jan 1910, Bothwell)

O'Neill, John, 35, brusher, 15 Dixon St., Blantyre, **ch. 3**. (W, Mary Dawson, & 3 ch)

Orrick, Henry, miner, *13*

Oselies, Andrew, 24, miner, 1 Bellgowan Terr., Glebe St., Bellshill, *155*. (B: Fri, 21st Jan 1910, Bothwell)

Ostler, David, miner, Russell's Land, Newarthill, *142*. (Died at home)

Ovens, Robert, 21, miner, 12 Hall St., Blantyre, **ch. 2**. (B: Wed, 7th Nov 1877, Blantyre)

Owen, John, overseer, *92*

P

Park, Alexander, 55, bencher, Park Pl., Greengairs, **ch. 6**

Park, John, 34, miner, Kirkton, Blantyre, **ch. 2**. (B: Fri, 9th Nov 1877, Blantyre)

Pate, George, miner, *7*

Paterson, James, 36, sinker, Millheugh, Larkhall, *72*. (W & 5 ch)

Paterson, John, miner, *12*. (W & 3 ch)

Paterson, Joseph, fireman, *31*

Paterson, William, 38, fireman, Earnock Colliery Rows, *139*. (W & ch)

Patrick, James, 27, miner, Dunn's Land, Udston, *124*. (B/o Robert)

Patrick, Robert, 23, miner, Dunn's Land, Udston, *124*. (B/o James)

Penman, Thomas, 20, pony driver, High Dykehead, **ch. 4**. (B/o Walter)

Penman, Walter, 22, pony driver, High Dykehead, **ch. 4**. (B/o Thomas)

Pollock, Hugh, 48, miner, *64*. (B: Bothwell)

Pollock, Robert, 49, miner, Drumbreck, Eastfield, Airdrie, **ch. 6**. (W, Annie Busby. F/o Robert)

Pollock, Robert, 15, drawer, Drumbreck, Eastfield, Airdrie, **ch. 6**. (S/o Robert)

Potter, John, 24, miner, *33*. (W. B/o Thomas)

Potter, Thomas, 19, miner, *33*. (B/o John)

Price, Aaron, 50, stone worker, 71 Redbrae Rd., Hillhead, Kirkintilloch, **ch. 8**

Price, Robert, 47, stone worker, 40 Waverley Cres., Hillhead, Kirkintilloch, **ch. 8**

Primrose, William, 17, chainman, Blantyre Works, **ch. 2**. (B: Tue, 6th Nov 1877, Blantyre)

Pritchard, George, 13, brusher, 9 Gladstone St., Burnbank, Hamilton, *100*. (Died at home, 11.40 pm that night)

Q

Quate, Taylor, miner, Calder St., Whifflet, *179*. (D: Thu, 16th Aug 1934, Glasgow Royal Infirmary)

Queen, John, 59, miner, Brick Row, Darngavil, Airdrie, **ch. 6**. (Widower, ch)

Quinn, Michael, 21, miner, Causeystanes, Blantyre, **ch. 4**. (W & 1 ch)

R

Rae, James (supposed name), 35/40, miner, **ch. 2**. (B: Tue, 6th Nov 1877, Blantyre)

Rae, Robert, 54, miner, St David's Pl., Macneill St., Larkhall, *68*

Ramsay, Robert, redsman, Mavis Valley, **ch. 5**. (W & 3 ch. B/o William. B: Wed, 6th Aug 1913)

Ramsay, Thomas, 25, miner, Pilot Acre, Blantyre, **ch. 2**. (Widower of Sarah Agnew. B: Sun, 28th Oct 1877, Blantyre)

Ramsay, William, redsman, Mavis Valley, **ch. 5**. (B/o Robert. B: Wed, 6th Aug 1913)

Rankin, William, 20, onsetter, *136*

Rankine, Andrew, 19, miner, **ch. 1**. (B: New Monkland?)

Reevie (or **Revie**), Alexander, 19, miner, Dixon's Rows, Stonefield, Blantyre, **ch. 2**. (S/o John. B: Tue, 6th Nov 1877, Blantyre)

Reevie (or **Revie**), John, 59, miner, Dixon's Rows, Stonefield, Blantyre, **ch. 2**. (W, Jane Scobbie. F/o Alexander. B: Tue, 6th Nov 1877, Blantyre)

Regan, Joseph, 55, miner, 7 Watson St., Blantyre, *172*. (Widower, 3 ch. B: Blantyre)

Regan, Patrick, brusher, Drummond St., Lambhill, **ch. 5**. (W & 3 ch. B: Wed, 6th Aug 1913)

Reid, James, 13, miner, Gladstone St., Burnbank, Hamilton, **ch. 2**. (B/o William. B: Mon, 29th Oct 1877, Blantyre)

Reid, John, 24, miner, 24a Beckford St., Hamilton, **ch. 4**. (W & 2 ch)

Reid, John Stark, 41, fireman, Bank Rd., Coatbridge, *175*

Reid, John, 21, miner, *193*

Reid, William, 27, miner, Gladstone St., Burnbank, Hamilton, **ch. 2**. (W, Agnes Gemmell. B/o James. B: Mon, 29th Oct 1877, Blantyre)

Reilly, Charles, fireman, 14 Park Pl., Maryhill, **ch. 5**. (W & 7 ch. B: Wed, 6th Aug 1913)

Rennie, Matheson, miner, *93*

Renwick, George, 48, miner, **ch. 2**. (W, Margaret Kerr. B: Baillieston)

Reynolds, James, 43, miner, Wishaw, **ch. 7**

Richardson, William, 17, miner, Kirkton, Blantyre, **ch. 2**. (B: Sun, 28th Oct 1877, Blantyre)

Richmond, James, 58, miner, Station, Blantyre, **ch. 4**. (Widower, 2 ch)

Roberts, Moses, 17, miner, 60 Hall St., Blantyre, **ch. 2**. (B/o William, Thomas & Samuel. B: Mon, 5th

Nov 1877, Blantyre)

Roberts, Samuel, 14, miner, 60 Hall St., Blantyre, **ch. 2**. (B/o William, Thomas & Moses. B: Mon, 5th Nov 1877, Blantyre)

Roberts, Thomas, 20, miner, 60 Hall St., Blantyre, **ch. 2**. (B/o William, Moses & Samuel. B: Mon, 5th Nov 1877, Blantyre)

Roberts, William, 24, miner, Larkfield, Blantyre, **ch. 2**. (W, Margaret Forsyth. B/o Thomas, Moses & Samuel. B: Mon, 29th Oct 1877, Blantyre)

Robertson, Daniel, 15, drawer, Auchentibber, **ch. 4**

Robertson, James, 28, miner, 48 Calder Pl., Bothwellhaugh, *181*

Robertson, Robert, 35, pony driver, 229 Low Waters, Hamilton, *165*. (W, Mary Johnstone [or Easson])

Rodger (or **Cochrane**), Cecilia, *168*

Rooney, Terence, 55, miner, Auchentibber, **ch. 4**. (W)

Ross, Richard, 30, miner, Auchinraith, Blantyre, **ch. 2**. (B: Mon, 5th Nov 1877, Blantyre)

Roy, Gilbert, brusher, Hamilton Rd., Flemington, Cambuslang, *182*. (W & 3 ch)

Rundell, John, 36, miner, 111 Muir St., Larkhall, *180*. (W & 3 ch)

Runn, Richard, 36, brusher, Barnhill, Blantyre, **ch. 3**. (W, Christina Hunter, & 6 ch)

Russell, Edward, 18, labourer, native of Donegal, *40*

Russell, John, 20, miner, Kirkton, Blantyre, **ch. 2**. (B: Fri, 2nd Nov 1877, Blantyre)

Russell, Thomas, miner, Victoria St., Larkhall, *164*

S

Samuel, George, miner, *30*

Sawyers, George, 24, miner, Kirkton, Blantyre, **ch. 2**. (W, Martha Lang. B: Fri, 9th Nov 1877, Blantyre)

Scott, Alexander, pithead worker, Law, *83*. (W & 3 ch)

Scott, Hugh, 45, contractor, 30 Low Waters, Hamilton, *165*. (W, Annie Harvey. Body never recovered)

Semple, George, 32, miner, Auchinraith, Blantyre, **ch. 2**. (W, Marion Nimmo. B: Blantyre)

Shanks, David, 45, miner, Auchentibber, **ch. 4**. (W & 4 ch. F/o David)

Shanks, David, 13, miner, Auchentibber, **ch. 4**. (S/o David)

Sharp, Alexander, 34, coal stripper, 119 Easterhouse Rd., Glasgow, **ch. 8**

Sharp, James, 40, miner, 48 Calder St., Dixon's Rows, Blantyre, **ch. 2**. (S/o William. B: Tue, 6th Nov 1877, Blantyre)

Sharp, William, 63, miner, 48 Calder St., Dixon's Rows, Blantyre, **ch. 2**. (W, Elizabeth Burns. F/o James. B: Tue, 6th Nov 1877, Blantyre)

Shaw, David, 28, engineman, Lochfauld Cottages, Cadder, *62*. (W & 4 ch)

Shaw, John, miner, Newmains, *66*

Shaw, John, 22, miner, 136 Eddlewood Rows, Hamilton, *165*. (Body never recovered)

Shearer, James, 24, brusher, 32 Bothlyn Rd., Chryston, *173*. (B: Sat, 24th Jan 1931, Bedlay)

Shevlin, John, 46, oncost worker, 20 Coronation Pl., Mount Ellen, Chryston, **ch. 8**

Shields, Patrick, 21, miner, Blackfaulds Row, Rutherglen, *58*

Shiveral, William, 24, fireman, New Waverly Pl., Bothwell, *147*

Shorthouse, George, 63, miner, 10 Gladstone St., Burnbank, Hamilton, *172*. (B: Hamilton)

Siddens, John, miner, *22*. (D: Tue, 10th May 1859)

Sime, Peter, 21, pony driver, *146*

Simpson, James, 24, miner, 20 Larkfield, Blantyre, **ch. 2**. (B: Thu, 25th Oct 1877, Blantyre)

Simpson, Robert, 60, roadsman, Burnbank, Hamilton, **ch. 2**. (Widower of Agnes Buchanan. B: Bellshill Ch/yard)

Simpson, William, miner, *44*

Skilling, William, 53, oncost worker, 5 Chriss Ave., Eddlewood, Hamilton, **ch. 8**

Smith, Edward, 22, miner, Larkfield, Blantyre, **ch. 2**. (B/o Patrick. B: Sat, 3rd Nov 1877, Dalbeth)

Smith, James, 35, miner, Dixon's Rows, Stonefield, Blantyre, **ch. 2**. (W, Catherine Richards. B: Sat, 3rd Nov 1877, Dalbeth)

Smith, James, 23, brusher, 29 Alexandra Pl., Muirhead, *173*. (B: Sat, 24th Jan 1931, Bedlay)

Smith, John, miner, *7*

Smith, John, 34, miner, Larkfield, Blantyre, **ch. 4**

Smith, Louis, 26, miner, 1 Stewart St., Mossend, *187*. (D: Sun, 14th May 1939, Glasgow Royal Infirmary)

Smith, Patrick, 40, miner, Larkfield, Blantyre, **ch. 2**. (W, Mary Ann Connelly. B/o Edward. B: Thu, 1st Nov 1877, Dalbeth)

Sneadon (or **Sneddon**), Robert, oversman, *18*

Sneddon, James, 39, miner, Auchinraith, Blantyre, **ch. 2**. (W, Elizabeth Archibald. F/o John [19] & James. B: Blantyre)

Sneddon, James, 16, miner, Auchinraith, Blantyre, **ch. 2**. (S/o James, B/o John [19]. B: Sat, 10th Nov 1877, Blantyre)

Sneddon, James Munro, 14, drawer, Back Row, Greengairs, **ch. 6**

Sneddon, John, 19, miner, Auchinraith, Blantyre, **ch. 2**. (S/o James, B/o James [16]. B: Tue, 30th Oct 1877, Blantyre)

Sneddon, John, 31, miner, McCracken's Place, Greengairs, **ch. 6**. (W, Jeanie Gray)

Spiers, George, 16, miner, Barnhill, Blantyre, **ch. 2**. (B/o John [15]. B: Mon, 5th Nov 1877, Blantyre)

Spiers, James, 38, miner, Old Calderwood, East Kilbride, **ch. 4**. (W & 5/6 ch)

Spiers, John, 15, pony driver, Barnhill, Blantyre, **ch. 2**. (B/o George. B: Mon, 5th Nov 1877, Blantyre)

Spiers, John, 13, miner, 9 Miller St., Blantyre, **ch. 2**. (B/o William. B: Thu, 22nd Nov 1877, Blantyre)

Spiers, William, 28, miner, Kirkton, Blantyre, **ch. 2**. (W, Magdalene Wright. B/o John [13]. B: Sat, 3rd Nov 1877, Blantyre)

Sprott (or **Sproat**), William, 42, fireman, 2 Auchinraith Terr., Blantyre, *172*. (W & ch. B: Blantyre)

Stark, John, 29, miner, Annsfield Pl., Hamilton, **ch. 2**. (W, Mary Anderson. B: 31st Oct 1877, Blantyre)

Stark, John Mack, 23, coal stripper, 36 Bridgend, Chryston, **ch. 8**

Steele, James, 36, miner, Flemington, Cambuslang, **ch. 2**. (W, Elizabeth Steele. F/o Robert. B: Fri, 9th Nov 1877, Blantyre)

Steele, Robert, 13, miner, Flemington, Cambuslang, **ch. 2**. (S/o James. B: Fri, 9th Nov 1877, Blantyre)

Steen, Adam, miner, West Merryston, *95*

Stenzel, Theodore, 32, engineer, *194*

Stevenson, ?, miner, *11*

Stevenson, Alexander, 42, miner, 15 Govan St., Blantyre, **ch. 2**. (W, Margaret Porter. F/o John & William [14]. B: Sun, 28th Oct 1877, Blantyre)

Stevenson, John, 19, miner, 15 Govan St., Blantyre, **ch. 2**. (S/o Alexander. B/o William [14]. B: Mon, 29th Oct 1877, Blantyre)

Stevenson, William, mining engineer, *73*

Stevenson, William, 14, miner, 15 Govan St., Blantyre, **ch. 2**. (S/o Alexander. B/o John. B: Mon, 29th Oct 1877, Blantyre)

Stevenson, William, 51, miner, 51 Calder St., Whifflet, *140*. (W & ch)

Stewart, George, 29, miner, 187 Low Waters, Hamilton, *165*. (W, Mary Connell. Body never recovered)

Stewart, James, 19, miner, 34 Hall St., Blantyre, **ch. 2**. (B/o Robert [17]. B: Blantyre)

Stewart, Malcolm, 15, miner, 52 Calder St., Dixon's Rows, Blantyre, **ch. 2**. (B: Tue, 6th Nov 1877, Blantyre)

Stewart, Robert, 17, miner, 34 Hall St., Blantyre, **ch. 2**. (B/o James. B: Mon, 29th Oct 1877, Blantyre)

Stewart, Robert, 21, roadsman, 21 Austin St., Cadzow, Hamilton, *176*

Stirling, Allan, 22, miner, New Houses, Earnock, Hamilton, **ch. 4**

Stokes, Thomas, 32, oncost worker, 60 Bridgend, Chryston, **ch. 8**

Strain, Anthony, 17, pithead worker, Bothwellhaugh, *185*

Summers, John, 19, miner, *63*. (W & 1 ch)

Swan, James, miner, *29*

Symington, Alexander (Ed), 24, brusher, Larkfield, Blantyre, **ch. 3**

T

Tait, Francis, 25, gummer, 24 Baillie's Causeway, Hamilton, *152*. (W, Elizabeth Tonner, & 5 ch. D: Glasgow Royal Infirmary)

Taylor, Alexander, 16, miner, Ferniegair, *125*

Taylor, William, 23, miner, Whitedyke Cott., Glenboig, *153*. (W & 1 day-old child)

Templeton, George, 37, miner, Low Meadow Head, Airdrie, **ch. 6**. (W, Minnie Barclay)

Tennant, Henry, 17, McAlpine's Buildings, Stonefield, Blantyre, *132*

Thom, William, under 18, miner, *71*

Thompson, John, miner, 36. (W & ch. D: Sat, 18th Jan 1862)

Thomson, John, miner, Woodlands Sq., Law, *169*. (W. F/o John)

Thomson, John, miner, Woodlands Sq., Law, *169*. (W & ch. S/o John)

Thompson, Neil, 25, miner, *33*. (W)

Thomson, Edward, 35, brusher, Hunthill, Blantyre, **ch. 3**. (W, Mary Watson, & 3 ch)

Thomson, John, 17, ostler, Larkfield, Blantyre, **ch. 2**. (B: Sun, 28th Oct 1877, Blantyre)

Thomson, Thomas, miner, *2*

Tinlin, John, 21, pithead worker, 125 Brandon St., Palace Colliery Rows, *151*

Todd, George, 43, ostler, Kirkton, Blantyre, **ch. 2**. (W, Margaret Mann, B: Thu, 25th Oct 1877, Blantyre)

Tokenies, Adam, 25, miner, McCann's Land, 276 Main St., Bellshill, *155*. (B: Fri, 21st Jan 1910, Bothwell)

Tollson, William, 20, miner, **ch. 1**. (B: New Monkland?)

Tonner, Charles, 15, drawer, 13 Calder St., Dixon's Rows, Blantyre, **ch. 2**. (S/o Hugh. B: Sat, 3rd Nov 1877, Blantyre)

Tonner, Hugh, 48, miner, 13 Calder St., Dixon's Rows, Blantyre, **ch. 2**. (W, Margaret McIntyre. F/o Charles. B: Sat, 3rd Nov 1877, Blantyre)

Torley, Alexander, 26, fireman, Udston Rows, Hamilton, **ch. 4**. (W & 1 ch)

Torley, Felix, 43, miner, Udston Rows, Hamilton, **ch. 4**

Wilson, Alexander, miner, *28*

Wilson, Andrew, miner, *54*. (W, Agnes Russell, & 4 ch)

Wilson, Hugh, 36, miner, 55 Calder St., Dixon's Rows, Blantyre, **ch. 2**. (W, Mary Burns, & 4 ch. F/o William & James [14]. B: Mon, 29th Oct 1877, Blantyre)

Wilson, James, 17, miner, Larkfield, Blantyre, **ch. 2**. (S/o Thomas [45]. B/o Thomas [21]. B: Sat, 10th Nov 1877, Blantyre)

Wilson, James, 14, drawer, 55 Calder St., Dixon's Rows, Blantyre, **ch. 2**. (S/o Hugh. B/o William. B: Sat, 10th Nov 1877, Blantyre)

Wilson, James, 40, miner, 50 Udston Rows, Hamilton, **ch. 4**. (W & 7 ch)

Wilson, John, 17, drawer, 19 Muir St., Hamilton, *61*

Wilson, John, 25, brusher, Causewayshot, **ch. 3**. (W, Mary Grimson)

Wilson, John, 20, miner, Udston Rows, Hamilton, **ch. 4**

Wilson, Peter, 31 Roman Row, Hamilton Palace Colliery, *148*. (W & 1 ch)

Wilson, Thomas, 45, miner, Larkfield, Blantyre, **ch. 2**. (W, Rebecca Welsh. F/o Thomas & James [17]. B: Mon. 29th Oct 1877, Blantyre)

Wilson, Thomas, 21, miner, Greenfield, Hamilton, **ch. 2**. (S/o Thomas [45]. B/o James [17]. B: Tue, 30th Oct 1877, Blantyre)

Wilson, William, 17, miner, 55 Calder St., Dixon's Rows, Blantyre, **ch. 2**. (S/o Hugh. B/o James [14]. B: Blantyre)

Winning, John, sinker, *56*

Winters, Walter, 22, drawer, Udston Rows, Hamilton, **ch. 4**

Wood, William, 51, miner, Springfield Terr., Blantyre, **ch. 2**. (W, Angeline Connell)

Worthington, John (Jack), redsman, Blackhall Row, Summerlee, **ch. 5**. (W & 3 ch. B: Wed, 6th Aug 1913)

Wotherspoon, William, miner, *7*

Wright, James, 49, fireman, 3 Priestfield Terr., Blantyre, **ch. 2**. (W, Jane Marshall. F/o John. B: Episcopalian Church, Broadlees, Baillieston)

Wright, John McEwan, 17, pony driver, 3 Priestfield Terr., Blantyre, **ch. 2**. (S/o James. B: Episcopalian Church, Broadlees, Baillieston)

Y

Young, James, putter, *46*

Yuille, John, 62, miner, Wishaw, *160*

Bibliography

Primary sources:

Children's Employment Commission – Mines – Appendix Part 1, C 381 (HMSO, 1842).

Report by Messrs. Ralph Moore, T.E. Wales, and James Willis, Inspectors of Mines (preliminary report on the Blantyre disaster, 22nd October, 1877) C 1915 (HMSO, 1878).

Report on the Blantyre Colliery Explosion by Robert MacLean, Esquire, of Edinburgh, Advocate, and Joseph Dickinson, Esquire, of South Bank, Pendleton, Manchester, one of Her Majesty's Inspectors of Mines, C 1916 (HMSO, 1878).

Copy of Special Report to the Secretary of State on the Blantyre Colliery, dated the 31st day of October 1878, by Messrs Joseph Dickinson and Ralph Moore, Inspectors of Mines. Report 350 (HMSO, 1879).

Report on the Blantyre Explosion by William Alexander and Ralph Moore, Esqrs, Inspectors of Mines, dated 24th July 1879. C 2497 (HMSO, 1879).

Explosions (Udston Colliery). Report to the Secretary of State for the Home Department by J. Dickinson, HM Inspector of Mines, and C.C. Maconochie, Advocate. C 5192 (HMSO, 1887).

Report to the Secretary of State for the Home Department on the Circumstances Attending an Explosion at Udston Colliery, Hamilton, on the 28th May, 1887 by Ralph Moore, HM Inspector of Mines (HMSO, 1887).

Report of a Formal Investigation under Section 83 (1) of the Coal Mines Act, 1911, of the Accident which occurred at the Cadder Colliery on Sunday, August 3rd, 1913, and of its Causes and Circumstances by Sir Henry Cunynghame, K.C.B. Cd 7133 (HMSO, 1913).

Report on the Causes and Circumstances attending the Accident at Stanrigg & Arbuckle Colliery, Lanarkshire, on the 9th July, 1918, from an Inrush of Moss by W. Walker, C.B.E., HM Acting Chief Inspector of Mines. Cmd 146 (HMSO, 1919).

Report on the Causes of and Circumstances attending the Explosion which occurred at Cardowan Colliery, Lanarkshire, on the 16th November, 1932 by Sir Henry Walker, C.B.E., HM Chief Inspector of Mines. Cmd 4309 (HMSO, 1933).

Report on the Causes of, and the Circumstances attending, the Underground Fire which occurred at Auchengeich Colliery, Lanarkshire, on 18th September 1959 by T.A. Rogers, C.B.E, HM Chief Inspector of Mines and Quarries. Cmd 1022 (HMSO, 1960).

Auchengeich Colliery Disaster: Brief Summary of the Proceedings of the Court of Inquiry into the fire at Auchengeich Colliery, Lanarkshire, on 18th September, 1959, compiled on behalf of the Executive Committee, Scottish Area, National Union of Mineworkers, (Scottish Area, N.U.M, July, 1960).

Reports of HM Inspectors of Mines and Quarries for 1960: Scottish Division by Henry Hyde, Divisional Inspector of Mines and Quarries. (HMSO, 1961).

All underground plans, and passages quoted directly from HMSO documents, appear by kind permission of Her Majesty's Stationary Office, London.

Contemporary newspapers:
Airdrie and Coatbridge Advertiser
Coatbridge Express
Colliery Guardian
Daily Record and Mail
Evening Citizen
Glasgow Courier
Glasgow Herald
Hamilton Advertiser
Kilsyth Chronicle
Scotsman
Scottish Miner
Sunday Herald
The Times

Historical injury data supplied by the Health & Safety Executive, Bootle, Merseyside. Thanks also to Ian Winstanley for much additional information from the Coal Mining History Resource Centre and Picks Publishing, Wigan (www.cmhrc.pwp.blueyonder.co.uk).

Secondary sources:
Abel, Sir Frederick, *Mining Accidents and their Prevention*, New York 1889.
Arnot, R. Page, *A History of the Scottish Miners from the Earliest Times*, London 1955.
Barrowman, James, *A Glossary of Scotch Mining Terms*, Hamilton 1886.
Benson, John, *British Coalminers in the Nineteenth Century: a Social History*, London 1989.
Blantyre Miners' Welfare Charitable Society & Social Club 40th Anniversary 1960–2000, Hamilton 2000.
Bolton, Wilma S., *Black Faces and Tackety Boots: True Stories from the Coal Mines of Lanarkshire*, Hamilton 2006.
Calder, Jenni, *Scotland in Trust*, Glasgow 1990.
Dron, Robert W., *The Coal Fields of Scotland*, Glasgow 1902.
Duckham, Helen & Baron, *Great Pit Disasters; Great Britain, 1700 to the Present Day*, Newton Abbot 1973.
Duncan, Robert, *The Mineworkers*, Edinburgh 2005.
Dunn, Matthias, *A Treatise on the Winning and Working of the Collieries*, Newcastle upon Tyne 1852.
Durland, Kellog, *Among the Fife Miners*, London 1904.
Galloway, Robert, *A History of Coal Mining in Great Britain*, London 1882.
Galloway, Robert, *Annals of Coal Mining and the Coal Trade*, Newton Abbot 1971.
Hutton, Guthrie, *Mining, Ayrshire's Lost Industry*, Cumnock 1996.

Bibliography

Hutton, Guthrie, *Lanarkshire's Mining Legacy*, Cumnock 1997.

Keay, John & Julia, *Collins Encyclopaedia of Scotland*, London 1994.

Kerr, George L., *Elementary Coal Mining*, London 1902.

Lewis, Brian, *Coal Mining in the Eighteenth and Nineteenth Centuries*, London 1971.

Lythe, S.E.G. & Butt, J., *An Economic History of Scotland: 1100–1939* (Glasgow, 1975).

Mason, E., *Practical Coal Mining for Miners* (2 vols.), London 1951.

Nimmo, William, *The History of Stirlingshire*, Glasgow 1880.

O'Hare, Larry, *The Stanrigg Pit Disaster*, Airdrie 1987.

Paterson, Andrew, *A Blast from the Past*, Airdrie 2005.

Smith, Robin, *The Making of Scotland: A Comprehensive Guide to the Growth of its Cities, Towns and Villages*, Edinburgh 2001.

Smout, T. C., *A History of the Scottish People, 1560–1830*, London 1969.

Terris, Ian, *Twenty Years Down the Mines*, Ochiltree 2001.

Whatley, Christopher A., *The Industrial Revolution in Scotland*, Cambridge 1997.

Glossary

The following definitions have been taken from several sources, in particular Barrowman's glossary (see Bibliography).

afterdamp – the mixture of gasses (mostly carbonic acid, or carbon dioxide) resulting from an explosion of *firedamp*. It is non-combustible, colourless, odourless and (unless in large quantities) tasteless. In such quantities it can be highly poisonous. Heavier than air, it tends to accumulate in low places such as dip workings and sumps. 1% in the air will cause shortage of breath, 8% will put out a flame in still air, and 10% causes death. Also known as *blackdamp* or *chokedamp*.

air crossing – a construction situated at a point where the two air currents, intake and return, have to cross each other without intermixing, one being built over the top of the other. See also *overcast*, *undercast*.

bailing tank – see *chest*.

bank *(pit bank)* – the pithead.

banksman – a pithead worker responsible for loading and unloading the cage at the surface.

bench – a junction (usually floored with an area of steel plating) where hutches can be transferred from one road to another.

bencher – a workman employed to transfer the hutches.

blackdamp – see *afterdamp*.

blaes – bituminous shale, normally found in strata above the coal seam.

blind pit – underground, a short shaft linking one level and another either above or below, sometimes fitted with stairs and used either to conduct air or for escape purposes.

boiler shell – a large steel pipe, placed on end and wide enough for men to work inside. Normally used for sinking a narrow shaft, the men excavated the ground inside while the shell was gradually lowered, forming a strong steel wall around them and preventing collapse of the sides. Additional shells were added as the shaft went deeper.

bottomer – a workman in attendance at the bottom of the shaft, the miners' link with the surface. Among his tasks is to supervise the loading of hutches onto and out of the cages and to signal the winding engineman at the surface.

brakesman – a workman who operates the brakes on a wagons.

brattice screen *(bratticing)* – a temporary screen, usually comprising a wooden frame overlaid with canvas or cloth, which is placed roof to floor lengthways along the centre of a passage as a division to conduct a current of air into and out of confined areas such as working faces in *stoop-and-room* workings.

brushing – the removal of waste material from either above or below a coal seam in preparation for the production shift. The workmen (brushers) also re-cut the roofs of passageways that have sunk and sides in need of widening or repair, a process called back-brushing.

buntons – in the shaft, the cross-members of the framework holding the slides, between which the cage travels.

carbon dioxide – see *afterdamp*.

carbon monoxide – see *whitedamp*.

checkweighman – a worker who takes account of the coal raised (on behalf of the miners).

chest – a large open-topped tank, made of wood or iron, used to bail out flooded shafts. Also known as a *bailing tank*.

chokedamp – see *afterdamp*.

clipper – a workman who attaches (clips) hutches to an endless rope haulage.

coked/coking – the partial carbonisation of coal or coal dust on the surface (of timbers, etc.) facing the source of an explosion, as a result of intensive heat.

crosscut – a secondary road driven through the intervening strata between two major roads.

cube – (in older pits) the ventilating furnace situated near the bottom of the upcast shaft which draws fresh air down the downcast shaft (or the downcast division of a single shaft) thus ventilating the workings.

cundy – (in steep *longwall* workings) a narrow roadway down which mineral is rolled, to be loaded into hutches at the bottom.

dook – a dip or incline in a coal seam.

downcast – the shaft down which fresh air travels into the pit workings.

drawer – a workman whose task it is to move hutches manually from the coalface to the haulage roads. Compare with *putter*.

drift mine – a passage driven from the surface and following underground the course of an outcrop. Underground, also used of certain return airways, as in furnace drift.

fan drift – a sealed passage of wood or metal leading from the top of the *upcast* shaft to the extractor fan (and enclosing both) to guide the spent air drawn from the workings.

fast place – a cul-de-sac or dead end, for example a working face in *stoop-and-room* workings.

fathom – the standard measurement of depth in mining, equal to six feet (1.8 metres).

feeder – a small issue of water or gas, usually firedamp, from a fissure in the solid coal.

firedamp – a highly combustible gas, chiefly methane and carburetted hydrogen, which has been trapped in the seam since its formation. Being much lighter than air, accumulations tend to form in higher places such as the roofs of passageways, at the face, or in the inaccessible waste areas of abandoned workings, from where it can sometimes be dislodged by movement of the waste or by a sharp drop in barometric pressure. The cause of many explosions, *firedamp* has no colour, taste, or smell. Also known as marsh gas.

gauton – a narrow ditch or drain cut along the side of an underground pavement to collect water and conduct it to the pumps.

gin – a pulley-type device, driven by horses or water, formerly used for winding men and materials up and down the shaft.

gummer – a workman who cleans out the 'gum' (small cuttings and dross) from the cut left by a coal-cutting machine.

haulage – a railed road used for hauling coal or waste to the pit bottom.

head frame – the tall framework built over the

shaft on which the pulley wheels, used to raise and lower the cages, are hung. Also known as head gear.

hill – the pithead.

horse road – a roadway on which the haulage is carried out by horses.

hutch – a box-type container of steel or wood which runs on rails like a miniature railway wagon. Used for transporting materials underground and carrying coal or waste to the surface. Sometimes called a tub.

inbye – towards the workings, away from the pit bottom. Compare with *outbye*.

intake – the road along which fresh air travels into the workings. Compare with *return*.

kettle – a large bucket made of wood, or more commonly iron, used for lifting or lowering men or materials inside the shaft, especially during sinking operations.

lamp cabin – (before electric lights) a room underground where safety lamps are stored.

lamp station – a room where safety lamps can be opened and trimmed, beyond which no naked lights can be taken.

lampman – a worker whose job it is to repair, trim and text the miners' lamps.

longwall – a system of coal extraction where (a) following the seam, all the coal is worked from the shaft outwards to the boundary of the royalty (advancing), or (b) a road is driven from the shaft directly to the boundary and the coal extracted working back towards the shaft (retreating). In both cases the space left behind is packed with leftover waste material. By the early 1900s this work was increasingly being carried out using coal-cutting machines which were much more economical.

manhole – an 'inshot', or recess, in the wall of a passageway, designed as a passing place, or a refuge in the event of, for example, runaway hutches.

man-riding haulage – (in later collieries) an underground transport system for miners consisting of a series of bogies, fitted with seats, which is pulled either by endless haulage rope or engine.

metals – a general name for the strata in which minerals are found.

midwall – in a shaft, a wall, usually of wood, dividing the shaft into two sections; in bratticing, a wall of brattice screen, placed roof to floor, from the main airway to a working place to direct a current of air around the face.

oncost – a workman who is paid by the shift.

onsetter – a workman whose job it is to load and unload the cage at the foot of the shaft.

outbye – towards the pit bottom, away from the workings. Compare with inbye.

outcrop – the edge of a coal seam which has broken the surface.

overcast – the higher of two air courses at an air crossing. Compare with *undercast*.

oversman – the foreman in charge of underground operations.

pavement – the floor of any underground passageway.

pricker – a device (e.g. a needle) for raising or lowering the wick in a safety lamp.

prop/pit prop – a wooden post, cut to size, used underground for supporting the roof. Also known as a tree.

pumpman – a water pump attendant.

putter – (in earlier years) a drawer, usually a young boy or girl, who was harnessed or chained to the hutch and made to pull its weight from the coalface to the haulage road or even to the pit bottom. Another, again usually a young boy or girl, assisted the putter by pushing the hutches from behind.

rake – (of hutches) several, a train.

redsman – a workman employed to clear rubble, spilled coal, etc., from the roads to keep them clear.

return – the path along which spent air travels towards the upcast shaft. Compare with *intake*.

rise pit – workings that follow a rising seam.

roadsman – a workman who repairs the rails, etc. in the haulage road.

royalty – the area licensed for coal extraction.

shothole – a hole drilled for explosives in blasting operations.

sinker – one of a squad of men employed to dig or 'sink' mine shafts.

sit – an area where the surface, usually in a liquid or semi-liquid state, has collapsed into the workings.

slides – the vertical guides, usually of wood, between which the cage travels up and down the shaft.

snibbling – thrusting a metal or wooden pin (a 'snibble') through the spokes of hutch or wagon wheels to bring them to a halt.

stone drift – see *stone mine*.

stonedusting – the process of spreading non-flammable material (e.g. silica dust) to cover deposits of fine coal dust lying in roadways and at working faces. This is done to inhibit the ignition of such dust in the event of an explosion.

stone mine – a passageway driven through the intervening, usually barren strata from one level to another. Also known as a *stone drift*, or a dipping mine.

stoop-and-room – a system of coal extraction, in which passages (rooms) are cut through the solid coal seam in a grid-work leaving large rectangular blocks of coal (stoops) which are later extracted.

stooping – the removal of the stoops or blocks of coal.

stopping – a barricade of brickwork (or wood and brattice cloth, if temporary) blocking off from the ventilation flow a road which is out of use.

sump – a hole excavated at the bottom of a shaft below the level of the cage landing into which water drains and is pumped out.

tacksman – a lessee, the person who holds the lease to mine coal.

tally (*tallow*) **lamp** – a naked flame lamp comprising a small tin resembling a miniature watering can with a lid that snapped down to seal in the oil. From the end of the spout a wick protruded measuring about a quarter of an inch in diameter. Normally worn on the miner's cap, in the early days the tally was preferred because it gave out the best light – regardless of the danger of explosion.

througher – a passage cut directly between two rooms to section-off the formed stoop and assist ventilation.

throw – the displacement of a seam, up (upthrow) or down (downthrow), caused by a fault, or faults, in the strata.

tree – see *prop*.

undercast – the lower of two air courses at an air crossing. Compare with *overcast*.

upcast – the shaft up which return (spent) air travels out of the pit workings.

weighting – (of a roof) sagging under pressure from above.

whitedamp – carbonic oxide, or carbon monoxide, gas. It is combustible, colourless and tasteless, but possesses a faint odour when present in large enough quantities. Rarely found naturally in mines, this gas is present only under exceptional circumstances such as underground fires, etc.

winding engineman (or *engineman*) – workman who operates the engine for winding the cage up and down the shaft.